Democratic Theory and Causal Methodology in Comparative Politics

Barrington Moore bequeathe ~~to reconcile his causal claim~~ with his normative "dream of a free and rational society." ~~In this~~ book, Mark I. Lichbach harmonizes causal methodology and normative democratic theory, suggesting that the Moore Curve – the more external the causal methodology, the thinner the democratic theory – governs democratization studies. Using a dialogue among four specific texts, Lichbach advances five constructive themes. First, comparativists should study the causal agency of individuals, groups, and democracies. Second, the three types of collective agency should be paired with an exploration of three corresponding moral dilemmas: ought/is, freedom/power, and democracy/causality. Third, at the center of inquiry comparativists should place big-P Paradigms and big-M Methodology. Fourth, as they play with research schools, creatively combining prescriptive and descriptive approaches to democratization, they should encourage a mixed-theory and mixed-method field. Finally, comparativists should study pragmatic questions about political power and democratic performance: in building a democratic state, which democracy, under which conditions, is best, and how might it be achieved?

Mark I. Lichbach is Professor of Government and Politics at the University of Maryland. He received a BA from Brooklyn College of the City University of New York, an MA from Brown University, and a PhD in political science from Northwestern University. He is the author or editor of numerous books, including the award-winning *The Rebel's Dilemma*, and of many articles that have appeared in scholarly journals in political science, economics, and sociology. His work has been supported by the National Science Foundation and private foundations. Lichbach has served as book review editor of the *American Political Science Review*; as editor of the University of Michigan Press's series Interests, Identities, and Institutions; and as chair of three political science departments: the University of Maryland, the University of Colorado, and the University of California–Riverside.

Democratic Theory and Causal Methodology in Comparative Politics

MARK I. LICHBACH

University of Maryland

CAMBRIDGE
UNIVERSITY PRESS

CAMBRIDGE UNIVERSITY PRESS
Cambridge, New York, Melbourne, Madrid, Cape Town,
Singapore, São Paulo, Delhi, Mexico City

Cambridge University Press
32 Avenue of the Americas, New York, NY 10013-2473, USA

www.cambridge.org
Information on this title: www.cambridge.org/9781107622357

© Mark I. Lichbach 2013

First published 2013

Printed in the United States of America

A catalog record for this publication is available from the British Library.

Library of Congress Cataloging in Publication Data
Lichbach, Mark Irving, 1951–
Democratic theory and causal methodology in comparative politics / Mark
I. Lichbach, University of Maryland.
    p. cm.
Includes bibliographical references and index.
ISBN 978-1-107-02581-3 (hardback) – ISBN 978-1-107-62235-7 (pbk.)
1. Comparative government. 2. Democracy. I. Title.
JF51.L525   2013
321.8–dc23

                                                        2012038746

ISBN 978-1-107-02581-3 Hardback
ISBN 978-1-107-62235-7 Paperback

Faye Marsha Lichbach

1952–2011

"Xs and Ys don't love you like I do."

Political theorists often fail to appreciate that arguments about how politics ought to be organized typically depend on relational claims involving agents, actions, legitimacy, and ends.

Ian Shapiro (2005: 152)

[W]e must develop and deploy a conception of what a democratic polity is which is appropriate to grasping its causal dynamics. This is overwhelmingly much harder to do than political scientists have yet fathomed.

John Dunn (1999: 138)

Normative and explanatory theories of democracy grow out of literatures that proceed, for the most part, on separate tracks, largely uninformed by one another.

Ian Shapiro (2003: 2)

[A] skeptical, historical approach ... sees normative categories as inexpugnable from the understanding of political causality.

John Dunn (1999: 137–39)

[T]he history of thought is a history of issues about which we, in the end, care. I find it thrilling to ask what we have learned about these issues from our empirical knowledge of political institutions and events. I think we did learn, we are wiser, and we often see things more clearly than our intellectual forefathers. Unless, however, we bring our knowledge to bear on the big issues, it will remain sterile.

Adam Przeworski (2010: xv)

Contents

Tables

Preface

Barrington Moore bequeathed to comparativists a problem: reconcile his causal claim of "no bourgeoisie, no democracy" with his normative "dream of a free and rational society." Most comparativists nowadays solve the problem by assuming it away. Believing that causal methodology and democratic theory are independent ingredients in inquiry, causal methodologists discuss comparative statics, constructivism, structural capacity, and mechanisms, while democratic theorists hold a separate debate about procedural, discursive, class-coalitional, and contentious democracy. Against the idea of two compartmentalized reading lists, this book argues that theory and method hold an elective affinity. The Moore Curve – the more external the causal methodology, the thinner the democratic theory – governs democratization studies.

To make its contrarian case, the book adopts a particular style of presentation. A dialogue among four specific texts allows the authors to speak in their own voices and yet represent general paradigms of politics. The analysis opens by comparing an exemplar of rational choice theory, Daron Acemoglu and James A. Robinson's *Economic Origins of Dictatorship and Democracy*, with an exemplar of constructivist theory, Lisa Wedeen's *Peripheral Visions: Publics, Power, and Performance in Yemen*. Commencing from Moore's causal claim of "no bourgeoisie, no democracy," Acemoglu and Robinson couple procedural democracy with comparative statics. Their thin democracy embraces internal choice subject to external constraints. Taking off from Moore's normative "dream of a free and rational society," Wedeen pairs discursive democracy with social constructivism. Her thick democracy endorses a release from external bondage to the environment. Perhaps a free and rational society requires a fit state that navigates between a thin democracy determined exogenously and a thick democracy fashioning its own future. Atul Kohli's *State-Directed Development: Political Power and Industrialization in the Global Periphery* offers a third synthesis of norms and empirics: a thin class-coalitional democracy tied to a powerful externalist etiology. While Kohli's fit state adjusts to the environmental constraints of world history and global order, it trades Moore's "dream of a free and rational society" for economic development. Finally, Charles Tilly's *Democracy* offers a pragmatic and pluralistic synthesis of democratic theories and causal methodologies. Tilly's contentious democracy is thinner than Wedeen's discursive democracy but thicker than Acemoglu and Robinson's procedural democracy. By democratizing complex social mechanisms and contingent political processes, Tilly's fit state flourishes in the midst of its environment.

Moving forward, offering solutions and not only characterizing problems, the book advances five constructive themes. First, while the texts examined here have strengths and weaknesses that can serve as complements and substitutes, comparativists should begin with Tilly's contentious-politics approach. The best way to advance democratization studies is to use Tilly as the springboard and the others as sounding boards to study the causal agency of individuals, groups, and democracies. Second, the book urges comparativists to pair these three types of collective agency with an exploration of three corresponding moral dilemmas: ought/is, freedom/power, and democracy/causality. Third, the recent focus on causal analysis should not push big-P Paradigms and big-M Methodology from the center of comparative politics. Theory and method offer creative heuristics that can stimulate studies of democratization. Fourth, while normative and empirical ideas coming from a research school bear a family resemblance, recognizing the elective affinities of theory and method leads to its undoing. Comparativists who play with research schools can turn the connections between prescriptive and descriptive approaches to democratization into creative tensions. As comparative politics becomes a mixed-theory and mixed-method field, democratic theorists and causal methodologists become allies rather than adversaries. Finally, as comparativists develop the observable implications of different methods and theories, creative play with paradigms must be constrained by the empirics of regime fitness. Because democracies operate in the midst of environmental constraints, comparativists should study pragmatic questions about political power and democratic performance: in building a democratic state, which democracy under which conditions is best, and how might it be achieved? In returning to this core concern of the 1960s, today's comparative politics can renew its past and strengthen its future. As comparativists address Barrington Moore's ought/is dilemma of causal collective human agency in democratization, they come to understand how alternative modernities challenge liberalism; how state building occurs amid contentious world politics; and how institutions arise, persist, and change.

When I began the book, I did not know that this book was the book that I would write. Brian Barry's four-decades-old *Sociologists, Economists, and Democracy* had captured an exhilarating moment in the history of comparative politics, and I sensed a similar intellectual ferment today (Lichbach 2003, 2005, 2009, 2010; Lichbach and Kopstein 2009; Lichbach and Lebow 2007; Lichbach and Seligman 2000; Lichbach and Zuckerman 2009). Rather than again writing generally about contemporary scholarly debates, I decided to follow Barry's example and write a book about a very small number of specific books, exploring path-breaking exemplars of different approaches to comparative politics. While I quickly decided on the texts, my theme about the Moore Curve (Table 2) only emerged in the midst of things – just as the great comparativist Alexis de Tocqueville had said. With the Moore-Curve heuristic firmly in mind, I worked out its meaning and significance, working forward toward its observable and unobservable implications and working backward toward its causes and origins. My writing was constrained by an imaginary reader's problem situation. I had in mind a graduate student interested in the causal origins of democracy. While attracted to rational choice institutionalism, partly because of its modernist appeal and partly because of its dominance in the field, he or she is reflective enough to be skeptical about the theory and thoughtful enough to be interested in the models and foils of multitheory and multimethod research. To these inquiring minds, here is my message: before comparativists prefer socialism to capitalism, they insist on studying real existing socialisms. Before preferring social constructivism or historical institutionalism to rational choice, graduate students should study real existing constructivisms and institutionalisms. I am reminded of an old joke: a king judges an operatic contest, and after hearing the first singer he gives the prize to the second.

As I wrote and rewrote, Daron Acemoglu, Colin Elman, Jeff Kopstein, Margaret Pearson, Sid Tarrow, and Ian Ward offered important suggestions and valuable encouragement. Lisa Wedeen commented on several drafts, and her insights were particularly valuable. Lew Bateman, that masterful academic editor, was a joy to work with. He provided two very helpful reviews. I also want to thank the several generations of graduate students in my comparative politics courses. Their curiosity convinced me that the book would find a receptive audience. Finally, I want to thank my department colleagues and several deans. They allowed me to perform my administrative responsibilities as department chair while continuing to enjoy reading scholarly works and writing academic prose.

During the three years I was writing this book, my life changed forever. My first mentor in graduate school, Alan Zuckerman, passed away from pancreatic cancer. Alan taught me what comparative politics should be: substantively relevant, theoretically rich, methodologically sophisticated, and philosophically attuned. We became coauthors and friends, sharing things professional and things personal. I miss Alan very much.

During these years my wife, Faye Lichbach, passed away from metastatic breast cancer that turned into bone cancer, liver cancer, and brain cancer. I was her principal caregiver, attending to her daily needs. Faye was a blessing to all who knew her. Our children, Sammi Jo and Yossi, and I love her very much. She lives with us forever.

I

Methodology's Problem, and Democracy's Too

People fight for democracy. The fall of communisms, the Color Revolutions, and the Arab Spring are recent popular struggles about democratization. If collective human agency causes democracy, two questions arise: what type of democracy do people want? How is their collective agency causal for democracy?

Comparativists studying democratization advocate democratic theories and advance causal methodologies. This book will discern an elective affinity of theory and method. The Moore Curve – the more external the causal methodology, the thinner the democratic theory – governs democratization studies. However, most comparativists never stop to reflect on the relationship between normative and empirical questions of collective human agency. They inevitably slight concerns about how their prescriptive theories and descriptive methods cohere.

The way forward in comparative politics to more fully anthropomorphize people and insert them into the ought/is debate. Desired outcomes Y face the opportunities and constraints of historical conditions X. To deepen normative appreciation and empirical understanding of democracy, to join why-Y normative visions of democracy with if-X-then-Y causal models of democracy, comparativists should thicken their conceptions of collective human agency. Complexifying agency allows comparativists to reconcile different normative theories of democracy with different empirical approaches to causality. A new and different understanding then emerges: because collective agency is the causal force behind democracy, the freedom and the power of collective agency become the core dilemmas of democratization. With these ideas in hand, comparativists can address the crucial practical problem of democratic performance: in building a democratic state, which democracy under which conditions is best? Democratic theory without causal method is empty; causal method without democratic theory is blind. Only in unison can knowledge advance about the causal collective human agency behind democratization.

To develop these themes, I first examine Barrington Moore's problem situation (Section 1.1) and his core problem (Section 1.2). I then explore the democratic theories and causal methodologies used by today's comparativists (Section 1.3). Next, I argue that the elective affinities of theory and method result from research schools in comparative politics (Section 1.4). The constructive aims of the book connect causal collective human agency with democratization (Section 1.5). Finally, I summarize the chapters (Section 1.6).

1.1. THE BARRINGTON MOORE PROBLEM SITUATION

The search for the causes of democracy begins with Barrington Moore's *Social Origins of Democracy and Dictatorship: Lord and Peasant in the Making of the Modern World*. In 1966, Moore offered the UrTheory of modern comparative politics: "No bourgeoisie, no democracy." Outlasting a hundred qualifications and a thousand equivocations, here was a pithy narrative, pregnant with morals and methods, that was powerful enough to animate the field. Moore's proposition held significant implications for what Ira Katznelson (2009) calls the big structures of liberalism: a secular national culture, pluralist civil society, capitalist economic market, procedurally responsive governing institutions, limited state bureaucracy, and an international order facilitating peace and trade among states. Since its inception, "bourgeois" liberalism, Moore reminded us, was a core political tradition of the West. Under siege in bipolar and multipolar worlds, the tradition was challenged by major powers pursuing counterhegemonic modernities that offered religious and ethnic, authoritarian and statist, alternatives.

One reason for Moore's enduring success arises from his vivid descriptions and concrete explanations of the various paths to modernity. Capturing variation in the historical experiences of the early developers in the West – England and France – he also depicted the diversity of the follow-up experiences of middle-developer Japan and late-developer China. Drawing comparisons to cases not often thought about – America as an early developer and India as a late developer – was a stroke of genius. By not including chapters on Germany and Russia he forced comparativists to rethink the development experiences of these crucial cases.

Moore's narratives were also successful because they told and foretold the dramatic political battles of world politics. Believing that the key protagonists were the crown (bureaucracy and army), aristocracy (landowners), lower classes of ordinary peoples (peasants and workers), and the bourgeoisie, he portrayed the strange political bargains that were struck. To capture the state and direct its development, a rising bourgeoisie could ally with an old rural elite, or a peasantry could join a working-class party. Understanding the protagonists as class-bound actors did produce somewhat of a fairy tale. Nevertheless, Moore correctly argued that during the twentieth and now twenty-first centuries, contending constellations of historical forces – carrier groups and their associated ideas and organizations – advanced their domestic and foreign policy agendas through attempted revolutionary and reformist changes in regimes. Collective human agency was thus causally connected to the interstate conflicts and internal wars of the 1920s and 1930s, producing the clash of democracy, fascism, and communism. In the post WWII period, the old colonial order was opposed by domestic coalitions in new states seeking national liberation from various empires. During the Cold War, states pursuing varieties of authoritarian communism fought states pursuing types of democratic capitalism. After the Cold War, as states in the West attempted to reorganize their democracies and markets, variations of liberalism and neoliberalism, and modifications of conservatism and neoconservatism, found domestic and global champions. Since the Iranian revolution, political Islam has been an alternative development strategy pursued in the postcolonial world. After Deng Xiaoping replaced Mao, China showed late-late developers that a communist party could be the vanguard of state-led capitalist economic development. During the 1990s and afterward, certain states in the global south did not pursue any recognizable path of development. Usually predatory and sometimes genocidal, they often collapsed into civil war and bred transnational terrorism. And throughout the post-Moore years, various worldwide political projects emerged from global civil society. Collective actors, advocating socialism with a human face, universal human rights, cosmopolitan peace and justice, and liberation theology proposed regime organizations and global institutions that challenged the hegemony of "bourgeoisie" liberalism.

In sum, Moore effectively captured the problem situation of contemporary comparative politics: in competitive international environments, contending social formations (with preferences, beliefs, endowments, and strategies) construct state institutions that produce policy regimes that, in turn, influence economic development. Today's comparativists typically propose midrange theories about the coevolution of parts of Moore's story. Challenges to the state are global. Ruling coalitions are key factuals. Potential governing coalitions that never form are important historical counterfactuals; causal claims explore, for example, why a German-type authoritarian coalition did not have sufficient collective agency to dominate American politics. World politics is about the conflict over institutional frameworks for constructing and reconstructing states. States pursue policy regimes for economic development, and public policies are judged by their economic consequences.

Moore was also successful because his story built on a core question of social and political thought: how do conflicts create institutions and how do the institutions then manage the conflicts?

The tradition of studying the static covariance and dynamic coevolution of institutions and conflicts extends from Plato (1974) and Aristotle (1981); to Montesquieu (1989) and Machiavelli ([1514] 1961); to Hobbes ([1651] 1988), Locke (1988), and Rousseau ([1762] 1968); to Hamilton, Jay, and Madison ([1787–1788] 1961); to Marx ([1869] 1963) and Weber ([1924] 1968); to Easton (1953) and Almond and Powell (1966); to Linz ([1975] 2000), Eckstein and Gurr (1975), and Huntington (1968); and beyond Moore to Skocpol (1979) and Lijphart (1999). Part of this long tradition, Moore understood domestic battles over state building as entailing more than disputes about today's decision-making processes and tomorrow's allocation strategies – "who gets what, when, and where" questions (Lasswell 1950). Institutions are long-run patterns of authority over peoples and territories that undergird resource extraction (taxes and conscription) and societal regulation (laws and rules). They create power, or "the ability to get someone to do something they wouldn't otherwise do" (Dahl 1957). Structures of domestic governance therefore become the objects of power struggles over alternative paths of development. By following Moore, comparativists could study contentious world politics as the perpetual bargaining in a state over the "*monopoly of the legitimate use of physical force*" (Weber 1946a: 78, emphasis in original) and "the authoritative allocation of scarce values" (Easton 1953). Today's comparativists could thus join generations of social and political theorists in searching for the well-functioning and high-performing structures of politics and government. By following Moore, they could address big questions about deep institutional arrangements. Laying at the interstices of global governance, state structures, and popular participation, these governing regimes create the patterns of conflict and systems of conflict resolution that animate world politics.

Moore thus remains a cornerstone of comparativists studying how collective human agency manifests itself in the political contention surrounding state institutions. In other words, domestic and international actors, and their associated interests, ideas, and organizations, contend for power. Political demands and collective claim making construct characteristic patterns of domestic politics. Paraphrasing Charles Tilly (1975: 42), one of Moore's most famous students, internal war made the state and the state made internal war. Political contention over development manifests itself as peaceful dissent, social movements, protest demonstrations, and political strikes. Violent ethnic riots, terrorist campaigns, military coups, guerrilla insurgencies, civil wars, and social revolutions are additional possibilities. Because internal wars over grand strategies of state building produced powerful sovereign states in some places and Hobbesian state breakdowns elsewhere, political contention influences the types of political order that prevail in particular historical eras.

Finally, Moore was successful because he challenged the never-dying theory of universal modernity. Marx's materialism and Hegel's idealism diagnosed the master levers of systemic change and placed them at the cores of progressively unfolding historical narratives. Their essentialist and historicist perspectives could be tragic and yet ultimately redeeming: holding short-lived bumps on the way to happy endings, they held that social life is governed by blind forces producing resolvable contradictions. A widely accepted moral framework for political thought, modernization's current manifestation is global democracy and cosmopolitan human rights: the everywhere and everytime culmination of the millenniums-long moral development of virtue and enlightenment. Instead of a relentless modernist project – one grand teleological model of organic, stable, and harmonious development – Moore invited us to see bloody battles over science and secularism, nationalism and pluralism, markets and planning, democracy and dictatorship, limited and statist bureaucracies, and international order and global anarchy. He thus taught us that these struggles over "bourgeois" liberalism are endless. While winners claim victory and then in good fractal fashion fragment (Abbott 2001), losers, rather than receding into history, politicize new dimensions of conflict (Riker 1982). As new institutions yield new conflicts, popular agency reinvents itself.

So here are the grand concerns Barrington Moore bequeathed to comparative politics: alternative modernities and the challenges to liberalism; state building and contentious world politics; and the origins, operations, and outcomes of political institutions. At the center of comparative inquiry, Moore placed the question of causal collective human agency as the motor of historical change.

I.2. THE BARRINGTON MOORE PROBLEM

Given his influence, it is surprising that comparativists have forgotten Moore's (p. 508) concluding reflections: "Whether the ancient Western dream of a free and rational society will always remain a chimera, no one can know for sure. But if the men of the future are ever to break the chains of the present, they will have to understand the forces that forged them." His conclusion was doubly ironic.

Moore's historical narratives had shown that utopian dreams of moral purity transcending politics inevitably confront real-world empirical realities. Moore (p. 427) thus distinguished among the people who begin a revolution, those who carry through the revolution, and the ones who profit from a revolution. In other words, real historical actors never enjoy the benefits of the grand philosophical systems that they try to implement. As would-be makers of revolution adopt incoherent ideologies, offer confused programmatic blueprints, and pursue unstable political strategies, their political actions hold unintended, unwanted, and unexpected consequences. For example, Moore (p. 505) thought that revolutionary violence was needed to produce democratic outcomes, and was often worth the costs. Moreover, local actors never think of themselves as historical agents taking sides in this historical mishmash. While it might seem that "the making of the modern world" entails glorious ideals, giant projects, grand strategies, and great revolutions, Moore's histories were far more complex. Hence, the irony: even if "the men of the future" could "understand the forces that forged" the present, implementing "the ancient Western dream of a free and rational society" could never be straightforward. Moore's most penetrating historical reflections had revealed the disillusioning facts, intractable tradeoffs, and distasteful compromises that plague would-be state builders.

Moore's second irony was contained in his argument that material structures determine political regimes. While he polemicized against cultural theories – "To explain behavior in terms of cultural values is to engage in circular reasoning" (p. 483) – his concluding remarks appear to say something quite different. If people could grasp their architectonic system as a whole, and if they could thereby come to see the laws that drive human affairs, Moore seemed to suggest that their understandings of themselves and of their place in the system could turn a nation-in-itself into a nation-for-itself. Never mind the burdens of history – the grind of path dependence and the trap of causal determinism. While men and women always face rigid economic, social, and political structures, they can turn hidden opportunities into creative possibilities. Alternative modernities, while never infinite, are always greater than at first you believe. Yet once Moore asked people to stop and think about their politics, he had placed normative conceptions of democracy at the core of the causal human agency behind democratization.

Can collective human agency trump structuralist teleology and fashion democracy? Can citizens overcome billiard-ball causal constraints, manipulate environmental counterfactuals, and invent "a free and rational society"? By pitting collective human agency against structural finalism, modernist dreams against genealogical realities, Moore had problematized the relationship between normative theories advocating a democratic state and causal methodologies seeking the origins of democracy.

The Barrington Moore Problem: reconciling the causal claim "no bourgeoisie, no democracy" with the normative "dream of a free and rational society."

Modernity, Moore tells us, is an unfinished project fraught with challenges and crises. In analyzing struggle, comparativists should bring their moral commitments to their academic work. Using the analytical powers of social science, they should preserve and protect, defend and extend, the Enlightenment's liberal values of a free and rational political order. Nevertheless, Moore also led comparativists to wonder: given the causal dynamics behind multiple paths to the modern world, can the dream of a free and rational society be salvaged? Is it possible to employ realistic empirical methodologies and simultaneously defend normative commitments to democracy? Put otherwise, under the causal conditions of modernity, can a self-organizing community of free and equal citizens create a rational society as proclaimed by the Enlightenment? Or do the conditions of economic industrialization and technological development unleash the destructive capacity of collective human power that outweighs its creative potential?

It is important to recognize the Barrington Moore Problem as part of a 1960s problematique (Katznelson 2003). Just as in the 1930s, and even earlier at the turn of the twentieth century, in the 1960s democratic practices challenged democratic theories. As the new realistic empiricism coming out of political science undermined the long-standing desiderata cherished by political theorists, the West seemed unable to defend its commitments. Caught between the specter of academic relativism and the fear of real-world absolutism, defenders of a free and rational society rallied against irrationality and autocracy.

Offering a dynamic twist on a debate concerned with equilibrium outcomes, Moore studied class alignments and revolutionary violence as historical agents of the West's democratization. Unfortunately, Moore never elaborated a theory that connected cause and cause, that is, moral cause with empirical cause. If bourgeois capitalist industrialization began the process of democratization, his bourgeoisie remained a messy and contested ethical force behind change. Without an explicit etiology of collective human agency, his analysis raised as many questions as it answered. The task of reconciling the ought/is dilemma of democratization was bequeathed to future comparativists.

1.3. COMPARATIVISTS TODAY

Moore's concluding remarks have been forgotten, allowing today's comparativists to benefit from a division of labor. While they elaborate alternative visions of causality – comparative statics, constructivism, historical-structural typologies, and mechanisms and processes – they leave the task of specifying alternative visions of democracy to political theorists. Passions and commitments – the hopes and dreams for a democratic politics based on electoral procedures, a national community, economic development, and peaceful contention – are for others.

In the nearly five decades since Moore wrote, comparativists devised new methodologies for causal analysis. Their methods permit them to explore new situations confronting new actors possessing new forms of agency. However, the deepening of empirical methods have come at the cost of ignoring Moore's core problem of moral agency in a causal world. Today's comparativists never stop to think about how their answers to the question "What causes a democratic state?" depend on what they mean by *cause*, depend on what they mean by *democratic state*, and depend on the elective affinities of their answers. In short, comparativists never address democracy as *both* normatively *and* empirically relevant to today's novel problem situations.

To study how the Barrington Moore Problem arises in today's comparative politics, four questions should be addressed:

1. What is the problem situation in which the Moore Problem arises?
2. Which type of democracy is advocated?
3. How is the research methodology causally relevant?
4. Who provides the collective human agency that solves the Moore Problem?

In other words, comparativists must begin with their understanding of the world-historical problem situation, propose normative theories of democracy, and advance research methodologies. The problem of collective human agency – the cause behind a cause – then arises. As normative theory and research methodology interweave, potentially fruitful elective affinities are brought to the various problem situations under investigation.

This book shows how these four questions are addressed by four research paradigms, or overall visions of politics, that have gained prominence since Moore wrote (Table 1). Rational choice

TABLE 1. *Paradigms, Democracy, and Causality*

	Democracy	Causality
Rational Choice	Procedural	Comparative Statics
Social Constructivism	Discursive	Social Constructivism
State-Society	Multiclass	Structural Capacity
Contentious Politics	Contentious	Dynamic Mechanisms

theory has emerged as a principal approach to reconstructing Moore's edifice. In a book whose title – *Economic Origins of Dictatorship and Democracy* – plays on his classic, Daron Acemoglu and James A. Robinson advance a causal claim about democracy that builds on Moore:

Given certain particulars of a nondemocratic environment – the power of its elite, the collective action problems of its citizens, the specifics of its institutions, and the level of its economic inequality – coercive bargaining among key political-economic actors can produce an institutional equilibrium among classes that results in procedural democracy.

Procedural democracy – popular voting in free elections – thus results when strategic bargaining between autocratic elites who control wealth and dissidents who specialize in violence share the rents of economic progress. With this set up, Acemoglu and Robinson employ comparative statics to examine the generative powers of the environment. Assuming that public policies follow mechanically from voting procedures, and that political preferences result automatically from material position in the political economy, Acemoglu and Robinson conclude that forward-looking players submit to the brute facts of democratic politics. When exogenous factors shift bargainers's attributes, the bargainers obey the material structure of the political economy and make different choices for or against the empowerment of voters. As fixed givens generate compulsory preferences, and as preexisting forces create causal necessities, repeatable patterns and common paths of democratization result. Significant political implications follow from this vision of causal collective human agency: procedural democracy coupled to comparative statics yields a particularly "thin democracy." Pushed and shoved by its environment, democracy's "free and rational society" is severely constrained. As a causal methodology, comparative statics also yields the conclusion that countries couple thin democracy to a weak state.

Constructivism, a more recent paradigm to enter comparative politics, disparages procedural democracy's constitutionalism, institutionalism, and formalism. Preferring their "free and rational society" participatory and deliberative, constructivists seek a democracy in which local communities possess the collective agency to constitute self-governing politics that reach the national level. A discursive democracy's practices and performances, driven by the power of its ideas and words, allow citizens to enjoy the power of their social constructions. As they fashion social identities holding normative authority, citizens discover new patterns of politics and novel paths of democratization. The origins and outcomes of the democratic state are open-ended. Rather than focusing on the generative powers of the environment, constructivists thus follow Moore's dream and discover citizens who can liberate themselves from the exogenously binding factual causality of arbitrary external conditions. Lisa Wedeen's *Peripheral Visions: Publics, Power, and Performance in Yemen* therefore offers a different causal claim about democracy:

Even given seemingly unfavorable environments, for example a weak semi-authoritarian state emerging from civil war, discursive practices and performances, driven by the power of words and ideas, can allow citizens to construct deliberative democracy.

Constructivism's democracy-causality connection – call its vision of causal collective human agency "thick democracy" – thus involves the generative powers of democracy fashioning its own possibilities through endogenous chains of self-creating dynamics. Absent a focus on such state institutions as bureaucracies, courts, and parties, a thick democracy appears to be a weak state with a limited capability of imposing its will on a large and recalcitrant nation.

Does the best possible democracy manifest a "free and rational society," thereby maximizing human freedom and creativity? Or does the most feasible democracy "understand the forces" forging it, thereby appreciating its institutional grounding, recognizing its exogenous causal constraints, and accepting limits on political engineering? Acemoglu and Robinson and Wedeen tilt toward different horns of the dilemma raised by Moore. Other comparativists have suggested that a free and rational society requires a fit state, or one that navigates between a thin democracy determined exogenously and a thick democracy fashioning its own future. A third paradigm of politics has thus also been at the core of contemporary comparative politics. Channeling Marx and Weber through Moore, many comparativists study how different kinds of state-society relations are behind the historical development of the different kinds of state institutions that produce the different kinds of economic outcomes. In *State-Directed Development: Political Power and Industrialization in the Global Periphery*, Atul Kohli retains Moore's focus on patterns of state authority and alternative developmental pathways to the modern world. Kohli's typology involves three kinds of late-late developing states and their characteristic outcomes. In a cohesive-capitalist state, a top-down ruling coalition successfully organizes capitalism from above. Penetrating, controlling, and mobilizing society, such a state is capable of promoting economic development. In a neo-patrimonial state, personalistic authoritarian leaders, unconstrained by bureaucratic norms, fail to articulate clear state goals and never implement consistent public policies. Unable to penetrate society, the state is weak, corrupt, and predatory – and of course unable to spur economic development. A third type of state – fragmented multiclass – embodies the contradictions of a society that is both "free" and "rational." In this type of state accountable political leaders seek legitimacy by maximizing public support. However, constructing a broad class alliance, and thereby trying to satisfy the different goals of multiple constituencies, produces an inefficient and ineffective state:

Given a late-late developing state with a certain type of colonial experience, a broad multiclass coalition can produce a fragmented multiclass democracy that is unable to bring about economic development.

In fiercely competitive external environments, popular participation and democratic deliberation, says Kohli, are luxury goods. Given powerful military and economic rivals, managed democracies or authoritarian capitalisms can employ state-led networks to successfully tie single-minded ideological visions to command-and-control procedures. Kohli's focus on structural capacity or political power as a causal methodology thus yields an important conclusion: in the late-late developing world, the stronger the state the thinner the democracy but the greater the economic development. His focus on the state capacity's to do things – structure economics, manage society, and control politics – is the antithesis of Wedeen's vision of causal collective human agency lodged in a democratic society.

In sum, three social-scientific approaches express different norms of a "free and rational society" and advance different causal explanations of democracy's origins. Acemoglu and Robinson stress the comparative statics of procedural democracy, Wedeen the social construction of discursive democracy, and Kohli the colonial origins of fragmented multiclass democracy. It is easy to see a rationalist-culturalist-structuralist triangle emerging from Moore. Acemoglu and Robinson draw on a rationalist Moore: no bourgeoisie rationality (political coalitions), no democracy. Wedeen draws on a culturalist Moore: no bourgeoisie culture (national public sphere), no democracy. Kohli draws on a historical-institutional and state-society Moore: no bourgeoisie structures (civil society tied to political society), no democracy.

Charles Tilly's *Democracy* pairs another type of democracy with another type of causality. While Moore's work grows out of the twentieth century's world wars and great revolutions, Tilly's analysis addresses the twenty-first century's state breakdowns and civil wars. Tilly is thus concerned with people power and popular revolution, with dissident mobilization and rebel resistance. His problem situation of contentious politics (Tarrow 2011; Tilly and Tarrow 2007) involves challenges to the state from below. Tilly's contentious democracy is thus constituted by struggles among the networks of interest and identity claims mobilized by state construction. He argues that citizens of a state hold multiple ties and connections and that they engage in manifold interactions and transactions. Social relationships in political society unleash open-ended and dynamic mechanisms and processes that influence the accountability of rulers to the ruled. Studying how civil society organizations are empowered, he explores the rich and vibrant social capital that checks and limits state power. Tilly is also concerned with ethnicity and diversity: fundamentalist religious and nationalist movements that contest democratic paths of development. Tilly thus advocates a particular type of political order: ceaseless and perpetual contentious democracy. To study the messy social mechanisms behind this messy democracy's messy democratization and messy dedemocratization, he employs mixed theories and mixed methods.

In short, Tilly's theory of causal collective human agency involves a mobilized civil society engaged in protest and rebellion. Only contention, for example, participatory revolutionary politics and networked transnational activism, can create and sustain democracy. While endless battles against state power can achieve contentious democracy, states and regimes also result from the exogenous causal constraints that structure their contentious politics. A methodological focus on complex – contingent and dynamic – processes allows Tilly to vary environment and democracy simultaneously, and thereby to advance this causal claim:

> Given a particular state-building environment – its underlying political-economy structures of coercion, capital, and commitment and the exogenous shocks of revolution, conquest, confrontation, and colonization – specific mechanisms and processes – the integration trust networks into public politics, the insulation of public politics from categorical inequalities, and the subordination of autonomous power centers to public politics – can generate contentious democracy.

Tilly's jargon will be explained shortly. The important point for now is that his contentious democracy is a prudent compromise between factual and artifactual causation, or between decisive preexisting givens (as in Acemoglu and Robinson's tilt toward Moore's aim to "understand the forces") and reflexive human constructions (as in Wedeen's tilt toward Moore's hope for a "free and rational society"). Echoing Kohli, Tilly's ideal state is a "fit democracy" that adapts to and shapes the opportunities and constraints posed by its environment. However, Tilly turns Kohli's compromise on its head: strong states and thick democracies go hand in hand.

1.4. THE PARADIGMS: A ROAD MAP TO THE BOOK

Causal claims about democratic states thus disagree about democracy and about causality. After Moore wrote, comparativists developed several different models of democracy: democracy as a major bargain, agreement, or contract that results from a balance of power among classes and that establishes a thin democracy with a weak state (Acemoglu and Robinson's rational choice theory); democracy as quotidian discussions that construct everyday practices and local performances that guide a thick democracy and a weak state (Wedeen's constructivist theory); democracy as a state-society multiclass coalition that operates a thick democracy and a weak state (Kohli's state-society or state-capacity theory); and democracy as adversarial confrontations between citizens and the state that couple a thick democracy to a strong state (Tilly's contentious-politics theory). When bargains, discussions, coalitions, and struggles endure, democracy – procedural, discursive, fragmented, and contentious – becomes a self-reproducing political order. As comparativists pursued theories of the democratic state, they elaborated their explanatory programs's causal powers. Causal methodologists analyzed empirical aspects of the democratic state, such as conditions of possibility and contexts for change. Many alternative causal methodologies became popular: rational choice theorists studied the comparative statics of exogenous shifts in the causal forces that disturb equilibrium; constructivists examined the endogenous causal construction of social phenomena; state-society theorists investigated the causal structural capacity of class coalitions and the state; and contentious-politics theorists explored the complex – contingent and dynamic – mechanisms and processes that underlay causal social relations.

To study democratization, comparativists thus link normative theories of democracy with causal methodologies. The resulting paradigms or approaches are proposition-generating machines. Each produces a distinctive type of thick description and explanatory system that accounts for the origins of specific types of democratic states: rational choice theory's comparative statics produces exogenous propositions about the origins of procedural democracy (a thin democracy in a weak state); constructivism offers endogenous propositions about the sources of discursive democracy (a thick democracy in a weak state); state-capacity theory develops structural propositions about the historical causes of capitalist coalitional democracy (a thin democracy in a strong state); and contentious-politics theory yields process propositions about the bases of contentious democracy (a thick democracy in a strong state).

This book investigates the connections between four causal methodologies and four normative theories that address the democratic state. Comparativists nowadays think of themselves as pragmatic pluralists, mixing methods and theories as needed, and drawing on Moore as required. Nevertheless, in the current scholarly division of labor, causal methodology and democratic-state theory have become compartmentalized research traditions. Narrowly bound and tightly constrained, the traditions seem designed to avoid overlapping – and hence big and messy – questions. Yet comparativists couple the kinds of democratic state they theorize to the kinds of causality they deploy.

- Comparative-statics methodology discovers a thin (procedural) democracy and a weak state in which the environment has the power and self-governing democracy loses its freedom.
- Social-constructivist methodology finds a thick (discursive) democracy and a weak state in which democracy has the freedom to overcome the power of its environment, but the institutions required to implement its will are undefined.
- Structural-capacity methodology unearths a thin (multiclass coalition) democracy and a strong state that is fit enough to shape its

TABLE 2. *The Moore Curve*

		Causal Methodology		
		Internal	Mixed	External
	Thick	Wedeen		
Democratic			Tilly	
Theory	Mixed			
			Acemoglu and Robinson	
	Thin			Kohli

environment and thus has the power to produce economic development.

• Contingent-process methodology locates a thick (fit) democracy and a strong state in which democratic freedoms take advantage of environmental opportunities to overcome constraints.

Comparativists who advance causal claims about democratic states therefore ultimately wrestle with Barrington Moore's ought/is dilemma of democratization. Their work reveals an elective affinity between the choice of a causal methodology and the choice of a theory of the democratic state. The Moore Curve – the more external the causal methodology, the thinner the democratic theory – governs democratization studies (Table 2).

I.5. THEMES AND THESES

If Barrington Moore were here today, he would probably respond that the point is to change social science, not merely to describe and explain it. Comparing explanatory programs should spur critical and creative investigations of causal claims. The elective affinities of normative theories of the democratic state and research methodologies of causal analysis can indeed be the basis of a creative art of discovery. This book offers explanation sketches that allow comparativists to identify the generative principles behind paradigms of politics that can be mixed and matched. Comparativists can use the sketches to develop innovative avenues of inquiry that could unearth new and important causal claims about democratic states. My own sympathies lay with Tilly. Tilly hits the sweet spot between structure and action, the golden mean of working within constraints while reflecting upon one's preferences and beliefs. Contentious democracy is thus the best entrance into the supermarket of ideas. Comparativists can then pivot to procedural democracy's claims about the grand exogenous structuring of politics and subsequently move to discursive democracy's local creative dynamics. The structural capacity of fragmented multiclass democracy can be investigated next. All dyadic comparisons can eventually be drawn. Similar efforts, for example reconciling rational choice theory with ethnographies of social construction, or accounts of causal mechanisms with narratives of the historical development of capable state institutions, are also available.

The book thus endorses Tilly's contentious-politics approach as a starting point. Tilly examines how people fight for democracy. He believes that the struggle is worthwhile and the goal attainable. By persuading comparativists to study how citizens experience democracy and causality, Tilly indeed makes the best case for democracy as a valuable political order. In addition, by showing comparativists how to study collective agency as the causal force behind democratization, Tilly's analysis reveals how the power and freedom of collectivities, as well as the limitations and constraints on their agency, are connected to the affinities of democratic theories and causal methodologies. Finally, by mixing big-P Paradigms, and big-M Methods, his work also best stimulates studies that evaluate the political performance of regimes.

The concluding chapter therefore uses Tilly as the springboard and the others as sounding boards to develop a positive approach to democratization studies. The way forward is to begin with ideas about contentious politics and explore collective agency as the causal force behind democratization. All the comparativists studied here indeed begin with the moral facts of causal collective human agency. In Acemoglu and Robinson's view, as lower-class voters pursue economic redistribution and upper-class elites seek political stability, the contending social forces turn autocracy into procedural democracy. When actors talk in the public sphere, Wedeen sees the possibility that their discourses become the actualities of democratic performances. Kohli's state-class coalitions have developmental aims and accordingly seek state power in a thin democracy. Tilly's dissidents in civil society aim to reform and revolutionize governments, thereby thickening democracy and strengthening the state. Collective moral agency is thus a central theme of each text. In other words, the comparativists studied here advance approaches to causal collective human agency that address norms/facts or ought/is questions about democracy in a causal world. Comparative politics indeed needs the internal perspectives of participants – people's own normative self-understandings of democracy – to explain democratization and dedemocratization.

Comparativists also advance external perspectives on collective agency, studying how the environment offers opportunities to citizens and poses constraints on people's aims. By mixing internal and external perspectives, the authors come to defend their particular versions of democracy in the face of their empirical analyses. Hence, the freedom and the power of collective agency are the core dilemmas of democracy and causality. While citizens in a democratic state seek freedom from interference and the power to fashion their lives, comparativists locate causes that are free from obstruction and that have the power to affect outcomes.

Moving forward, offering solutions and not only characterizing problems, the book therefore advances five constructive themes elaborated into twelve theses. First, while the texts examined here have strengths and weaknesses that can serve as complements and substitutes, comparativists should begin with Tilly's contentious-politics approach. The best way to advance democratization studies is to use Tilly to study the causal agency of individuals, groups, and democracies.

Thesis 1. Individual and Agency. Adopt an internal perspective on the self-understandings of agents struggling for democracy: individuals hold values and beliefs, are moved by intentions and motives, and make strong evaluations and political judgments.

Thesis 2. Collectivity and Agency. Demonstrate how collective human agency, or the freedom and power of actors in the face of complexity and ambiguity, results from the unintended and unwanted, unpredicted and unexpected, and unstable and incoherent consequences of their interactions.

Thesis 3. Democracy and Agency. Defend contentious democracy as the last best hope for a free and rational society, because it encourages pragmatic critical reason, creative problem solving, and political adaptability.

Second, the book urges comparativists to pair the three types of collective agency with an exploration of three corresponding moral dilemmas: ought/is, freedom/power, and democracy/causality.

Thesis 4. Ought and Is. Reconcile normative commitments with causal claims.

Thesis 5. Freedom and Power. Reconcile group agency with causal social structure.

Thesis 6. Democracy and Causality. Reconcile democratic theory with causal methodology.

Third, the recent focus on causal analysis should not push big-P Paradigms and big-M Methodology from the center of comparative politics. Theory and method offer creative heuristics that can stimulate studies of democratization.

Thesis 7. Big-P Paradigms and Comparative Politics. Use paradigms as creative heuristics.

Thesis 8. Big-M Methodology and Comparative Politics. Use methods as creative heuristics.

Fourth, while the normative and empirical ideas coming from a research school indeed bear a family resemblance, recognizing the elective affinities of theory and method leads to its undoing.

Comparativists who play with research schools can turn the connections between prescriptive and descriptive approaches to democratization into creative tensions. As comparative politics becomes a mixed-theory and mixed-method field, democratic theorists and causal methodologists turn into allies rather than adversaries.

Thesis 9. Research Schools and Elective Affinities. Recognize that the ostensibly different ideas coming from a research school bear a family resemblance, thereby appreciating the elective affinity between democratic theories and causal methodologies: the more external the causal methodology, the thinner the democratic theory (The Moore Curve).

Thesis 10. Research Schools and Creative Tensions. Recognize that the ostensibly different ideas coming from a research school contain creative tensions between democratic theory and causal methodology that can be used as heuristics to energize comparative politics.

Finally, as comparativists develop the observable implications of different methods and theories, creative play with paradigms must be constrained by an examination of the empirics of regime fitness. Because democracies operate in the midst of environmental constraints, comparativists should study pragmatic questions about political power and democratic performance: in building a democratic state, which democracy under which conditions is best, and how might it be achieved? In returning to this core concern of the 1960s, today's comparative politics can renew the field's past and strengthen its future. As comparativists address Barrington Moore's ought/is dilemma of causal collective human agency in democratization, they can come to understand how alternative modernities challenge liberalism, how state building occurs amid contentious world politics, and how institutions arise, persist, and change.

Thesis 11. Democracy, Causality, and Power. Recognize how power is central to democracy and causality.

Thesis 12. Democracy and Performance. Address the key practical problem of democratic performance: in building a democratic state, which democracy under which conditions is best, and how might it be achieved?

In sum, the inspiration for the book is my dissatisfaction with democratization studies for slighting the ought/is problem. I express my strongest admiration for Tilly's placement of contentious politics at the core of democratization studies. I then take the best from the other authors. I borrow Acemoglu and Robinson's use of rational choice methodology, Wedeen's focus on constructing national identities from local groupings, and Kohli's concern with viable state strategies for development. Learning from these seminal texts, I suggest that collective agency is the causal force behind democratization, that democracy and causality are about the freedom and power of collective agency, that placing big-P Paradigms and big-M Methodology at the core of comparative inquiry creatively energizes the study of democratization, and that in building a democratic state, the core question is which democracy under which conditions is best.

1.6. THE CHAPTERS

Part I explores rationalism and constructivism. Chapter 2 begins with two democratic theories, procedural democracy and discursive democracy, and then analyzes Acemoglu and Robinson's and Wedeen's causal theories. Rational reconstructions of generative principles reveal how comparativists use their methodologies to think and to work. Chapter 3 compares two causal methodologies, comparative statics and constructivism. Chapter 4 combines the theoretical domain of democracy and the methodological domain of causality to explore the problems of thin and thick democracy. Part II explores state-society and contentious politics approaches to democratization. Chapter 5 discusses Kohli's practical compromise: a fit state with the structural capacity to generate economic development. Chapter 6 discusses how a democratic theory – Tilly's adversarial or contentious democracy – coupled to a causal methodology – complex contingent processes – pragmatically studies fit democracy. Part III shows the final fruits of exploring the ought/is dilemmas of Acemoglu and Robinson, Wedeen, Kohli, and Tilly. Chapter 7 explores the problem of agency, Chapter 8 the question of paradigms, and Chapter 9 the centrality of power and performance to comparative politics.

This book therefore examines four contemporary comparativists who address the key questions Moore bequeathed to contemporary comparative politics: in the competitive international environment facing the global south, which alternative modernities challenge liberalism? How do social forces contend, democratic states arise, and policy regimes matter? And what are the origins, operations, and outcomes of state institutions? In examining the answers to these questions, the book connects the current interest in causality among methodologists with political theorists' long-standing concerns about the democratic state. Focusing on four important texts allows the book to explore how paradigms of politics link theories of the democratic state to causal methodologies.

Acemoglu and Robinson display a love of the paradoxes of choice and bargaining, Wedeen a love of the endogeneity of dialogue and construction, Kohli a love of the historical development of state capacity, and Tilly a love of the dynamic mechanisms and processes behind the struggle for democracy. Their excitement is contagious. The authors so effectively demonstrate the power of their theoretical and methodological approaches that their books are Kuhnian "exemplars" (Kuhn 1970). These "killer apps" exemplify the principal contemporary causal approaches to the democratic state. Most important, they illustrate how post-Moore comparative politics can place normative theory and causal analysis, and big-P Paradigms and big-M Methodology, at the center of the field.

PART I

RATIONALISM AND CONSTRUCTIVISM

2

Where Democracy Is To Be Found and Why

Though Przeworski et al. (2000) found that wealth is the principal requirement for remaining a democracy, other comparativists have found that there is no one path to democracy, nor one manner in which all democracies operate, nor one outcome that all produce. Democracies are thus highly variable, inviting investigation into various causal questions. This chapter connects the different understandings of democracy to diverse causal stories.

2.1. WHERE IS DEMOCRACY TO BE FOUND?

If "democracy" is not a single type of politics, what is the thing called "democracy" that concerns Acemoglu and Robinson and what is the other thing called "democracy" that concerns Wedeen? How exactly do the authors think these things work?

2.1.1. Procedural Democracy

According to Acemoglu and Robinson, regular voting and fair elections lead the government in a procedural democracy to be responsive and accountable to its citizens. Elections, in turn, are driven by redistributive class politics: political preferences result automatically from material position in the political economy, and public policies flow mechanically from voting procedures.

Because democracy entails bargaining over grand questions of
political economy, the key controversy surrounding democratization is political inclusion. Enfranchisement of citizens is
achieved coercively: election-oriented agents in civil society and
in the government negotiate, using threats and promises backed
by force. Democratic regimes are therefore equilibrium institutions that
aggregate coercive bargaining relations into stable balances-of-
power. Many virtues result. First, because it creates incentives
for politicians and parties to aggregate citizen preferences, to
represent various constituencies and to serve the public good,
Schumpeterian competition for power checks and constrains
elites. Second, competition buttresses constitutionalism – a public
sphere of laws and institutions that secure the rights, liberties, and
freedoms required for electoral participation. Third, although
people disagree about the good life, holding widely different conceptions of what is worthwhile, equilibrium procedural democracy can maintain political order by constituting a minimalist
bargain about the good polity. The equilibrium state is thus an
inclusive and neutral baseline institution that allows private lives
to develop in families, organizations, and markets. Procedural
democracy is consequently instrumental for managing pluralism,
containing conflict, preventing violence, supporting legitimacy,
and assuring stability. Finally, by encouraging civic peace and
restraining civil war, equilibrium procedural democracy promotes
economic prosperity.

2.1.2. Deliberative Democracy

Yemen? Foreign travelers have often discovered democracies that
are attractive but puzzling. Alexis de Tocqueville ([1850] 1969)
thought democracy in America bewildering, just as Norway's
democracy confounded Harry Eckstein (1966) and democracy in
the Netherlands perplexed Arend Lijphart (1975). If Acemoglu and
Robinson find the slow growth of democracy in England a causal
puzzle, the very existence of democracy in Yemen is a causal puzzle
for Lisa Wedeen.

Yemen's weak state is the source of the problem. Recently emerging from civil war and newly unified from two parts, Yemen's national political institutions are underdeveloped. Quasiauthoritarian or semiautocratic, the country barely holds together. Its citizenry is heavily armed, and public authorities are often unable to control violence and provide security. Yemen's fragmentation makes it appear one step from state breakdown and internal war, the typical fates of weak sovereignties.

Though a weak semiauthoritarian state emerging from civil war, Yemen nevertheless displays important features of democracy. "[P]eaceful, adversarial politics" (Wedeen, p. 2) and "a wide array of critical newspapers, and a plethora of political parties" (Wedeen, p. 2) can be found. "[G]eneral political battles are waged on local, intimate levels" (Wedeen, p. 47). These everyday discursive performances constitute local experiential practices of democracy. For example, qāt chews, which are discussion groups organized around the chewing of a mild stimulant, help fashion minipublics. Yemen's weak state thus offers nonstate actors the political space for public discussion. Enclaves of lively, vigorous, and open communication under its semiauthoritarian regime encourages popular discourse. A mobilized local public sphere thus allows Yemenis to enact and perform democracy. Wedeen therefore suggests that ordinary citizens in a semidictatorship can employ long-standing local institutions like qāt chews to deliberate collectively about the civic issues important to their lives. Social dialogue and public performance transforms preferences and beliefs, contributing to the manufacture of the public good. Political participation and public activism allows ordinary citizens to work together and contest existing forms of power. As the political process proceeds, citizens create new forms of commonality and new patterns of sociality, thereby thickening democracy. Wedeen (p. 18) concludes that Yemen's "deliberative democracy in the absence of contested elections" demonstrates that even "fragile authoritarian states (with weak capacities to generate national loyalty)" can provide "opportunities for widespread political activism and critical, public discussion" (p. 19).

Wedeen's democracy is therefore deliberative democracy: through discursive and agonistic debate, ordinary people meet, act together, and perform publicly in lived, every day, local experiences. As she (p. 3) puts it, "in the absence of fair and free elections, democratic persons are nevertheless produced through quotidian practices of deliberation. These acts are not embellishments of democracy independently existing. They are the thing itself." Wedeen's critical point is that these conversations are constitutive of democracy: "the political activity of discussing and deliberating is part of what a democracy does" (p. 141) and "part of what democracy means" (p. 142). Put otherwise, as discourse helps fashion preferences and as participation helps construct beliefs, public citizenship creates a shared life of common purpose and mutual action. Deliberative democracy is thus not only instrumental for other public goods; it itself is the common good.

Wedeen's (p. 119) fieldwork in fact reveals "qāt chews as sites of democratic practice in their own right." The "kinds of critical practices of deliberation taking place within public spheres," such as in qāt chews, turn out to "be intrinsically democratic" (p. 119) in several ways. First, deliberative social gatherings are part of Yemen's active civil society of charitable associations, protest movements, intellectual conferences, mosque sermons, village and "tribal" cooperatives, critical press, and journalist syndicates. Second, participants in these public gatherings "share information about political events" (Wedeen, p. 114), increasing citizen awareness and common understandings and thereby influencing the "meaning" and "significance" of democracy. Third, "qāt chews are democratic in substantive representational terms – less because they actually enable citizen control than because they facilitate a kind of political participation" (Wedeen, pp. 119–20). Fourth, deliberations produce the agreement and consensus that lends moral legitimacy to public policies. Fifth, deliberations contribute to "political self-fashioning" (Wedeen, p. 126) because "political subject formation … takes place through the practice of discussion" (Wedeen, p. 140). Hence, "the very activity of deliberating in public contributes to the formation of democratic persons" (Wedeen, p. 105). For those who remain skeptical of the equation of democracy with discussion, Wedeen adds one final observation: "actual policy decisions get made" (Wedeen, p. 113). Public gatherings promote regime responsiveness, or the responsibility of the rulers to the ruled. The discussions involve "negotiating power relationships between elites and constituencies in which elites are held responsible and are required to be responsive to the needs of the participants by guaranteeing goods and services or by advocating on behalf of the village, electoral district, or local group" (Wedeen, p. 114).

Procedural democracy is not inspiring, constitutionalism not exciting, and the rule of law not edifying. By demonstrating that even in the absence of a procedurally democratic regime qāt chews can be a vital element in a vibrant network of democratic practices and performances, Wedeen offers two powerful critiques of so-called "realist" democracy. First, the procedural apparatus of electoral democracy and representative government – political parties and elections – can legitimate economic unfairness, hide social injustice, and protect political authoritarianism. However, public citizenship and civic engagement, even in authoritarian systems, can create the social capital, civic assets, and collective capacity that empower people to become significant counterweights to state power. And local populist democracy, even under authoritarianism, can overcome national power structures and hierarchical institutions, allowing people to shape their lives. She foreshadows the Arab Spring.

Wedeen emphasizes a second shortcoming of procedural democracy: its focus on policy making at the peak of national politics and in the center of political power. While procedural democrats assume that the state is the guardian of economic well-being, pluralistic tolerance, and ethical community, a state-centered focus on market, society, and nation in fact narrows democracy. Much politics and problem solving occurs elsewhere. Local democracy thus involves bottom-up processes. Ongoing social interactions and community relationships allow citizens to turn public spaces, civil-society sites, political spheres, and discourse domains into opportunities for self-organized nonstate governance. As engaged citizens construct their local communities, they interface with the outside world, becoming embedded in complex multilevel structures of governance. Vertical and horizontal political orders begin to overlap. Given the limitations of procedural democracy, what explains its popularity among comparativists? Wedeen suggests that a Schumpeterian focus suits the broad crossnational coding of contested or competitive elections: "adoption of a thin, or minimalist, definition is, in part, a way of facilitating coding in the interests of scientific testing" (Wedeen, p. 110). In her (p. 112) view, the costs overwhelm the benefits: "As Wittgenstein shows us, the point is not that a methodologically driven or ideologically motivated definition of a concept, such as democracy as contested elections, is wrong, but that the assumptions underlying such an analysis miss something important about what we mean by the term." Hence, "this commitment to the scientific method comes at the cost of ignoring much of what is political and important about the practices of democracy" (Wedeen, p. 110). More specifically, by ignoring "democratic phenomena that exist outside of electoral and other formal organizational confines" (Wedeen, p. 3), by slighting "initiative, spontaneity, self-fashioning, revelation, ingenuity, action, creativity – which occurs *outside the domain of electoral outcomes*" (2004: 280, emphasis in original), the procedural approach to democracy "deflects attention from important forms of democratic practice taking place in authoritarian circumstances" (Wedeen, p. 105). Wedeen (2004: 286) thus elsewhere maintains that "there are different sites of the enactment of democracy, and a strong democracy needs them all." She (p. 145) concludes that a focus on procedural democracy "may be less helpful in thinking through why a regime like Yemen's is as democratic as it is in both electoral and substantive representational terms ... or in identifying vibrant forms of debate and disagreement that produce creative, contestatory publics in the absence of fair and free elections."

In sum, Wedeen shows comparativists who study democracy around the world what is at stake in Yemen. Her approach should not be confused with what the comparative politics of the 1960s called the Zanzibar ploy. She is not saying "things don't work that way in Yemen." Rather than setting Yemen up as an anomaly, Wedeen has more ambitious goals. She shows Yemen to be a perplexing case of democracy because it raises definitional issues that force comparativists to see if their concepts work. If comparativists focus on hierarchical state bureaucracies, Jacobin-Leninist national revolutions, and procedurally democratic institutions they miss the democracy occurring below their radar screen. They will not see a qāt-chew democracy, where a heterogeneous group of local citizens engage in face-to-face relations that help unify their nation and beget the spontaneous cooperation that leads to the self-management of communal affairs.

Comparativists have a long tradition of arguing that "[d]emocracy needs to be reconceived as something other than a form of government" (Wolin 1996: 43). Tocqueville's ([1850] 1969) community, Habermas's (1989) public sphere of discourse, Ostrom's (1990) self-organizing governance systems, Mansbridge's (1980) participatory forms of democracy, and Tilly's (2007) embedded trust networks rely on the social capital inherent in civil society to forge the social networks supporting self-help organizations. Nonstate religious organizations – monastic groups, Quaker communities, Israeli Kibbutzim, messianic communes – conduct experiments in cooperative living. Habyarimana, Humphreys, Posner, and Weinstein (2009) are concerned with local governments providing local public goods, and Tsai (2007) with local governments lobbying the national government for those goods. Comparativists also have a long tradition of studying such subnational institutions as free cities, neighborhood associations, town councils, rural parishes, provincial estates, and local parliaments. Rather than being rooted in civic culture – a set of ideas that float free of agents – democracy is rooted in spheres, places, and sites of communicative practices located outside of formal government institutions. In short, Wedeen views democracy through the lens of society.

2.2. TWO CAUSAL THEORIES OF DEMOCRACY

Different explanandums, different explanans. With their different dependent variables in place, the authors draw different explanation sketches.

2.2.1. Acemoglu and Robinson

Acemoglu and Robinson begin with Barrington Moore's core problem: class struggle over regime construction. The basic storyline about the origins of democracy is familiar: British industrialization advanced, economic hardships happened, and grievances escalated. Coercive bargaining between regime and opposition then proceeded: working classes mobilized, dissident organizations formed, riots and strikes occurred, and violence and repression followed. A solution was finally reached: political-economic elites conceded and enfranchisement under procedural democracy resulted. The upshot was that Britain avoided the sort of revolution that occurred in France, Russia, and China.

Overall, the picture that emerges from British political history is clear. Beginning in 1832, when Britain was governed by the relatively rich, primarily rural aristocracy, strategic concessions were made during an eighty-six-year period to adult men. These concessions were aimed at incorporating the previously disenfranchised into politics because the alternative was seen to be social unrest, chaos, and possibly revolution. ... Although the pressure of the disenfranchised was more influential in some reforms than others, and other factors undoubtedly played a role, the threat of social disorder was the driving force behind the creation of democracy in Britain. (Acemoglu and Robinson, p. 4)

The puzzle, of course, is why a nondemocratic elite pursuing state building would accept mass suffrage under procedural democracy. Here is Acemoglu and Robinson's causal story.

   1. Domestic class groups, with particular preexisting interests and identities, beliefs and ideas, and resources and capabilities, are the source of politics.

2. Because democracy allows the people to rule, and because classes vote their material interests, elections have consequences. Under full enfranchisement, the democratic class struggle results in promajority policies that redistribute wealth and income from the rich minority to the poor majority. In other words, procedural democracy is inherently promajority and propoor, and therefore systematically antielite and antirich.

3. Material preferences over wealth along with beliefs about elections generate political preferences over regimes: the rich (poor) prefer resource allocations under dictatorship (democracy). A Schumpeterian dichotomy between democracy and nondemocracy consequently implies that while rich elites prefer dictatorship to procedural democracy, the poor masses prefer procedural democracy to dictatorship (Acemoglu and Robinson, pp. 17–18). Put otherwise, the rich minority elite and the poor majority citizens hold different material interests, and hence prefer different governmental institutions for allocating political power and ultimately distributing economic resources.

4. Competing models of government – democracy and dictatorship – attract competing social classes. As material preferences over regimes generate a political struggle between self-conscious democrats and reflective autocrats, the rich and the poor articulate different claims about governance systems. The struggle over demands for economic distribution thus induces jockeying over political institutions.

5. Coercive bargaining – threats and promises backed by force – occurs. The dominant rich, democratic-resisting, class battles the subordinate poor, democratic-demanding, class. On one side, the majority brings its de facto political power to the bargaining table. Disenfranchised classes thus mobilize their available resources. The majority, hoping to democratize via enfranchisement, threaten the elite's dictatorship with protests and rebellions, strikes and insurgencies. On the other side, the rich employ repression. However, the

elite fears that their coercion could foment a mass revolution that forces them from power.

6. Because popular insurrection could impose great costs on the minority, the governing elite realizes that it must react strategically. One strategy is accommodation. Short-term policy concessions might involve, for example, some income redistribution. Because the majority knows that once the social unrest subsides the dictatorial elite will withdraw its concessions, the governing elite cannot contain popular upheaval with short-term policy relief. Quick-fix promises are ex-post unenforceable and hence not credible commitments. Elites can shirk or renege on their promises, and hence they must find another strategic response to mass unrest (Acemoglu and Robinson, pp. 136–42).

7. To contain the majority's potential for demonstrations and riots, the elite can also employ force. However, government repression entails considerable short-term and long-run costs to the elite. Questions of efficiency (e.g., economic growth) thereby affect struggles over equity (e.g., income distribution).

8. A third governmental response strategy is enfranchisement under procedural democracy. A transfer of political power from the minority to the majority offers the poor a credible commitment to sustainable promajority redistributive policies. More effective at forestalling revolution than noncredible policy concessions, less costly to elites than deadly repression, procedural democracy becomes the state-building compromise. As Acemoglu and Robinson (p. 349) put it, "there was a sufficient threat of revolution in predemocratic Britain and the elites could not defuse those pressures without democratization. They also did not find it beneficial to use repression to prevent democratization." The compromise can work: by threatening revolution, the disenfranchised poor in an autocratic regime can turn their current de facto political power into future de jure political power; by democratizing, the rich can avoid political and economic instability.

9. The extension of suffrage under procedural democracy is accompanied by additional intertemporal political contracts. By monopolizing the upper house of the legislature, the military, the courts, the banks, the corporations, and so on, traditional governing elites who enfranchise the poor can continue to dominate the polity.

10. Political crises and moments of social transformation can eventually stabilize into systems of rule. If democratizing elites lack the incentives to mount a coup, procedural democracy consolidates and institutionalizes.

Acemoglu and Robinson's causal story deepens liberal-individualistic theories of democracy. Compare it, for example, to theories that simply claim that socioeconomic status (SES) influences voting. In several ways, Acemoglu and Robinson offer a more macro- or system-level perspective.

First, they recognize social class. Inequalities among social classes drive democratic governance. Second, they understand institutional structures. Institutions confer comparative advantages that determine public policy. Third, they appreciate the possibilities of revolution. Building on the Tocquevillian fear of a *bourgeoisie* overpowered by *citoyen*, they theorize about how the mass politics of *classes dangereux* could lead to mob rule, or how the poor might use political disorder to make a violent revolution that confiscates the wealth of the rich. Fourth, Acemoglu and Robinson place the coercive power of the state to redistribute wealth at the core of democratic politics. Following Moore (1978: 473), they recognize that elite repression greases political agreement: "Suppression prepared the way for negotiation and bargaining. For the weaker contestants gradualism was not the virtue in its own right that it became for the dominant classes; it was a virtue forced upon them by necessity."

Most important, Acemoglu and Robinson view politics contractually. Democratization is at base a struggle over the franchise. Democratic politics is the institutionalized wager or gamble that you could lose an election but that your opponents will only govern for a time. The political equilibrium is therefore stable because elections are unstable. The problem of establishing a legitimate opposition is thus the problem of alternating in office via elections. A democratic equilibrium involves mutual guarantees and restraints between ins and outs. A workable agreement between classes that reforms the predemocratic system, electoral democracy grants power to the poor and provides security for the rich. Harmonizing interests, democracy is thus a pragmatic and practical compromise. Acemoglu and Robinson thus offer an interesting twist on liberal thinking. The conventional wisdom holds that while democracy resolves social conflict and then stabilizes a nonviolent balance of power, democratization upsets the existing autocratic balance of power and thereby generates violent social conflict. Acemoglu and Robinson argue that while democracy involves social conflict between the rich and the poor, democratization can immunize autocratic politics against violent social conflict and thus create a harmonious balance of political power.

Finally, Acemoglu and Robinson overturn Marx's idea that capitalistic inequality and democratic governance are incompatible. Because the two can be married and the resulting state stable, majority voting becomes the opiate of the masses and economic inequality turns out to be the unexpected ground of democratic stability. Rather than forging a Marxian raw deal, class protagonists can fashion a rational bargain in the collective interest.

While Acemoglu and Robinson have told a telling tale, one wonders if things are always like that. Schmitter (2007: 326) suggests that the elite's fear of the masses – the story's driving component – is socially constructed and hence historically contingent:

We have since learned that democratizing is easier, yet also much less consequential in socioeconomic terms, that we used to think. Today, the non-elite groups that historically struggled for democracy make compromises where they accept a great deal less than they would have in the past, perhaps because of previous failures and a process of collective learning. As a result, inequitable systems of property rights survive many transitions to democracy without a scratch. And in some cases, for example, in Eastern Europe, income inequality has even gotten worse – deliberately worse – after democratization. So, democratizing is easier today precisely because it's less consequential. This is not terribly heartening. It's not what the people who struggled for democracy had expected. They compromised and accepted maybe even their third best alternative, because they had learned that going for the first best option by pushing immediately for socioeconomic redistribution can bring disaster.

The door is open for an approach that is completely different.

2.2.2. Wedeen

Holding another conception of democracy, Wedeen offers an alternative causal explanation of its origins. Given that most comparativists are unfamiliar with the subtle and complex set of mechanisms that underlie her constructivist approach, more than soundbites are needed. Allowing Wedeen to speak for herself will help fashion an explanation sketch with content and substance.

1. Meanings (concepts) are neither natural nor inevitable ways of conceiving and classifying social objects. While Sancho-Panza can get a laugh by asking who invented sleep – it seems natural and normal, and hence has always been there – constructivists maintain that classifications, and hence distinctions among classes, arise discursively. Without the words that give humans the ability to talk about a thing, the thing does not exist as an experience in consciousness. Concepts are thus artificial inventions of language, historically positioned ways of thinking and talking that situated agents use to address problem situations.

2. Collectivities are embedded in the relational categories of language: "group identifications exist in relation to other group identifications. In the U.S. context, for example, we may say that there is really no such thing as blackness independent of whiteness" (Wedeen, p. 150). Groups are thus neither objective nor natural but rather contingent and constructed with respect to one another: "categories ... exist within distinct political orders. These orders are themselves reproduced and maintained, in part, through category-based knowledge" (Wedeen, p. 150).

Categories therefore construct groups: "Categories are not groups, but they do make groups thinkable and legible, and indeed help constitute groups as objects available for self-identification" (Wedeen, p. 170).

3. Because group classifications are manufactured logics – structural idioms for managing and organizing the world – "Borders are by definition artificial, artifacts of historical events, power relationships, and political considerations" (Wedeen, p. 37). Rather than real, boundaries between groups are thus imaginary.

4. The existence of conceptual boundaries lead people to reify, objectify, naturalize, and fetishize groups. A group's exterior environment can thus appear alien, hostile, and threatening.

5. A human construction, classification becomes a conceptual iron cage: the way we talk about X produces rigidities of thought about X. When objections arise, classifications provoke debates about the group boundaries that, in turn, are behind the classifications.

6. Actors and their identities are similarly artifactual constructions of discourse. For example, "elites who write nationalist tracts or are represented in them do not somehow exist outside of the conditions that have enabled their emergence as elites. Rather, elites and ordinary citizens are coformed in a discursive context, in which the language and symbols involved are continually being both absorbed and created anew" (Wedeen, p. 64). Social entities are thus the results of human powers and the products of human action. Rules and practices are historical objects, and nominal universals names for clusters of particulars sharing historical contiguity.

7. Interests and ideas are also constructed: "interests are no less historical or 'constructed' than are ... ideas, and they are constructed in a critical sense in tandem with ideas. What counts as an interest will be mediated through the worlds of meaning making within which people act" (Wedeen, p. 56). Because "ongoing strategic concerns

operate under broader meaning-making conditions, which help determine what counts as a strategy or concern" (Wedeen, p. 55), "[t]he interplay of political interests and semiotic circumstances makes attempts to isolate instrumental (or purportedly 'material') motivations from identity-derived or identity-aspirational ('ideational') ones" . . . problematic (Wedeen, p. 56). Rather than interests coming first and discourses second, interests and discourses are thus mutually coconstructed: "many studies also regard discourses as epiphenomenal, as somehow outside of the material interests that actually determine solidarities and conflict. But material interests might be fruitfully viewed not as objective criteria but as being discursively produced: in other words, what counts as a material interest is mediated through our language about what 'interest' means and what the material is" (Wedeen, p. 183).

8. Constructions – actors, and their associated interests, identities, and ideas – present themselves to others. Presence, not contaminated by anything – grounds, foundations, or preconditions – outside of itself expresses itself in the instant of time that separates past and future. The performance, without historic or contextual entanglements, conveys an impression to an audience. The audience interprets the performance much as they would understand a theatrical play. The spectacle appears as tragedy, comedy, drama, and so on.

9. Social constructions are path dependent. Actors, and their associated interests, identities, and ideas, become historically sticky: "Such categories may have long, enduring histories or they may be of more recent origin. They are rarely fabricated out of thin air" (Wedeen, p. 170).

10. As citizens participate in everyday performative practices, they disseminate ritualistic public enactments that help stabilize categories of thought and action. Routines of theatre and spectacle thus contain symbols and signs that "disseminate category-based knowledge about people,

places, and things" (Wedeen, p. 176). For example,
"When scholars or on-the-ground protagonists invoke
terms such as 'the Zaydis' they are also calling these
groups into existence" (Wedeen, p. 170). Another example: "poetry worked as a performative, summoning into
being nationalists by evincing the commonalities that
could create them" (Wedeen, p. 48). More generally, language, custom, and dress are constitutive of groups,
because they make various identifications – nation, piety
group, and democracy – seem thinkable and desirable,
natural, and permanent.

11. The institutionalization of categories therefore occurs
through a dialectic of discursive group categories and
everyday local practices that occur "under particular historical and strategic circumstances" (Wedeen, p. 170).
Consequently, "categories and the material practices
instantiating them operate dialectically, separable ultimately neither from each other nor from group formation
itself" (Wedeen, p. 170).

12. The institutionalization of categories also occurs
through a dialectic of (material) institutions and (ideational) discourses: "Discourses and institutions are
defined and generated in reference to each other"
(Wedeen, p. 49). Because institutions and discourses
reciprocally determine each other, they "can come into
conflict, both conceptually in their meanings and causally in the world, so that the only way of handling such
material is by considering their analytic synthesis – that
is, by maintaining an overview that includes each without stifling the conflict or denying the logical incompati-
bilities" (Wedeen, p. 49).

13. Because constructions made are constructions believed, the
imagined does not remain imaginary. Artificial but stabilized category-based knowledge has real and important
consequences: "classificatory systems help determine the
contours of group membership, the self-understandings of
actors, the mobilization strategies of leaders, and the

political claims of citizens" (Wedeen, p. 177). The thinking and imagining that occurs through categories are responsible for the production, construction, and constitution of objects "because language and other symbolic systems both organize and exemplify the conceptual universe through which action ... takes place" (Wedeen, p. 184). Language thereby creates and generates, shapes and molds, experience. The meanings on which we act (re)make the social world.

14. Because discussion groups, for example qāt chews, contribute to "political subject formation" (Wedeen, p. 11) they thereby contribute to democracy. During discussions, people share "the experience of knowing about and participating in a common political project" (Wedeen, p. 41). As they "disseminate category-based knowledge about people, places, and things" (Wedeen, p. 176), local debates and everyday discussions can fix imaginations on democracy. Life imitates art. The fate of the nation – also a discursive construct – is wrapped up with the fate of its democracy.

Wedeen's essentialist foil, which could well be Acemoglu and Robinson, maintains that a group "exists outside of the historical conditions and contexts that allow these categories to make sense – and that permit the interpretive communities they index to thrive" (Wedeen, p. 157). Focusing on actors as archetypical structures – abstract, ideal, and transcendental – that display teleological development, Acemoglu and Robinson study actors as the protagonists of history. Groups are the keys to democratization, and their agency appears as categories professing mini-theories of causation. Terms such as "urban rebellion," "Kurdish protest," "class conflict," and "Sunni dissent" thus imply causality. While such phrases might be useful shorthand indices, in reality the codes have only weak causal properties: "The deployment of categories can be generative without being totalizing. Categories have the capacity to define aspects of selfhood while foreclosing others, even though no category exhausts the ways in which people view themselves or act politically"

(Wedeen, p. 150). In other words, a group's shorthand belies the differentiated historical memories and traditions, diverse positions and commitments, multiple relationships and organizations, and heterogeneous practices and performances that characterize its members. Ongoing debates and discussions can produce schisms that leave the group contested. As interpretive communities are not monoliths, analysts should not conflate categories with unified actors or with stabilized agents who undertake directed activities. Because meanings are not uniform across society, an internally coherent pattern embodying fixed rules or norms, "the working class" is a collectivity whose meaning is contingent, disparate, and diverse – and therefore contested.

Processes of actor construction thus "need to be historically contextualized: their meanings and importance change over time and according to situation" (Wedeen, p. 157). Because constructivists claim that groupness becomes meaningful under particular conditions, they study "the processes through which particular identifications get mobilized and groups made" and thus how "particular categories of group affiliation become politically salient" (Wedeen, p. 157). As agents modify or transform meanings in use, collective identities, organizational affiliations, political ideologies, and joint activities change swiftly. Like fads, they come and go, form and reform, as actors are mobilized, demobilized, and remobilized. Wedeen thus emphasizes the fluidity of group life. While Acemoglu and Robinson's contractualism implies that individuals remain at a fixed distance from each other, Wedeen's constructivism implies that individuals are historically interpenetrated and dynamically interrelated.

More generally, while concepts can be generalized and become universal, their expression and interpretation – whose justice is important, what democracy means, where equality is good, when discourse is true, how participation should be cultivated, and why nationalism exists – varies from time to time, place to place, society to society, and situation to situation. Democracy and nation are thus socially constructed in particular historical contexts.

The constructivists's point is well taken. If the world is "without form and void" (*Genesis* 1: 2), where there are no intrinsic human needs such as survival (Darwin), pleasure (Mill), or power (Nietzsche); no basic social natures such as a working class, an ethnic group, or a religious community; and no universal existential problems such as finding allies, arranging marriages, feeding families, and balancing individual and society, then creation and construction, naming and bounding, are indeed the imperatives of social order.

3

When Causality Is To Be Found and How

To recapitulate: while Acemoglu and Robinson are concerned with procedural democracy as a grand bargain aggregated among market interests, Wedeen cares about discursive democracy as a performative local consensus tied to national identity. Now consider the tough social-scientific question of how these theorists turn invisible principles of political order into causal methodologies that hold observable implications. In gist, rationalists and constructivists generate observable implications in five similar ways: weaving problem situations into core problems, shaping concepts into observations, fashioning hypotheses into causal mechanisms, turning cases into units of analysis, and converting environments into contexts. Although they address the same problems of research design, rationalists and constructivists adopt different causal methodologies.

3.1. COMPARATIVE STATICS

Acemoglu and Robinson mold Moore's problem situation of distributional struggles over competing grand strategies and alternative paths of development into a core problem of democracy and dictatorship. Their democracy is a grand balance-of-power, a compositional collectivity in which contracting parties share sovereignty. What brings the bargainers together? How does a bargain become self-regulating and self-reproducing, thereby persisting against the available alternatives? And what is the source of the partial adjustments needed to prevent revolution? To address these questions and thereby move their game theory beyond science fiction, Acemoglu and Robinson begin (pp. 2–14) and end (pp. 349–55) with ideal types and exemplars: high inequality yields unstable autocracy (South Africa) and unstable democracy (Argentina); medium inequality yields slow and permanent democratization (Britain); and low inequality yields stable autocracy (Singapore). They also turn their central concepts – class, democracy, and coercive bargaining – into brief narrative observations.

For example, they suggest that in the British case coercive bargaining produced the Reform Act of 1832, Second Reform Act of 1867, Third Reform Act of 1884, and the Representation of the People's Act in 1918. Legislation to end corruption and to institute the secret ballot was also significant. Other "turning point[s] in the history of the British state" involved labor-market regulation, health and unemployment insurance, government-financed pensions, minimum wages, redistributive taxation, and primary and secondary education (Acemoglu and Robinson, pp. 63–64).

Acemoglu and Robinson probe the observable implications of their causal argument in another way. Using classic techniques of economic modeling, they transform the vague environments surrounding their cases into units of analysis operating in concrete contexts, thereby generating testable propositions.

The outcomes of one or more episodes of coercive bargaining are equilibrium institutions. Interacting groups thus turn their balance of power into the institutional equilibria – social contracts and political compromises – of a game. Equilibria in game theory are indeed best understood as political institutions and governing regimes that control conflictual interactions and determine co-operative ones. Perhaps the earliest statement of this important idea can be found in Schotter and Schwödiauer (1980: 482):

Von Neuman-Morgenstern game theory is, in sum, the theory of the emergence of stable institutional arrangements or 'standards of behavior' in a given physical situation or game. In other words the theory tries to predict what stable institutions form will emerge from a given economic background and what the resulting value relationships will be. As a result, the theory does not assume that any particular institutional arrangement exists at the outset, as does the neoclassical (economic) theory, but starts out by describing the states and technologies of the agent in an institutional "state of nature" for which it predicts what stable institutional arrangements or standards will evolve. Social institutions can be seen as the equilibrium outcomes of games of strategy whose descriptions are given by the physical capability of the agents of the game – the empirical background. They are an outcome of the game, rather than an input into it.

Given that different stable institutions correspond to different endogenously created equilibria, game theorists ask where a particular equilibrium of agent interactions came from, what sustains it, and where it can head – precisely Acemoglu and Robinson's questions.

Nowadays a game-theoretic equilibrium means that actors or agents with interdependent beliefs, resources, and strategies follow Nash behavioral norms: the preexisting rules of the game, which remain constant and unalterable, create the players' opportunities and constraints; exogenous variables – both observable and unobservable – then determine a Nash (self-enforcing) equilibrium of strategic interactions. In short, given an equilibrium outcome or institution, everyone is acting optimally. The equilibrium thus limits every actor's ability to unilaterally change strategies. All are prevented from altering course, because everyone has already chosen their optimal response to the given situation. All are deterred from changing strategies, because everyone fears retaliation. From an individual's perspective, an equilibrium is a natural and stable point of cooperation, a place where no one has an incentive to change strategies. From the collectivity's perspective, an equilibrium is a natural and stable point of coordination, a place where there is a tacit understanding on which actors focus. An equilibrium has authority in the sense that actors believe in it as an outcome and defend it by pursuing their self-interests. If suboptimal, however, it might lack legitimacy in the sense that people need not value it as a norm. Nevertheless, even in the absence of a higher authority serving as an enforcement mechanism, the equilibrium is self-enforcing because everyone has an incentive to not break the agreement that is implicitly behind the equilibrium. Subject to trends, cycles, and shocks, a game's environment is always changing. Moreover, at any one point in time the environment is complex and diverse. Interested in variables and not constants, Acemoglu and Robinson thus study the comparative statics of the equilibrium, or the contextual factors that cause the interactions that produce particular outcomes of the game. In other words, Acemoglu and Robinson employ comparative statics that address causal questions about equilibrium selection, persistence, and change. The idea comes from Paul Samuelson (1947): if a utility function is maximized and an equilibrium found, exogenous changes can shift the equilibrium outcome. For example, if consumers optimize a utility function, equating marginal benefits and marginal costs, exogenous shifts in price influence the quantities consumed. The approach thus explains observed behaviors, such as the emergence of cooperative and noncooperative equilibria, by isolating the structural conditions of the environment that combine with the underlying rules of the game to produce outcomes. Comparative statics thus link normative optima to observable quantities, suiting positivist cannons of testability and falsifiability.

Acemoglu and Robinson thus search for the most basic form of causality: something causes something else. "Nothing arises from nowhere" and "everything comes from other things and gives rise to other things" (Bohm in Kurki 2008: 16). Put otherwise, nothing can cause, move, or change itself. Self-cause, self-motion, and self-change are not possible. Because nothing by itself can bring about its own existence, causes must be external to effects, and cause and consequence necessarily separate and distinct. Rather than explaining phenomena "in and of themselves," explanation focuses on how phenomena vary as a result of contextual factors situated in time and space. Rorty (1982: 199) puts the idea as follows: "[Y]ou can't know anything about Y without knowing a lot about X." He (1982: 199) elaborates: "[C]ast around for some way of making sense of what had happened by looking for a vocabulary in which a puzzling object is related to other, more familiar, objects so as to become intelligible." Hence, "one needs to bring the object into relation with many other different sorts of objects in order to tell a coherent narrative which will incorporate the initial object" (Rorty 1982: 200).

For example, democracy is a social object situated in a nexus of relationships with other social objects. Democracy can only be known by understanding how its relationships operate in diverse situations. Put otherwise, democracy's qualities only become publicly known when they react to other things under various conditions. Because "democracy arises when inequality is sufficiently high that the disenfranchised want to contest power but not so high that the elites find it attractive to use repression" (p. 218), Acemoglu and Robinson's core proposition is that "intergroup inequality should have an effect on the equilibrium of political institutions and thus on the likelihood that a society ends up as a democracy" (pp. 58–59). By investigating how the fixed parameters, reflecting diverse situations and various conditions, of their models affect the variable decisions of the rich and the poor, Acemoglu and Robinson's comparative statics generates testable hypotheses about the origins of procedural democracy. For example, they suggest that "as an economy develops, factors of production accumulate, and per capita income rises, it is the change in the structure of the economy toward a more capital-intensive endowment of assets that leads to democracy and its consolidation" (p. 318). Acemoglu and Robinson's etiology of preexisting forces includes the history of political institutions such as parliament; the character of economic institutions such as property rights, markets, and gentry-merchant connections; the structure of land, labor, and capital in the economy, which, in turn, are affected by such factors as urbanization, the factory system, and industrialization; the strength of civil society, especially the middle class; the collective action problems of the poor and disenfranchised, or their organizational strength and militancy; the concurrent political and economic crises surrounding reform episodes; and the form and extent of globalization. This rich inventory of exogenous factors, the book's principal substantive concern, allows Acemoglu and Robinson to assess the costs and benefits of bargaining. Varying one thing at a time, trying to do it well, and then moving on to the next thing, they trace the dynamics of promises and threats, constraints and opportunities – the causal mechanisms behind their propositions – to fixed antecedent situations and noninteracting prior conditions.

In sum, Acemoglu and Robinson argue that procedural democracy and political economy are external constraints on agents and then demonstrate how the comparative statics of the agents's environment generate the observable implications of their ideas. They thus model the incentives deriving from exogenous social formations and external political structures that have solidified over decades. While their game theory seems to operate best in the longer run of fixed preferences and stable beliefs, Acemoglu and Robinson's book holds our interest because their comparative statics generates valuable regression experiments. They evidently address big questions, falsifying the charge that rational choice theory works only in trivial situations, or when it is least needed. Nonetheless, if comparativists care about the shorter run, the more prospective causal dynamics surrounding the intended and unintended consequences of agency – actors coming and going, learning and adapting, identifying and joining – they must look elsewhere. Such an alternative approach to causality would emphasize that "[t]he motor of history is endogeneity" (Przeworski 2007: 168).

3.2. SOCIAL CONSTRUCTION

Wedeen's rich theory of identity construction and reproduction employs such a method. She molds the problem situation of Yemen's democracy into core problems of citizen activism, civil society, and local democracy. Because causal relations refer to invisible worlds, Wedeen, similarly to Acemoglu and Robinson, ties her explanatory framework to research strategies that generate observable implications. For example, Wedeen deepens the study of Yemen by converting the case into units of analysis. She attends approximately 170 group discussions, each an episode in the construction of the group identities behind democracy. Once there, Wedeen studies "observable practices" and "observable conventions" and is concerned with such "observable political effects" (Wedeen, p. 15) as "public speech and action" (Wedeen, p. 16). Ignoring unobservables like intentions, a point discussed later, Wedeen pursues a descriptive/positivist constructivism. She aims to turn the concepts and principles of social construction into phenomena that can be investigated empirically.

Most important, Wedeen adopts a causal frame: "Not all performance practices produce either national consciousness or democratic persons, of course. This book explores the questions of which ones are likely to do so and how we know when they do" (Wedeen, pp. 3–4). Similarly to Acemoglu and Robinson, Wedeen also fashions general environments into observable causal contexts.

For example, Wedeen (p. 161) is interested in the observable impacts of national events and crises: "Because political identifications are a product of specifiable historical, political, and discursive circumstances, they are subject to modification as those circumstances change. Times of crisis may make people more aware of or invested in their own particular identifications, as part of actors' attempts to make sense of chaotic or confusing developments." Her (p. 19) empirical work in fact suggests that "national belonging may actually be shared in the breach of state authority – in the moments when large numbers of citizens, unknown to each other, long for its protection."

Another example: Wedeen (p. 161) studies how the construction of Yemen's nationalism, piety, and democracy may be traced to "some form of institutional intervention (whether by commission or omission) into the classificatory lives of ordinary citizens." She (p. 150) is particularly interested in how group- or category-based "knowledge is invoked and reiterated in the promulgation of laws; created and upheld through the classifications underlying the operation of specific state institutions or the strategies of particular regimes, or both; summoned into being and sustained through the work of intellectuals, clerics, and rhetoricians."

Another important causal claim she makes is that the discursive practices and performances of local civil society can construct a national public sphere. As qāt chews help fashion minipublics, local mobilization can lead to national solidarity. Political identity is thus fashioned through "diffuse points of shared reference" in which "participants often orient themselves to and receive information as part of a broader public of anonymous citizens" (Wedeen, p. 3). Even in the absence of face-to-face interactions, people living in geographically dispersed areas can thus "imagine themselves as inhabiting a world in common with like-minded, anonymous others" (Wedeen, p. 7). Ultimately, "people who were distant from one another [come] to conceive of themselves as part of a shared world of concomitant events" (Wedeen, p. 8), "as sharing the same experiences with unknown others" (Wedeen, p. 48). This imagined public community, consisting of common knowledge and shared consciousness, can become a national identity: "Even when discourses do not explicitly refer to nationalist ideas, people unknown to one another can come to share knowledge about events, actors, and places in ways that allow them to imagine themselves as members of discrete homogeneous collectivities, existing in calendric clock time within a spatially demarcated territory" (Wedeen, p. 10). Hence, by working through local communities "even a fragile state can instill in its citizenry intermittent attachments to a national community" (Wedeen, p. 18). The citizenry formed through a national poetry and a national sphere of discourse can then advance demands on the government: "in the absence of a robust network of state institutions, traumatic political events and the public discussions they inspire can produce conditions in which a putative 'nation' of citizens takes shape in the form of a demand for a state capable of protecting them" (Wedeen, p. 20). In sum, everyday local practices and the national public sphere are causally connected to the growth of nationalism in Yemen.

Wedeen (pp. 161–62) also finds that elites and organizations exert observable influences on group construction: "By characterizing events in terms of preexisting categories of political identification, organizations often amplify mildly constraining forms of affiliation into a more vigorous and active sense of urgency and commitment. This is not to argue that elites are deliberately manipulating ordinary citizens with titular categories. It just means that organizations do crucial work in making some categories more salient than others, effectively prescribing available self-identifications, so that citizens even tangentially related to the designation have little choice but to engage in everyday political conversation and action using this category – whether they believe in the classification's merits or not." Her (p. 161) empirical work even leads her to suggest that elites and organizations can potentially manufacture conflict among the groups they helped create: "political organizations or networks [can] play a critical role in transforming a point of disagreement – about religious doctrine or ritual, for example – into a motivation for hostile self-differentiation and political or military action."

Wedeen (pp. 176–77) also examines how the regime constructs the categories responsible for the boundaries between groups "that make groups seem quasi natural." She elaborates as follows: "Michel Foucault and Pierre Bourdieu inspired a plethora of work on how the modern state classifies its citizens, revealing how institutions underwrite the ways in which people understand themselves and each other. Categories of all sorts, whether of citizenship, race, religion, ethnicity, occupation, income bracket, property rights, sexuality, or criminality become salient, in part, through the state's ability to impose classifications on the world. States use documents of identification, such as driver's licenses and passports, as well as methods of sorting people across categories, such as censuses, to do significant 'organizational work.'" She clarifies even further: "The claim is not that the state creates these categories from scratch. But states do have the means to make these categories important by controlling how classificatory schemes and modes of social counting are put to practical use. State officials, judges, teachers, NGO workers, and local medical professionals, as well as others, make use of these categories in understanding their respective object worlds, in reaching decisions, ordering and apportioning populations, and reproducing the social conditions of their own expertise." She concludes that "Postcolonial countries, in particular, have also inherited the antecedent patterns of administrative classification devised under colonial rule, ones that may be undermined only partially by subsequent state-building processes or that may even be enhanced by the ways in which categories such as ethnicity or race or tribe are inscribed in a country's post-independence institutions." As elites and organizations that construct categories, the Yemeni regime can potentially manufacture conflict among the groups they help fashion: "the regime has been able to engage in divide-and-rule strategies that themselves reproduce and lend political salience to, if not create, categories of group membership – experiences of affiliation and possibilities for organization that have helped structure the current fault lines of Yemeni political life" (Wedeen, p. 180). Moreover, "it is primarily the regime's divide-and-rule strategies that have created the conditions under which passionate, contentious group-based solidarities thrive" (Wedeen, p. 178). There is a paradox here. Regimes adopt divide-and-rule strategies to survive politically: "By reproducing (if not always creating) spaces of ungovernability, the regime was able to exercise partial control over particular regions and thus limit the dominance of any one local organization" (Wedeen, p. 166). Yet by encouraging (or at least not preventing) disorder, the regime's strategies promote political durability at the cost of state construction: "Political rulers may not have incentives to build durable state institutions that can project power across territory in uniform, standard ways" (Wedeen, p. 179). Hence, "[v]iolence occurring within the nation–state's borders, or 'civil war onset,' may be prompted by an over-reaction on the part of a regime to demands made by organizations whose members were previously subject to a divide-and-rule system. A regime's efforts to bring the state into being by 'monopolizing' violence may actually generate more violence" (Wedeen, p. 185).

Finally, Wedeen argues that regimes and elites can set general parameters for the social construction of identities and discourse: "The available idioms through which experiences of common belonging to a people became institutionalized in this post-1970s world are a product of what regimes will tolerate and what Islamic movements have won. In some cases, this discursive latitude has enabled pointed attacks on corrupt leaders. But in almost all cases, expressions of Muslim piety go along with consensual understandings of anti-American and pro-Palestinian solidarities, and these are evident in both officials' speeches and in the voices raised in mass demonstrations. Islamic discourses put forth a coherent anti-imperialist doctrine and suggest ways of reestablishing community, offering visions of an equitable, just, socially responsible way of life, much as the now-discredited Arab national regimes of the 1950s and 1960s had done" (Wedeen, p. 189).

In sum, Wedeen is a causal theorist. Expecting discourse to unleash possibilities for social constructions, she uses ethnographic fieldwork to investigate the conditions responsible for the potentialities. She traces public performances of democracy, nationalism, piety, and conflict to national events and to institutional interventions by elites and organizations, especially those associated with the state, in the classificatory lives of citizens.

Nevertheless, Wedeen (p. 162, emphasis in original) repeatedly demurs from the sort of simple, direct, and powerful statements of exogenous causality found in Acemoglu and Robinson: "Divisive discourses do not *cause* violence, but they shape the conceptual space in which specific group solidarities become thinkable." Rejecting straight forward causal claims is indeed a central theme of her book. For example, she (p. 59, emphasis in original) dismisses causal claims linking regional diversity to political stability: "just as there was no *necessary* connection between the regional differences of North and South and the difficulties of unification, nor was there any necessary relationship between regional similarities and the likelihood of successful unity." Wedeen especially targets materialist cause-and-effect claims that do not come to grips with the social construction of discourses and performances. For example, when she explores contemporary Islamic movements, Wedeen emphasizes that their "transnational moral imaginary" (p. 187) is not caused by neoliberal economic reforms. She (p. 190) concludes that explanations of piety "cannot be reduced to economic determinations." As she (p. 210) puts it, "there may be a connection between neoliberal reforms and piety movements, but this relationship is not one of lockstep cause and effect." Hence, neoliberalism's "causal import is easily exaggerated" and analysts need to take into account numerous factors including "an increasing elective affinity between regime rhetoric and aspects of Islamic discourse, their close interaction and mutual historical constitution" (Wedeen, p. 189). Another complicating factor is anti-American "blowback": "Regime support of Islamic organizations and discourses, the fact of persistent U.S. intervention, and policies aimed at eliminating leftist opposition make it difficult to isolate economic reforms as the key variable or to establish a direct causal relationship between reforms and/or suffering, on the one hand, and Islamic political movements, on the other" (Wedeen, p. 191).

Yet Wedeen does not think that the key problem with materialist explanans is that they involve too many variables. Nor does she believe that the core difficulty is complex explanandums. And she (p. 14) does not hold that the problem is that competing understandings of "time, space, sovereignty, personhood and collectivity" coexist within heterogeneous modern nation–states. Materialist causality is troubling because exogeneity trumps endogeneity: "Although neoliberalism cannot be said to have *caused* movements of piety to develop, the ideas and consequences of neoliberal reform have become important subjects for debate and criticism within Islamic communities" (Wedeen, p. 201, emphasis in original). In other words, rather than operating in a straightforward input-output fashion, neoliberal policies operate indirectly through feedback dynamics: they fashion the possibilities that then generate the discourses that, in turn, shape further possibilities. As she (p. 190, emphasis in original) puts it, "These discourses not only reflect contemporary political conditions that go beyond economic causes but are also themselves generative of novel political possibilities. An alliance between regimes and some Islamic movements both institutionally *and discursively* has helped to define the shifting parameters of political expression it the Middle East."

Wedeen also rejects causal propositions about the direct impact of discourse. For example, she asserts that "there is no necessary connection between the claims of national solidarity and the likelihood of political stability, as such national

imaginings can be used to criticize or undermine current regimes
as well as to authorize them" (Wedeen, p. 66; also see p. 19).
Hence, "the mechanics of unity in Yemen were more difficult
than the convergence of discourses on a common national identity might suggest" (Wedeen, p. 57). Wedeen (p. 20) similarly
denies a noncircuitous causal connection between discourse and
national identity: "Public sphere activities facilitate nation-ness
to the extent that they create specific assemblages of fellow
participants who have come to share the everyday experience
of communicating with others within the limited, territorially
sovereign space of the nation-state. But the content of these
discussions does not necessarily presume a national identity or
use vocabulary suggestive of one. The Yemeni example shows
too that the public addressed in quotidian social gatherings can
be both broader and more indeterminate, or narrower and more
specifically local, than a national one." Another example:
Wedeen rejects the proposition that qāt chews can serve as a
safety valve for the regime, offering numerous criticisms of this
idea (pp. 119, 134, 135, 140, 151, 178). A final example: the
discourse of pious communities engaged in studying sacred texts
can lead to national solidarity or not, democratic practices or
not, liberalism or not, strong states or not, and instability/civil
war or not. As she shows in her chapter on Believing Youth, the
discursive public sphere, with its performances and practices,
ongoing enactments and theater, holds many possibilities.

Wedeen (p. 146; also see p. 3) similarly rejects a simple causal
connection between local discursive democracy and national procedural democracy: "The example of Yemen may show that there
is no necessary relationship either historically or theoretically
between agonistic disagreement, lively debate, rational-critical
thinking, temporary equality, and revelatory politics, on the one
hand, and either elections or liberal values, on the other. In short,
democrats can exist without procedural democracy. Democracy
(in substantive representational terms) may not even need the
ballot box." Hence, a vibrant public sector may or may not lead
to procedural democracy: "Proponents of civil society arguments
often ... [suggest] that a lively associational life can produce

effective governance or contested elections, or both. Yemen arguably has both a rich association life and spirited public sphere
practices, and yet no one would claim that the regime either
governs effectively or that its institutions generate alternation in
office. Although public spheres may represent a condition of
democratic possibility, they do not seem sufficient in themselves
to prompt Przeworski et al.'s contested elections. Or put differently, although qāt chews and other public sphere activities in
which people discuss their political worlds represent sites of
important political vitality, the lively and obvious presence of
such public arenas in the absence of fair and free contested elections suggests that such everyday practices may not be as instru-
mentally related to contestatory electoral arrangements as some
political scientists would claim – at least not in the short run"
(Wedeen, p. 118). Yet the absence of a direct causal connection
between popular discourse and procedural democracy does not
bother Wedeen (p. 145): "there is a range of valuable scholarly
activities to pursue without thinking about the instrumental value
of qāt chews for contested elections." After all, "the emphasis on
practices as performative does not fit comfortably into an
approach that privileges independent and dependent variables.
Qāt chews are enactments of democratic personhood, for example, but they do not cause a democratic regime (in the procedural
sense) to happen; nor do they require or necessarily promote
liberal values. Phrases highlighting how the circulation of discourses or the administrative routines of institutions 'make possible' or 'thinkable' new modes of political imagining (which may
or may not be deeply felt) do not provide us with a strong causal
story" (Wedeen, p. 216).

Even as she (p. 111) defines deliberation as "the widespread,
inclusive mobilization of critical, practical discourses in which
people articulate and think through their moral and material
demands in public," Wedeen (p. 125) adds that "[t]his is not
to argue that there is a one-to-one correspondence between
the frequency of qāt chewing and the liveliness of political
debate." When Wedeen (p. 152) suggests that "[t]he reasons for
the initial conflict and its escalation into a violent and persisting

showdown between the regime and al-Hūthī's followers remain unclear," the reader recognizes that she is once again rejecting "a strong causal story" that connects independent to dependent variables. Nevertheless, Wedeen theorizes about the power of discourse. Opening their eyes to the performative side of politics, she shows comparativists the value of seeing politics as theatre and spectacle. Moreover, she speculates about the preconditions or foundations of democratic discourse and performance. Her discussions of the history of Yemen and its potential future, given the introduction of new technologies such as televisions and cell phones, as well as her discussions of regime interventions, demonstrate an appreciation of causal contingency. Wedeen does think about the institutions and structures outside of the chew that permit them to become lively and/or effective. And she does think about internal organizations of the chew that enable and constrain its ability to fashion creative solutions to Yemen's problems. Yet Wedeen repeatedly argues against natural necessities; continually deconstructs the external constraints on autonomous communities deliberating their interests, identities, and ideas; doggedly unmasks the subjugation of conversation to heteronymous power; and over and over again disarms the purported causal powers of exogenous contexts (independent variables) over social phenomena (dependent variables). As such causal hypotheses about discourses are rejected and performances falsified, she advances causal mechanisms that ultimately destabilize the outside forces supporting regimes (Chapter 2), democracy (Chapter 3), and conflict (Chapter 4).

Wedeen therefore moves adeptly between two types of constructivism. The first is antirealist constructivism: "Antirealism consists of a kind of global critical constructivism applied to all our concepts. ... At times interpretivists suggest that the role of prior theories and traditions in constructing our experiences precludes our taking experiences to reflect a world independent of us. They suggest that we have access only to our world (things as we experience them), not the world as it is (things in themselves), and they conclude that we have not basis on which to treat our concepts as true to the world" (Bevir 2008: 61). The second is pragmatic constructivism: "[S]ocial concepts are vague; they capture family resemblances; they are conventional ways of dividing up continuums rather than terms for discrete chunks of experience. Yet, although pragmatic concepts do not refer to essences, they do refer to groups of objects, properties, or events. Social factors determine pragmatic concepts because they are innumerable ways in which we can classify things, and because it is our purposes and our histories that lead us to adopt some classifications and not others. Nonetheless, the role of social facts in determining pragmatic concepts does not mean that these concepts have no basis in the world. To the contrary, we might justify adopting the particular pragmatic concepts we do by arguing that they best serve our purposes, whether these purposes are descriptive, explanatory, or normative" (Bevir 2008: 61).

Wedeen is antirealist in that her repeated falsifications ultimately underdetermine all conditions of possibility. Yet Wedeen is also pragmatic in that her falsifications allow her to focus on what she takes to be – and what comparativists should also take to be – equally important: endogenously created enablers. Surely these creators of possibility deserve as much scrutiny as determinants of choice.

In sum, Acemoglu and Robinson's causality is built around elementary – plain and simple – components: one-way input-output relations. Independent variables move headlong into dependent variables, producing unbroken and uninterrupted consequences. Because snappy and terse explanans produce sharp and stark explanandums, clear and precise causal propositions result. While comparative statics is operational in its own subtle and sophisticated ways, Wedeen is suspicious of its type of causality. Such analyses typically offer too facile, gross, and crude an understanding of how the world is socially constructed. Since Wedeen believes that social causality is continually mitigated and refined through circuitous and cyclical endogenous feedback processes, she locates causality in more complexly dynamic social relations. Yet Wedeen does not feel that she is free to construct any theory she wants. Her important contribution to comparative politics is to demonstrate that her type of causality – social construction – is also operational in its own subtle and sophisticated ways. Like Acemoglu and Robinson, she too turns problem situations into core problems, concepts into observations, hypotheses into causal mechanisms, cases into units of analysis, and environments into contexts.

Wedeen makes another significant contribution to the field. In seeking the exogenous causal origins of things, she shows comparativists that they lose the charms of describing something being that thing and the delights of depicting that thing becoming some other thing. Comparative static exercises do not study being and becoming on their own terms, but rather reduce them to dependence on something else. If Acemoglu and Robinson show that comparativists can learn about a thing by examining its exogenous causal origins, Wedeen shows that comparativists can learn about a thing by studying its endogenous causal composition. The concomitants that define the elements that make up the thing are surely also worth investigating. Her approach to causality thus focuses on "the deep constitutive power of causal relationships" (Kern 2004). Constructivism is a form of *creation ex nihilo* that explores the freedom of the human imagination to design outcomes that are not subordinate to natural constraints. Its core idea is that people are not victims of their environment and hence that situations need not present them with insurmountable obstacles. As their dependence on circumstance is minimized, people become the empowered makers of their own history. Citizens who defend their liberty, and who quite possibly liberate themselves from their destiny, have the capacity to create the laws and structures that actualize the life of their community. Insisting that norms can become facts and that possibilities can become actualities, constructivists capture people cultivating their own tastes and judgments, fashioning their own ideas and understandings, and creating their own duties and obligations.

Nevertheless, Wedeen's constitutive causality does tend toward ontological indeterminism: she studies social objects that are constantly changing. Continually under construction, the thing is always process and never product. High-level abstractions therefore elude her. Though rather good at destroying the meta-physics of others, her continual deconstruction or falsification of exogenous causality means that she can only understand what people make of themselves. How the environment fashions people consequently also eludes her.

Yet environmental determinants exist. To paraphrase the U.S. military on the war in Iraq, "You go to democracy with the country you have, not the country you wish you had" (Friedman 2005). The weight of tradition and the limits of historical resources mean that there are possible impossibilities and impossible possibilities. People might want to change givens, but often cannot. Moreover, diminishing the significance of enduring conditions means more than marginalizing fixed constraints. Opportunities are also missed. Comparativists also want to study popular attempts to master restrictive circumstances by examining how people change supposed givens.

Acemoglu and Robinson's rejoinder to Wedeen is thus that causation is more than composition. While mutual constitution tends to conflate analytically autonomous objects that have their own internal logics, constitutive causality tends to muddle concrete historical subjects that have their own generative proper-ties. Surely constructivists want to avoid the essentialism of claiming that there is something intrinsic to X, and surely they would rather assert that X stands in certain types of relations to other things that make up the world. After all, many construc-tivists are pragmatists who want to do something with or to X: "For pragmatists, there is no such thing as a nonrelational feature of X, any more than there is such a thing as the intrinsic nature, the essence, of X" (Rorty 1999: 50). Moreover, the belief that everything is politically and socially constructed is itself a politically and socially constructed belief that obscures con-structivism's own conditions of possibility and overlooks its own enabling contexts. Finally, while constructivists recognize that the boundaries of a social entity are constructed, they should also recognize that conditions beyond boundaries influ-ence the causal processes invoked by boundary construction. Environmental context is thus partly responsible for the social entity's causal impacts. In sum, it is an ontological error to assume that a thing necessarily becomes part of another thing that it affects or that affects it. Comparativists must therefore distinguish between a thing and its causes and consequences.

The disjunctive relation "other than" yields "difference," leading comparativists to a fruitful exploration of the connective tissues behind elective affinities.

4

Two Western Dreams

Thin and Thick Democracy

Comparativists try to understand the forces (Chapter 3) behind two different types of "free and rational society" (Chapter 2). Wedeen's discursive democracy, subject only to its own discourses and performances, has autonomous agency and power. Acemoglu and Robinson's procedural democracy, a prisoner of its environmental constraints, is subject to economic markets, civil society, political culture, the bureaucratic state, and the world-historical situation. For example, is American democracy a free construction of European political theorists, the result of constitution makers enacting Enlightenment thought? Or is American democracy derivative of its circumstances, the consequences of a settler colony and frontier society with rich natural resources and ocean-delimited separation from the Old World? A pragmatic middle ground holds that the influence of democratic theories is contingent on their adaptations to changing environmental situations. For example, geographic isolation could have permitted political theories from the European Enlightenment to have safely taken root in America.

This chapter connects Chapters 3 and 4. It shows how rational choice's procedural democracy and its comparative statics jointly produce a dream of thin democracy, and how constructivism's deliberative democracy and its social constructivism jointly produce a dream of thick democracy. Here's the rub: both dreams are flawed. The following chapters then turn to Kohli's and Tilly's alternatives.

4.1. RATIONAL CHOICE'S THIN DEMOCRACY

Social-scientific efforts to establish causality confront the complexity of the empirical world. Explanations must take account of causal forces that are reciprocal and interactive, contextual and multilevel, uncertain and probabilistic, and dynamic and historical. Everything seems to depend on everything else – somewhere, sometime, and somehow. In short, positive and negative factors run amok (Eckstein 1980).

One way to control complexity it to locate a definitive starting point. One-way causality – input/output or stimulus/response etiology – connects a foundational and fixed explanan to a derivative and variable explanandum. Marxists thus distinguish superstructure from substructure, statisticians exogenous from endogenous variables, social theorists structure from agency, psychologists objective from subjective factors, and biologists environment from organism.

Weber's (1946b: 129) "pedantic political economist" begins with external conditions and then establishes meanings of action. Employing a deductive-nomological framework that separates constraint from choice, today's economists adopt several variations of this strategy.

- Microeconomics allows exogenous factors to shift endogenous prices and hence move demand curves.
- Standard economic analysis assumes lawlike theories operating under controlled conditions and uses comparative statics to derive predictions.
- Rational choice theory begins with the submission to facts that do not arise from human will and then adds motive: predetermined beliefs + predetermined preferences → strategic choices.
- Rational choice institutionalism makes a parallel argument at the macro level: institutions + preferences → policies.
- Game theory maintains that exogenously fixed rules + endogenously flexible strategies → outcomes.
- In a correlated equilibrium, common knowledge or shared beliefs about how the game is played is a function of a

correlating device that provides information to the players: a choreographer, common priors, or social norms thus coordinates strategies and determines outcomes.

Economists are evidently adept at finding unmoved movers. Modeling themselves on economists, comparativists nowadays adopt two gold standards: rational choice theory (RCT) coupled with randomized controlled trials (also RCT). RCT to test RCT, or $(RCT)^2$, is an deductive/inductive marriage made in heaven. When this blend cannot be fashioned, standard causal analysis in comparative politics begins with the natural environment: climate, soils, weather, oil, diamonds, mountains, neighborhoods, demography, or technology. In the absence of such natural givens, comparativists often begin at the beginning: historically concrete foundings, formative contexts, and genealogical origins. When beginnings cannot be fixed in time, comparativists begin with very large and hence seemingly very stable structures (e.g., political economy), institutions (e.g., democratic procedures), and variables (e.g., race, gender). Other comparativists begin with a selection equation that models how cases, for example revolutions or civil wars, enter a sample.

In seeking the holy grail of an unmoved mover X → democracy, comparativists who adopt various methods to assure one-way causality slight democracy's internal operations. Sometimes their findings are reduced to mechanical median-voter results. The explanandum of democracy then disappears in, or is subsumed by, the explanans of the environment. In other words, rational choice's procedural democracy becomes a dependent variable reduced to its environmental determinants. As exogenous realism yields radical externalism, fatalism descends on the internal political practices of democracy. When environment is destiny, democracy is a trifling superstructure derivative of its substructural circumstances. Merely a precipitate of its environment, median-voter outcomes shift as residues of circumstance. Why then should comparativists delve into the ebb and flow, the give and take, and the endogenous dynamics of democratic politics?

4.2. CONSTRUCTIVISM'S THICK DEMOCRACY

Such reductionism prompts constructivists to handle causal complexity differently. Offering a linguistic-interpretive analysis, they see the democratic collectivity as emergent. Theirs is a particularly thick version of democracy that thins environmental causes and thickens endogenous causality. Constructivists thus dream of a "free and rational society" that can facilitate its own construction, fashion its own practices, and produce its own performances.

Unger (1987: 17) isolates the logic behind thin environmental determinism: "Man is the infinite caught within the finite. His external circumstances belittle him." Since origins are arbitrary limitations and flawed hindrances to fashioning possibilities for change, thick democracy can explode supposedly fixed realities. By overcoming its exogenous environment, thick democracy can destabilize stagnant, routinized, and ossified institutions. Maintaining that there are no preexisting givens, only human choices and social constructions, constructivists argue that human energy and ingenuity can denaturalize society, thereby emancipating it from the conditions of the here and now. Freedom thus means freedom from exogenous causal constraints, the endogenous sovereignty and internal autonomy to transcend restrictions and become actual in history. Collective life is thus collective agency constructing collective fate, humanity's grand practical project.

Democracy and democratization, like civil war, is then a deeply "endogenous" process (Kalyvas 2006). Rather than X → democracy, democracy → democracy. In thick democracy, power is thus internal to the democratic collectivity. Imprisoned only within itself, democratic politics conquers its environment. Independent of social structure, thick democracy is free standing. Autonomous of world-historical context, thick democracy is sovereign. Driven only by its own causal forces, thick democracy is self-determining. In short, constructivism's radical internalism means that it's democracy all the way down.

Because thick democracy possesses endogenous causality, it fashions its own causal chains. As Gellner (1995: 76) puts it, "Once the engine is running, it feeds itself, it has no need for the starter motor." As thick democracy develops its own momentum, it becomes driven by its own path dependencies, developmental tendencies, and stages of development. In the absence of exogenous causation, thick democracy is self-organizing. Containing the seeds of its own constructions and reconstructions, thick democracy is self-caused: self-generating, self-inventing, self-originating, self-constituting, and self-designing. Thick democracy is also self-sustaining. Self-monitoring, self-regulating, and self-controlling, it is self-supporting and self-reproducing. In sum, thick democracy is all about itself.

The constructivists' thick democracy therefore rejects the inside/outside, intinsic/extrinsic, endogenous/exogenous, or inherent/contingent point of view: nothing is brute, given, and foundational. Not subject to an environmental milieu, thick democracy is an isolated or closed system lacking exogenous parameters that control or influence the system's response. The "because" is always an internal "being" and never an exogenous "cause." In gist, it's inside all the way outside.

Context smashing opens up the possibilities for deconstruction and rebuilding. If interests and identities emerge from within rather than being imposed from without, groups are blank slates ready for social (re)engineering. Malleable, anything can be written on them. Free, anything is possible and everything is permitted. Humans indeed have an endless ability to create new associations and combinations. Infinitely creative and expressive, humans have the collective capabilities and joint capacities, the common will and collaborative power, to continually innovate. Liberated from its environment and free from its circumstances, the collective imagination is freewheeling, unprogrammed, and unfettered. In the words of the slogan from the 1960s, "All Power to the Imagination." Societies that can be (re)imagined can be (re)made. After all, if society is a human artifact, the possibilities of change are endless; and if humans are self-transforming animals, collectivities can always begin again. Collective life thus can be made and remade endlessly: all laws can be transformed and all rules overturned.

Thick democracy thus involves rethinking, reconceptualizing, and redefining the possibilities that allow reconstructions and restructurings. Renewal, renaissance, and regeneration result. Thick democracies thus determine their own values and ends, interests and identities, associations and institutions, compromises and bargains, languages and reasons, goods and policies, capacities and capabilities, and practices and performances. The engine of change is public reason. Participation in public deliberation can produce a network of shared premises, a combination of social practices, and a set of performances that constitute power as legitimate and commitments as authoritative. The public goods of justice and fairness are thus shaped by the experience of practicing democracy. As legitimate authority grows out of performances that thicken the practices of democracy, the community gains social solidarity. Put otherwise, thick democracy is self-justifying and self-grounding.

Comparativists often think that old, big, and rich democratic states become more independent of their environmental contexts. Wedeen is telling comparativists that new, small, and poor local democracies can also be autonomous. This is why, as noted previously, so much of her book "deconstructs" materialistic and structuralist causal claims. Wedeen's message is that Yemen's future is more open than the conventional wisdom allows.

Constructivists deconstruct. By showing how they arise from social forces, critical constructivism denaturalizes taken-for-granted assumptions. And as indicated earlier, Wedeen is a master falsificationist. She dismantles the metaphysical premises underpinning inherited frameworks of thought and disrupts the ontological principles beneath traditional ways of thinking. Wedeen's unmasking of causality comes from a certain normative vision of democracy: people can realize the rational in the real, full human community is within their grasp, and humans can achieve freedom in the world. What does liberty mean if it cannot be manifested by a community's practices? The absence of external constraints implies the presence of the autonomy required to build the better institutions that can more effectively unleash creative human potential. Her relentless critique of exogenous causality is thus part of her continual resistance to prevailing structures of power and domination. Eliminate the external causality of contexts and you get the kind of democracy she wants.

4.3. COMPARING THIN AND THICK DEMOCRACY

Pulling together ideas from the previous two sections, note how the rationalist's thin democracy and the constructivist's thick democracy differ.

Causality:

> Thin democracy is driven or powered by thick exogenous contingent causes.
>
> Thick democracy is constructed or constituted by thick endogenous inherent causes.
>
> Thin democracy involves deterministic environmental foundations and bedrocks.
>
> Thick democracy involves self-determining performances and practices.
>
> Thin democracy's power is external or "out there."
>
> Thick democracy's power is internal or "in here."
>
> Thin democracy is hypothetical and conditional.
>
> Thick democracy is categorical and constitutive.

Statics and dynamics:

> Thin democracy is fixed by preexisting causal structures.
>
> Thick democracy features continually transforming movement.
>
> Thin democracy is a product: a world of nouns in which stable actors represent the essential nature of true things.
>
> Thick democracy is a process: a world of verbs in which fluid actions, ongoing makings and unmakings, create emergent outcomes.
>
> Thin democracy is an enduring and stable equilibria subject to comparative-static shocks.
>
> Thick democracy is constructed of continually reproduced relationships.

Origins, operations, and outcomes:

> Thin democracy has thick origins: exogenous constraints produce causally closed paths with few degrees of freedom.
>
> Thick democracy has thin origins: minimum environmental conditions of choice yield causally open paths with great opportunities.
>
> Thin democracy has thin operations, or minimalist democratic practices.
>
> Thick democracy has thick operations, or complex democratic performances.
>
> Thin democracy is a black box in which not much comes out.
>
> Thick democracy is a Pandora's box of discourses and deliberations.

Materialism and idealism:

> Thin democracy is thin on norms: materialistic social structures produce routine choice behaviors.
>
> Thick democracy is thick on norms: culture yields symbolic systems.
>
> Thin democracy has thick empirical foundations: held in place, it bends toward exogenous constraints.
>
> Thick democracy has thin empirical foundations: wandering anywhere, oughts force the environment to address needs.

Thin and thick rationality:

> Thin democracy features instrumental rationality: means-oriented reason grounded in environmental constraints.
>
> Thick democracy features value rationality: enlightened self-interest based on autonomous self-legislation that becomes self-grounding.

Individualism and holism:

> Thin democracy involves individuals and their choices.
>
> Thick democracy involves emergent collectivities.
>
> Thin democracy is passive; its abstract spectators or clients have predetermined goals and preferences.

Thick democracy is educative and transformative; its activist
citizens fashion their own values and ends.
Thin democracy contains private individuals who are victims
of social forces they cannot control.
Thick democracy contains public citizens whose intertwined
social dependencies constitute their collective fates.

Collective agency:

Thin democracy has weak collective agency: a reduction of
agency to its environment.
Thick democracy has strong collective agency: the autonomous
becoming of the collectivity.
Thin democracy is stimulus rich and response poor.
Thick democracy is stimulus poor and response rich.

Adaptation to environment:

Thin democracy is dependent on its environment; external
challenges produce outcomes that are derivative of context.
Thick democracy is emancipated from its environment; in the
face of external challenges, the collectivity separates outcomes
from context.
Thin democracy adapts to its environment.
Thick democracy adapts its environment to itself.

4.4. THE PROBLEMS OF THIN AND THICK DEMOCRACY

Each type of democracy has its flaws. The weaknesses of thin
democracy result from structural overdetermination. Reduction
to an environmental substructure turns democracy derivative. An
ideology or procedure that can be read off its environment
becomes abstract and reified. Radical externalism thus thins democratic practices. Moreover, pure exogeneity cannot yield the
freedom required for creative governance. Thin democracy is a
mechanical democracy that cannot adapt to its environment and
hence is unable to cope with hostile outside forces. Where everything democratic is a foregone conclusion, there is little scope for

innovative problem shaping and creative problem solving. Bonds and yokes, shackles and strait-jackets, cages and chains make thin democracy vulnerable and fragile. In the long run, such a democracy is not self-sustaining. If democracy rests on rigid foundations, a wiggle in one external driver or a wobble in an environmental factor brings about authoritarianism. Lacking the possibilities for creative reconstruction and reconsolidation, thin democracy ultimately turns out to be no democracy at all. Some comparativists thus look elsewhere for a "free and rational" society.

By emancipating people from the arbitrary power of their environment, constructivists maximize human autonomy. However, making perpetual context smashing the key to human liberation is "will-o'-the-wispish" (Shapiro 1990: 246). Groups and democracies are not free to construct anything they want. Effective political agents do not confuse constructing categories with changing the world. As Benhabib (1995: 679) writes, thick democracy tends toward manic or utopian idealism that overestimates the real possibilities of projects for change: "The distinction between social action and social structure, between agency and its constraining conditions, is an analytical one in social theory. Dissolve structure into chains of significance or patterns of representation and what you have is a form of cultural studies radicalism that thinks that all is possible in society under all conditions and at all times." Shapiro (2002: 250) agrees: "Conceding that politicized identities change and are socially constructed does not, however, generate the conclusion that they are infinitely malleable. ... Markets are human constructions, yet we may be unable to regulate them so as to operate at full employment without inflation for long periods of time. Ethnic hatred might concededly be learned behavior and hence by its terms socially constructed, yet we may have no idea how to prevent its being reproduced in the next generation. Proponents of social constructivism leap too quickly from the idea to the assumption of alterability; at best the two are contingently related."

Constructivist thinking thus becomes a self-fashioned iron cage that holds political dangers. As constructions lead a life of their own, they evade control. Too thick a democracy is self-undermining because it is self-absorbed with its own power. A thick democracy is therefore not necessarily a stable democracy because it produces unintended consequences: dictatorship or chaos. As thick democracy squashes differences, suppresses individuality, and homogenizes society, one possibility is that it becomes coercive authoritarianism. The tyranny of causal endogeneity leads to the tyranny of a political theory run riot. Thick democracy ends in no democracy at all. On the other hand, without foundations thick democracy is unstable. Politics becomes anarchical: infinitely malleable, anything goes. Evanescent and arbitrary, politics is changeable and tumultuous, and perpetually in motion. Winning and losing is localistic and particularistic. As politics becomes uncertain, it lacks intelligibility; as it becomes ambiguous, it loses meaning. Thick democracy again becomes no democracy at all.

Democracy consequently needs something prepolitical and predetermined to contain itself. As democracy operates within given fixed constraints, it stabilizes. Wedeen indeed includes causal stories about the construction of performances and discourses, for example about nationalist rhetoric and symbols. These causal stories can be used to unmask the power of qāt chews just as easily as they can be used to unmask the power of the environment: if something accompanies the qāt chew, like social well-being, one can ask whether it inheres in the logic of the qāt chew system or whether it emerges as a contingent outcome of the chew's environment. Two types of restrictions or limitations can discipline thick democracy: exogenous ones imposed from without and endogenous ones that are self-imposed.

Environmental factors induce people to participate in qāt chews. Habermas (1989) studies how historical conditions and structures led to the development of a public sphere in Europe. The expansion of markets and states was tied to the expansion of networks of discourse, the growth of civil society, and the emergence of civic associations. Wedeen (2004: 287) also adopts this causal perspective: "Different historical conditions of possibility from the ones Habermas specifies in Europe have allowed for the emergence of vibrant, politicized, critical communities of argument in Yemen." As has often been noted, if the ideal conditions for debate exist – if there is neither force nor fraud, fear nor deference, ignorance nor stupidity – then debate is probably not needed. Nevertheless, exogenous origins do contain thick democracy.

Internal forces can also discipline thick democracy. Collectivities that bind themselves, or institutionalize stable and ongoing rules to constrain their behavior, seemingly limit their power but actually increase their capability to shape outcomes (North and Weingast 1989). Moreover, constitution makers often rightly consider some things as beyond politics. Certain political practices are then not subject to the outcomes of particular public discourses. If human beings deserve certain natural or prepolitical rights, state institutions must protect them from social power – which can be as unfair, for example, as racist, sexist, and anti-Semitic – as governmental power. Since the Federalists wanted a democracy that even intelligent devils could run, the U.S. constitution imposes institutional and structural constraints on official's decision making. Democracy requires the self-restraint and the self-discipline produced by self-imposed constraints on self-expressed laws. By accepting the responsibilities and taking on the obligations of giving itself laws, democracy commits itself. By binding itself, democracy becomes constrained by its own self-imposed rules of the game. Its institutions and structures provide an inertial frame, center of gravity, or equilibrium point. Norms and rules then offer a sturdy and secure ground, an unassailable and indestructible bedrock, for governance.

Institutions that limit the discursive self-government of civil society include national executive, legislative, and judicial arrangements. The access of qāt chews to state-level political processes significantly affects their functioning. What rights and responsibilities within the larger political order do qāt chews possess? What are the origins of their constraints and the source of their opportunities? And how do these institutions influence a qāt chew's success as a thick democracy?

In sum, exogenous causal overdetermination destabilizes thin democracy and endogenous causal overdetermination destabilizes thick democracy. At a critical juncture the flaws of either system can generate a crisis. Self-destructive, self-defeating, and self-undermining, excessively thin or excessively thick democracy proves to be democracy's own worst enemy. The internal logics of thin and thick democracy may be likened to a cancer: something is fatally flawed in their conceptions, and growth cannot reach term or completion without self-annihilation.

Thin paradigm, thin democracy; thick paradigm, thick democracy. As rationalism is thin, so goes its democracy; as constructivism is thick, so goes its democracy. But if both types of democracies are decaying systems on suffocating treadmills, comparativists need a different approach to Barrington Moore's problem of reconciling democratic theory with causal methodology. They require, in other words, a practical way "to understand the forces" producing a "free and rational society." To navigate between a thin democracy determined by its environment and a thick democracy that determines its future, Kohli and Tilly offer paradigms that bring in the state.

PART II

STATE-SOCIETY AND CONTENTIOUS POLITICS

5

Pragmatic Theories of a Fit State: Kohli

In Atul Kohli's causal methodology, the state is a social object with an underlying structural capacity. In the face of environmental challenges, the state's organization – its institutions and patterns of authority – constitute its power to get things done. More specifically, "The role of the state has been decisive for patterns of industrialization in the developing world" (Kohli, p. 381). A democratic state's accountable political leaders seek legitimacy by maximizing public support and building a broad class alliance. Attempting to satisfy the different goals of its multiple constituencies, the leadership creates an inefficient and ineffective state. On the other hand, an autocratic government can fashion state-led social networks that tie single-minded ideological programs to command-and-control procedures. Since it can bring about economic development, such a state-society nexus constitutes a fit state.

Kohli's vision of the elective affinity of democratic theories and causal realities is therefore decidedly tragic: the global south can achieve Moore's goal of a "rational" society only at the cost of a "free" one. His causal methodology thus deflates democracy. Rather than state-building supporting democracy – Tilly's approach – Kohli's state undermines democracy.

Section 5.1 explores Kohli's democracy as a type of state. Section 5.2 discusses his causal theory. Finally, Section 5.3 analyzes Kohli's causal methodology: responding to specific world-historical challenges, ideal types of state capacities exercise their causal powers and fashion ideal types of industrialization, thereby producing observable correlations.

5.1. DEMOCRACY AS A TYPE OF STATE: CAPACITY, POWER, AND POLITICS

A state's potential for generating kinds or patterns of industrialization is a function of two dimensions of state capacity. The first is the state's capacity to set goals. The state can choose a political-economic ideology that defines its role as an economic actor. The second is the state's capacity to mobilize its resources. Kohli (p. 201) studies the "developmental capacities" of three types of states. Cohesive-capitalist, fragmented multiclass, and neopatrimonial states have different underlying causal structures consisting of different sets of causal powers.

5.1.1. Cohesive-Capitalist States

Cohesive-capitalist states, for example South Korea, couple a strong vision to a keen focus. Recognizing its competitive international environment, this type of state equates national security with economic development. The state's public purposes and political projects then involve the clearly defined goal of state-led industrialization. Put otherwise, the cohesive-capitalist state's economic ideology embraces activist state intervention and employs its available political instruments to shape the economy.

As a cohesive-capitalist state mobilizes its resources to accomplish its goals, it becomes an "efficacious economic actor" (Kohli, p. 56). In gist, politically powerful states intervene in the economy by promoting market-reinforcing behavior and encouraging investor profitability. Such states collect taxes and accumulate capital, channeling resources into priority areas and making public investments. Most important, the cohesive-capitalist state's directive economic activities alter the context within which firms operate. For example, by building the economic infrastructure that facilitates technology transfer, states shape the circumstances of private economic activities.

While high state capacity means that the state hopes to accomplish these tasks, it also means that the state actually gets them done. The state's capacity to reach its goals is a function of the state's power: "The fact that some states have been more successful than others at propelling industrialization suggests that successful states possessed a greater degree of power to define and pursue their goals" (Kohli, p. 20). Kohli stresses that power involves the political capacity to manage difficult circumstances and to turn constraints into opportunities: "Power is the currency that states use to achieve their desired ends" (Kohli, p. 20). Kohli (p. 418) continually hammers home this point: "The political economy problem of why state intervention helps to promote industrialization in some cases but not in others appears mainly to be a problem of political power. States with a certain type of power at their disposal, and more of it, are able to use it in a sustained way to promote economic growth."

Kohli (p. 420) believes that, at bottom, state power is a matter of politics: "The deeper reasons for why state intervention succeeds or fails have to do with the politics of the states. Some states are better at organizing power for use in a focused manner, while others are not." Politics generates power through a "centralized and purposive authority structure that often penetrates deep into the society" (Kohli, p. 10). In short, state power grows out of the politics of state-society relations.

The social relationships that affect a state's power to bring about economic development involve class. State capacity is thus rooted in the politics of state-class relations: "Any state's developmental effectiveness is a function not only of how well the state is organized but also of the underlying class basis of power" (Kohli, p. 384). A state-capital alliance, or a state-business ruling elite, lays behind the cohesive-capitalist state. Such a developmental coalition, where the state allies with producer or capitalist groups, generates the state's power resources. Kohli's approach to state power is therefore conditional but not reductionist: the cohesive-capitalist state does not swallow capitalist society, and neither does capitalist society swallow the state, but rather the state's power is a nonzero sum function of state and society. Kohli also offers an important caveat: state power can be based on fruitful, noncorrupt, state-private cooperation only if a state's bureaucratic elite is insulated from capture.

The state's power to resist capture is of course ultimately rooted in its potential to use its coercive force: "Power may be more or less legitimate, and it may be used positively as an incentive or negatively as punishment or threat of punishment" (Kohli, p. 20). The cohesive-capitalist state's bureaucracy thus creates a labor force and then exercises its authoritarian control by disciplining the workers: "The state penetrates society to incorporate and control the lower classes" (Kohli, p. 11). Hence, "repression was also a key component in enabling private investors to have a ready supply of cheap, 'flexible,' and disciplined labor" (Kohli, p. 13). The "brutal repression and systematic control of the lower classes in both the cities and the countryside" (Kohli, p. 27) produces a "disciplined, obedient, and educated work force" (Kohli, p. 33). Seeking political hegemony, the cohesive-capitalist state's policy of "extraction and control" aims to generate gains in economic productivity (Kohli, p. 59).

In cohesive-capitalist states, great elites decide grand matters of public policy. Because world-historical paths of development are chosen top-down, cohesive-capitalist states trade political democracy for economic development: "The narrow ruling coalition in these cases was a marriage of repression and profits aimed at economic growth in the name of the nation" (Kohli, p. 13). In Kohli's view, the search for democratic economic development in today's global south, the discovery of a developmental or modernizing democracy, is therefore a fool's errand. An administratively capable democracy, a Weberian bureaucratic state with the scientific and technological capacities to propel economic development, is impossible in the developing world. Democracy is thus a luxury good that low-income countries can ill afford: "Cohesive-capitalist states are likely to be authoritarian, and most developing country democracies are likely to be fragmented multiclass states" (Kohli, p. 301).

In stressing that the central explanation of successful economic development is long-term and deep-rooted state capacity, Kohli dismisses what he considers to be shallow factors. One such variable is political democracy. North and Weingast (1989) claim that in the West, state-society contracts traded revenue for representation. Put otherwise, strong parliaments enhanced state power. As argued earlier, Kohli rejects the idea that late-late developers can have strong democratic states. Another factor often offered to explain economic growth is technically correct, market-oriented policies that strengthen economic competitiveness and promote economic openness (i.e., an outward or export orientation). Kohli (p. 390) argues that in late-late developing countries, a self-limiting state whose policy only aims to prevent market distortions will not produce economic development: "The search for the magic set of policies that will produce rapid industrialization in the developing world may simply be in vain, as the effectiveness with which policies are pursued is deeply consequential." For example, "the roots of Nigeria's economic malaise are deep – having to do with the mutually reinforcing impact of an ineffective state and weak national capitalism – and not likely to be altered over the short term by any policy change" (Kohli, p. 360).

In sum, Kohli believes that in late-late developing countries, neither medium-term state institutions nor short-term public policies ultimately cause economic development. While acknowledging that "[A]t a proximate level of causation, the variety of contextual variables that might have influenced the relative success of development efforts included ... a set of institutional factors ... that are well recognized by economists and other social scientists and that often proved to be consequential in the analysis above included," Kohli (p. 418) insists that "[A]t a deeper level of causation, however, the comparative analysis above highlighted how, over time, more effective states have undertaken sustained actions that alter these and other contextual conditions."

In dismissing political democracy and capitalist markets as fundamental causes of economic development, Kohli repeatedly stresses that state-society relations offer a deeper and more satisfying causation. State power rooted in long-term, state-class relations thus determines economic development: "Cohesive-capitalist states have succeeded in facilitating rapid industrialization by promoting high rates and efficient allocation of investment and have done this better than other types of developing country states, mainly because they are able to mobilize, concentrate, and utilize power in a highly purposive manner" (Kohli, p. 390). In short, "[t]he resulting power gap is at the heart of why cohesive-capitalist states have proved to be so much better than" other types of states at facilitating rapid industrialization (Kohli, p. 420). Similar to Tilly's arguments to be discussed shortly, Kohli maintains that powerful states are not passive recipients of their environmental constraints. Kohli's state, just like Tilly's democracy, has political agency and thus coevolves with its environment.

5.1.2. Fragmented-Multiclass States

India, another type of late-late developing state, is led by accountable leaders who head a broad multiclass alliance. Rather than promoting economic growth, this state's principal goal is to achieve political legitimacy. Hoping to maximize public support, it attempts to satisfy its multiple constituencies. The fragmented-multiclass state thus pursues multiple goals: agricultural development, economic redistribution, welfare provision, national sovereignty, and so on. Kohli concludes that such a state's policies are inconsistent, its institutions incongruent, and its elites conflictual. While a real state, a fragmented-multiclass state's weak authority structure means that it has less political capacity to control labor and therefore to bring about economic development. Kohli offers evidence demonstrating that fragmented-multiclass states have a poorer record in producing development than cohesive-capitalist states.

5.1.3. Neopatrimonial States

Some late-late developing states, for example Nigeria, are run by personalistic leaders. Such neopatrimonial states never articulate clear public goals and, in any event, lack the political capacity to get things done. The consequences are as clear as they are unfortunate. The bureaucracy is of poor quality: neither modern nor rational, it is merely incompetent. Unconstrained by institutional norms, the private/public distinction blurs. Political corruption, clientelistic politics, and predatory state behavior then run rampant. Moreover, organizationally weak and politically incapable, the neopatrimonial state barely penetrates society. Centralized control exercised over a territory is either weak or nonexistent. Political instability then becomes a constant problem. Finally, a nominal democracy or a weak dictatorship, the neo-patrimonial state is not legitimate. The upshot is that neopatrimonial states achieve less economic development that even fragmented-multiclass states.

Kohli could be wrong about the type of postcolonial state best at producing economic development. Consider what scholars in Acemoglu and Robinson's rationalist tradition might call the Kohli Paradox: if cohesive-capitalist states succeed, they self-destruct. Industrialization produces the historical protagonists of change, and their preferences, beliefs, endowments, and strategies undermine the system. For example, capital and labor do not remain passive actors, but develop political agency. They adopt strategies to implement their own projects of state building, regime construction, and policy implementation. Seeking to control government, they attempt to implement the political arrangements that will secure their influence. Patterns of democratic corporatism, clientelism, and cronyism are thus inevitable concomitants of economic development. Hence, autocracy → economic development → democracy. Put otherwise, a bourgeois strata develops the structural, ideological, and instrumental power that facilitates its autonomy from the state. State-led industrialization undermines the state's autonomy, and state sponsorship of development opens the state to pluralist democratization. If autocracy is the prerequisite of economic development, economic development is then the prerequisite of democracy. Successful cohesive-capitalist governments therefore contain the seeds of their own demise. The economic development they produce transforms the societies that then push them aside.

On the other hand, cohesive-capitalist states might fail to generate economic development. Given that state bureaucracies are cumbersome and inefficient, such states could produce Keynesian catastrophes and welfarist fiascos. If they fail, they eventually self-destruct. After all, such autocracies only have the instrumental value that Kohli subscribes to them. Performance is everything, and if these states do not produce the promised results, they get replaced.

In sum, Acemoglu and Robinson would probably argue that cohesive-capitalist states in the modern world have increasing difficulties maintaining their authority. Whether run by leaders, cliques, dynasties, families, militaries, or parties, they eventually lose their legitimacy. Either economic success or economic failure undermines them and leads to their demise. These twin possibilities raise a series of questions.

With respect to autocracy: do state-organized societies in the global south generate economic development? Do strong developing states always turn out to be fit – autonomous and coherent, legitimate and stable, adaptive and enduring, effective and efficient – agents of development? Do hierarchical bureaucracies, not responsible to the general public, always guard the national interest? Are cohesive-capitalist states always economically effective mobilization regimes? Can such modernizing dictatorships always reorder their social strata into constituencies that support economic development? Is the cohesive-capitalist state always the best enlightened despotism? Might strong states that control civil society and constrain mass populations not produce political security and material welfare, and therefore only pay the costs of economic inequality, social injustice, and political coercion?

With respect to democracy: can fragmented multiclass democracies be economically successful? Could such a postcolonial democracy offer a rational path to economic development, or does such a state always perpetuate economic backwardness and presage state failure? Is such a democracy capable of governing successfully, either economically or politically? Are there no subtypes of fragmented multiclass democratic states that offer effective development? In short, can democracy and economic development coexist in the global south? Is economic development and political liberalization correlated in postcommunist states, for example?

5.2. A CAUSAL THEORY OF DEMOCRACY AND THE STATE

Kohli (p. 408) thus asks: "How and why developing countries acquired different types of states and how and why these states produced a range of economic outcomes." Kohli's answers emphasize historical specificity. Concerned with the structural capacity and developmental dynamics of types of states under specific conditions, Kohli stresses historical sequences of development. For example, he (2004: 8) argues that early and more spontaneous industrializers like Britain were "caused" by "several strands of underlying changes" and that middle, late, and late-late industrializers were "caused" by the joint initiatives of private capital (i.e., banks) and states.

To understand why some countries grew so much more rapidly than others, Kohli (p. 300) thus urges comparativists to explore specific historical origins: "Scholars of comparative development often do not assign significant weight to different starting points when assessing development performance across countries or regions. Instead, there is a tendency to treat all preindustrial, low-income developing countries – especially since the Second World War – as having been at a more or less similar starting point." The problem with this view is that "states acquired some of their core characteristics well before they become activist states, ready to pursue deliberate industrialization" (Kohli, p. 16).

The key difference among late-late developing states is colonialism. Kohli maintains that patterns of colonial experiences are responsible for the patterns of state construction that ultimately influence patterns of economic development:

types of colonial experiences → types of states → types of economic outcomes

To forge their empires, imperial powers used their states's power to reconstruct their colonies's power structures. Different colonizing powers adopted different strategies of rule. While colonial Korea resulted from the specific form of Japanese imperialism, colonial Nigeria and colonial India resulted from case-specific forms of British imperialism. Brazil's dependence during the nineteenth century was of a still different character. More generally, Kohli (p. 17) suggests that "in most developing countries states are the product of colonialism, and their respective forms were molded decisively by this encounter with more advanced political economies." Colonial institutions have persisted and have had enduring impacts: "Colonial constructed political institutions, in turn, proved to be highly resilient, influencing and molding the shape of sovereign developing country states" (Kohli, p. 409). Hence, countries that "inherited more effective state institutions have been better situated to propel their economic progress than those who inherited relatively poorly constructed states" (Kohli, p. 412).

In suggesting that "[c]olonialism has proved to be the most significant force in the construction of basic state structures in the developing world" (2004: 409), Kohli advocates "an analysis that goes deeper into the causal chain, to uncover why the state did what it did" (2004: 84) and thereby arrives at a "deeper causal variable" (2004: 216). By taking a "long historical view of the evolving world political economy" (2004: 123), and thereby uncovering a "distant level of causation" (2004: 222), Kohli argues that comparativists can begin to appreciate how world-historical time frames the politics of state-class relations and thereby determines economic outcomes.

5.3. CAUSAL METHODOLOGY: IDEAL TYPES WITH STRUCTURAL CAPACITIES

Kohli could be wrong about the types of states that are strong and the types that are weak. Scholars of Moore's generation thought that the USSR was a strong state and the United States a weak state. Kohli could also be wrong about the types of states in the global south that promote economic development and the types that do not. India is not the stagnant state that scholars once thought it to be. And Kohli could be wrong about the roots of state strength. Perhaps colonial history is not destiny.

Kohli pursues a causal methodology – ideal types with structural capacities and causal powers that operate under specific circumstances to produce observable correlations – that can evaluate his claims.

5.3.1. Ideal Types

Cohesive-capitalist, fragmented-multiclass, and neopatrimonial states are ideal types "not found in pure form. . . . Instead countries in specific periods exhibit more of one tendency than another." In other words, the "[r]eal historical records of actual countries . . . seldom reveal state types in their ideal-typical forms; states instead tend more toward one set of characteristics than another" (Kohli 2004: 12). Throwing a battery of ideal types at a single case yields complex and subtle analyses. For example, most states in the developing world are mixed states that emerged from political struggles, particularly the "classic battle between cohesive-capitalist and fragmented-multiclass political tendencies" (Kohli, p. 192). Because the potential for a fragmented multiclass state exists within a cohesive-capitalist state, the counterfactual alternative must have been rejected at key historical junctures.

Kohli (p. 12) can also think and work in terms of the variables composing ideal types: "When comparing and analyzing state types empirically one generally needs to focus on some state characteristics as leadership goals, degree of centralization of public authority, downward penetration of public authority, political organization of the mobilized political society, scope of state intervention in the economy, and quality of the economic bureaucracy." However, he is a classic comparativist who can see patterns in his variables and types of relationships in his cases. Kohli thus never describes similarities without being alert to differences, and never discusses identity in isolation from otherness. He approaches causation through static categorization (cohesive-capitalist, fragmented-multiclass, neopatrimonial) and dynamic periodization (precolonial, colonial, postcolonial).

5.3.2. Structural Capacities

State types are characterized by structured institutions and configured organizations. State-society relations consist of networks of connections and webs of interactions. Intertwined and patterned, types of states and types of state-society relations are complexly stratified at multiple, overlapping, and intersecting levels. One level is material. Structures of collective or shared interdependence are patterned forms of solidarity that arise from social relations, roles, and positions. Another level is ideational structures and shared representations. A common culture, collective norms, and public language fashion values and beliefs, preferences and ideas, interests and identities. A third level is collective or shared action. Common behavior in formal or informal organizations produce ongoing practices. Material structures, ideational languages, and everyday actions constitute potentials or capacities.

5.3.3. Causal Powers

The three levels of state-society relations are self-organizing and self-governing, self-sustaining and self-reproducing. State structures thus have dynamic lives of their own, with imminent properties, inherent tendencies, and integral logics. The result is internal feedback dynamics: historical phases, dynamic paths, and time sequences of self-referential, self-reinforcing, and self-regulating behaviors. Path-dependency can also involve self-destructive dynamics: inefficiency and inequity, dysfunction and disequilibrium, incoherence and contradiction, tension and dilemma, and ultimately crisis and disintegration, A state's built-in causal powers are thus responsible for its transformation, both its dynamic growth and its diachronic decay. Morphology creates phylogeny, taxonomy genealogy, and structure genesis.

For example, Kohli's starting point, the key source of different types of states, is colonialism. Once origins are set in place, capacities exert their causal powers: internal mechanisms and processes produce sequences of development. Historical patterns of state construction thus result from the path-dependence of self-generating and self-reproducing state structures. Since continuity of precolonial, colonial, and postcolonial politics marks the state, Kohli's (p. 376) causal methodology involves the "careful tracing of historical processes."

Common material, ideational, and action capacities of types of states and of types of state-society relations are causal. They generate real effects, especially success at economic development. The three interrelated levels form tightly integrated systems such that the parts are subordinate to the whole. The parts are specifically defined in terms of their functional role in producing economic outcomes. The state's structural capacity can thus be likened to a machine with a set of characteristic causal mechanisms and processes that are responsible for its outputs.

The state's causal powers define the nature of the state and constitute its causal agency. Its inner principles make the state an efficacious causal force. The state's deep causal powers and dispositional capacities, moreover, are rooted in the assembly and composition, configuration and structure, form and function, of its component state-society relations.

5.3.4. Circumstances

Because the structural capacities, intrinsic propensities, and causal powers of various types of states make things like economic development happen, piecing together causal mechanisms and processes allow predictions of observables. Properties and behaviors, concrete events and sequences of happenings, are thereby amenable to empirical study.

However, capacity is only one-half of the causal story. In Aristotle's sense, causes arise out of the potentiality of matter. Capabilities are thus only opportunity sets and causal capacity merely a latent potential not yet actualized. Causal capacity interacts with constraining and permissive conditions – the degrees of freedom for action in a given environment. Capacities are therefore exercised circumstantially. Given certain antecedent conditions, triggering stimuli, energizing environments, appropriating contexts, and relevant populations, causal properties become actual causal forces. In other words, state capacity only generates possibilities that, under specific environmental incidentals, become actuals. Environmental factors thus condition structural capacity, constraining and enabling, precluding and making possible, limiting and resourcing, yet-to-be realized powers. Endogenous causal powers generate tendencies for observable outcomes in the real exogenous world. Yet capacity yields outcome only under the right circumstances, leading to sometimes true theories and occasionally true laws. Because the number of actuals is always less than the number of possibles, negative facts – counterfactual dogs that do not bark – confound understanding of appearances. Kohli's causal methodology therefore involves more than the accumulation of stochastic probabilities. Theories of state capacity indeed offer a unique understanding of statistical correlations.

5.3.5. Correlations

Eschewing either inherent dispositions or fundamental essences, Kohli avoids reification. Examining testable capacities and operational faculties, he avoids tautology. Underlying Kohli's thinking is therefore the idea that a relatively enduring and stable capacity to make things happen, carried from situation to situation, produces Humean lawlike regularities. Put otherwise, he believes that structures have the capacity or causal power to produce the correlational laws that can be observed as measureable relationships among observables. Social entities with causal mechanisms and processes thereby yield nomological regularities seen as visible effects, results, and outcomes. Causal mechanisms manifesting themselves in correlations allow comparativists to make sense of the recorded empirical regularities – randomness, spontaneity, eventfulness – of the world. Cartwright (1989: 181) thus writes that structural capacities are fundamental and empirical associations secondary: "What is important for the project of taking capacities as primary is that these models show how it is possible to begin with capacities and to end with probabilities that describe the associations in nature as a consequence." Since causal capacities involve causal mechanisms that ultimately support causal claims, Cartwright (1989: 218) maintains that "the key to explanation is not subsumption, or derivability from law, as it is in the conventional deductive-nomological account. Laws ... may play a role in helping to trace causal processes, but what explains phenomena in typical theoretical explanations are the structures and processes that bring them about." In arguing against deductive theories like Acemoglu and Robinson's, she suggests that "laws themselves are generally pieces of science fiction, and where they do exist they are usually the objects of human constructions, objects to be explained, and not ones to serve as the source of explanation. Causes and their capacities are not to play a role alongside laws in scientific explanations, but – at least in many domains – to replace them altogether."

Correlational laws – if X is present in a population, the probability of Y in the population rises – therefore cannot be discovered by straightforward empiricism. Reducing structural causes to probabilistic regularities via statistical inspection does not work because other entities or things have their own causal mechanisms and processes. Each social object interacts with other social objects that are part of its environment, produce overlapping outcomes. The multiplicity of causal powers thus exist in complex interaction, constraining and enabling each other, and thereby producing observable empirical correlations, or the concrete actual events of the world. Kurki (2008: 296) thus refers to "[a] complex web of interacting and counteracting causal powers and structures of social relations." Observable manifestations, such as statistical correlations among events or variables, involve the inherency of one social entity deflected by the contingency of another social entity producing the chaos of the empirical world. The struggle among the causal powers of social objects therefore determines observable outcomes.

How then can comparativists discover causal laws? Cartwright (1989: 182) writes that "[n]ature, as it usually occurs, is a changing mix of different causes, coming and going; a stable pattern of association can emerge only when the mix is pinned down over some period or in some place ... laws of association are in fact quite uncommon in nature, and should not be seen as fundamental to how it operates. They are only fundamental to us, for they are one of the principal tools that we can use to learn about nature's capacities; and, in fact, most of the regularities that do obtain are ones constructed by us for just that purpose." Comparativists therefore construct local causal truths, measurements of the fixed causal influence of X on Y, relative to particular test conditions. Because excluded variables – those outside of the artificial situation – have the causal potential to influence outcomes, shielding makes the nomological machines work. Comparativists thus devise ways of allowing the inherent powers of social objects do their work of producing observable results (i.e., correlations). Causal understanding is more a matter of intervention in the world than of representing it (Hacking 1983). As long as comparativists take account of the circumstances surrounding their construction, correlations can be reliable indicators and adequate representations of stable causal laws.

Three approaches allow comparativists to infer causes from correlations and deduce causal laws from probabilistic relations. Like natural scientists, comparativists conduct experiments. Using treatment and control groups, they construct artificially closed systems. When interventions are not possible, comparativists substitute statistical controls. If causal laws dominate particular space-time domains and produce a system's stylized facts, statistical regression experiments can probe the lawlike regularities of open systems. The parameter estimates of regression equations, in a properly constructed causal domain, then become important indicators of the underlying causal mechanisms contained in social objects. Classic comparativists like Kohli adopt a third alternative: the historical experiments thrown up by the world. Carefully parsing causal and confounding variables through dynamic and static comparisons, they use the causal capacities of social types to explain observable relations.

In sum, Kohli's causal methodology can be represented as follows: under certain circumstances – environments that activate causal properties – states and state-society relations have causal powers that produce economic outcomes.

> Under conditions Z,
> a type of state or state-society relations X,
> with basic, natural, intrinsic property P,
> is disposed to produce output reaction R (create event E or outcome O),
> in reaction to input stimulus S (event C or input I).

In other words,

> Given Z,
> P confers the
> latent disposition or power on X
> to actively cause R to S.

Hence,

> E (O) is counterfactually
> dependent on C (I)
> due to law L
> and mechanism M.

Under the appropriate circumstances – specific time-space co-ordinates – social entities or objects therefore have the causal powers required to generate empirical laws, statistical generalizations, and stylized facts.

For example, under the right conditions, mass confers the power to resist acceleration; given the appropriate circumstances, the fragility of glass confers the power to shatter when struck; and taking into account the required environmental factors, volume and pressure confer the power to affect temperature. More to the point, given certain colonial experiences, under the right internationally competitive environment a certain type of state capacity confers the power to produce patterns of economic development. In response to historically specific environmental challenges, the state, crystallizing its social forces, exercises its political powers. Comparativists can therefore use observable correlations to help explain deep structural patterns.

Because his democracy responds to environmental challenges in a different way, Tilly offers a different solution to the Barrington Moore Problem of reconciling democratic theory with causal methodology. While Kohli tilts toward the "rational" side of a "free and rational society," Tilly slants in the "free" direction.

6

Pragmatic Theories of a Fit Democracy: Tilly

To navigate between a thin democracy determined exogenously and a thick democracy fashioning its own future, a free and rational society requires a fit state. After presenting Tilly's contentious democracy (Section 6.1), this chapter discusses his causal claims (Section 6.2). It then explores his causal methodology: complex contingent dynamic processes (Section 6.3). Since it is able to deal with environmental challenges, Tilly's contentious democracy is also a fit democracy (Section 6.4).

6.1. CONTENTIOUS DEMOCRACY

Suppose that there is no common currency of politics and no scheme to rank all social values. Further suppose that there is no single Good Life simultaneously manifesting the best of all moral goods and no one doctrine of Practical Reason on which all interests converge. Finally, suppose that there is no unitary Big Answer that makes all of the above consistent with one another. With no overarching principle to arbitrate or resolve conflicts, values inevitably come into conflict with one another. Rawls (1993: 129) thus writes that rather than being contingent, "reasonable pluralism is a permanent condition of public culture under free institutions." Even if a citizen is neither misinformed nor stupid, neither irrational nor obstinate, neither evil nor wicked, but rather is knowledgeable and smart, sincere and well-intentioned, and rational and cooperative, his or her own values could conflict. Among a set of citizens, values do not necessarily converge. Many distinct, well-reasoned, and intelligent positions can exist.

Following Arrow (1951), democracy must therefore cope with genuine clashes among political projects: conflicts of interests, different identities, alternative ideas, competing justifications for power, diverse constructions of the public good, and multiple worldviews (Zuckerman 1975; 1989). Democracy thus faces inescapable differences and ineliminatable otherness. Because partisan and ideological battles are inevitable, democracy must be agonistic, adversarial, and contentious. Social decisions invariably generate resistance by marginals and dissonance from losers.

Shapiro concludes that democracy must go beyond a minimal conception of the public good. It must provide more than peace and prosperity. It also must do more than turn coercive power relations into legitimate authority structures. Democracy should also offer "the best available system for managing power relations among people who disagree about the nature of the common good, among many other things, but who nonetheless are bound to live together" under some kind of constraining framework of laws and hierarchies (Shapiro 2003: 146). Finally, because it is instrumental, democracy must respect its constraints. A subordinate good that allows people to pursue superior goods such as family and religion, the arts and sports, democracy must be bounded: "The trick is to come up with ways to minimize domination with respect to the power dimension ... while keeping interference with the superordinate goals to a minimum" (Shapiro 2003: 148).

Adversarial democracy accomplishes these tricks of "devising ways to manage power relations so as to minimize domination" (Shapiro 2004: 11). The monster of state power is limited by vigorous participatory opposition to particular rulers, general policies, and regime structures. Adversarial democracy thus institutionalizes Arrow's (1951) tradeoff of dictatorship for transitivity and creates a "structured instability of power relations" (Shapiro 2003: 229). Citizens hold government responsible and accountable. By judging and evaluating, monitoring and inspecting, challenging and sanctioning, obstructing and vetoing, and compelling and pressuring, people influence their leaders. In a contestable democracy, consent follows from citizens's ability to challenge government decisions (Pettit 1997).

Tilly sets this general problem of democratic politics in the context of the specific challenges of state building. He argues that the redistributive politics that prompt and then accompany the enfranchisement of low-income voters involves more than cash transfers. A broad set of public policies and social services in fact accompany state construction. The core dilemma for democracy becomes, on the one hand, that building the state's sovereignty generates citizens's fears that they will lose power to the state, and hence that they will not be able to satisfy their superior goods, for example, family and religion. On the other hand, citizens also hope that building the state allows government to acquire the powers it needs to satisfy their claims, for example, regarding public education and public health.

Tilly suggests a way out of this trap. If democratic citizenship involves broad, equal, protected, and mutually binding consultations of citizens and state actors over policy questions, democracy can limit potentially unlimited government. Such a democracy involves "self-reproducing systems of control over states" (p. 40). Always a work-in-progress, such a democracy is maintained through adversarial struggles between a state that demands taxes and labor from its citizens and a citizenry that demands goods and services from its state. For example, warfare (desired by state rulers) is traded for welfare (desired by citizens), or external security is bartered for internal security. In the resulting political struggles, a mobilized and organized civil society forces state elites to conform to citizen demands. Public policy is thereby democratized.

Adversarial or contentious democracy is thus based on the freedom to oppose government, but only when that freedom is backed by widespread political mobilization. Decentralized networks and diffuse organizations, consisting of multiple spheres of publics and counterpublics, proliferate in a democracy's civil society. Popular deliberation, which is manifested as general public opinion, is facilitated by debate in the press and the media. Expert watchdogs, think tanks, and specialized pressure groups join the fray. Mobilized publics at national and local levels can confront legal forums for deliberation, such as legislatures, courts, and bureaucracies.

In a democracy, Tilly emphasizes, organized counterpower also involves unconventional political participation: protest politics, general strikes, street demonstrations, and social movements. Enclaves of excluded peripherals, marginalized citizens, and political outcasts use these types of popular mobilization to contest dominant and hegemonic elites. Mechanisms and processes of contentious politics – citizen-centered movements to overcome elite-selected paths of development – empower the unempowered. Outsiders can thereby overturn collective decisions and even governing arrangements.

Democratic governance is thus achieved through contentious pluralism: disparate interests and identities, as represented by mobilized groups claiming to speak on behalf of various sectors of society, forge agreements with the state. Rather than resulting from grand strategies of elite-determined development, paths of state building thus actually result from the piecemeal management and coordination of demand-influenced public policies. Tilly's state, though richly democratic, is thus a domain of ever-shifting and never-ending power struggles; a zone of fundamental political indeterminacy continually shaped by societal differences; and a public arena of endless cycles of state challenge, popular dissent, and state response.

Tilly's contentious democracy thus turns out to be quite Dahlian: contentious democracy involves the endless bargaining among social groups that constrains politicians. It is also very Madisonian: contentious democracy means that the power divided among multiple veto groups contains leaders. Democracy is thus a human contrivance of perpetual balances. Competing claims are juggled, different interests bargained, alternative identities coordinated, and conflicting ideas arbitrated. Democracy, a logic-in-use, thus always occurs in the midst of things, in the tangle of concrete power relationships. As Barber (1988: 209) puts it, "Politics is what men do when metaphysics fails." Tilly therefore joins Wedeen in criticizing the thinness and formality of procedural democracy. Elections neither assure popular consent, nor limit state power, nor command the responsiveness of politicians to citizens, nor guarantee that governments take account of the public's interests. In Tilly's view, a participatory and activist, insurgent and rebellious civil society is the continuing source of just and responsive, legitimate and effective, government. However, before power can be democratized by civil society, power has to be created by the state. States are indeed potential predators and rent-seekers. They prefer coercive and hierarchical patterns of state building. States are thus opposed from below by disenfranchised social movements seeking citizenship rights, by marginalized popular networks seeking governmental representation, and by aggrieved lower classes seeking political empowerment. From a negative point of view, democracy should be consistent with Pitkin's (1967: 155) nonobjection criterion: the citizen "does not object to what is done in" his or her name. From a positive point of view, the popular mobilization of civil society organizations creates the capacity and resources, and the initiative and autonomy, that erode authoritarian control of politics and thereby allow affirmative citizen claims regarding democratization to proceed.

6.2. A PRAGMATIC CAUSAL THEORY OF DEMOCRACY

If Acemoglu and Robinson begin with elite bargaining over rival blueprints for state building, Tilly begins with state formation and contentious politics. And if Acemoglu and Robinson begin with England as their exemplar of the gradual emergence of procedural democracy, Tilly (p. 33) begins with France as his classic case of political struggles producing regime experiments and political cycles: "France offers a fascinating challenge to common explanations of democratization and dedemocratization. It emphatically refutes any notion of democratization as a gradual, deliberated, irreversible process or as a handy set of political inventions a people simply locks into place when it is ready. On the contrary, it displays the crucial importance of struggle and shock for both democracy and its reversals." Over the centuries, Tilly shows, the French state built its capacity to control the people, resources, and activities within its territory. While certain French elites had much to gain from state building, ordinary French citizens had much to lose. The result: "State-citizen bargaining over state-sustaining resources" (p. 39) created "national dynamics of struggle" (p. 193) manifested in revolutionary situations that produced contentious adversarial democracy. In other words, "French democratization resulted from revolutionary struggle" (p. 37) in which states traded contentious democracy for citizen-controlled resources.

Tilly thus explores how reformist and revolutionary attempts at state building produce the internal violence, even civil war, that sometimes result in strong but democratic states. Here is an explanation sketch of the causal mechanisms buttressing his argument.

1. Observing that "all of Europe's historical paths to democracy passed through vigorous political contention" (Tilly, p. 35), Tilly's most fundamental causal claim is that "almost all of the crucial democracy-promoting causal mechanisms involve popular contention – politically constituted actors making public, collective claims on other actors, including agents of government – as correlates, causes, and effects" (Tilly, p. 78). By placing state-citizen struggles at the core of his analysis, Tilly stresses the centrality of contentious politics to government institutions – democracy and state capacity – and to public policies – social welfare, war, and international trade.

2. Tilly's Paradox of Democratization is hence that democracy is a method of nonviolent conflict resolution that originates in violence and struggle.

3. Unilinear political trends are not to be found: both democratization and dedemocratization are historical possibilities. Moreover, Tilly's Irony of Democratization is that "Democratization and dedemocratization turn out to have

been asymmetrical processes" in which dedemocratization "occurs more rapidly and violently" than democratization (Tilly, p. 71).

4. Popular contention is part of the bargaining between regime elites, local power holders, and ordinary citizens over resources. State leaders trade state-defined rights and obligations for citizen-controlled labor and capital: "When faced with resistance, dispersed or massive, what did rulers do? They bargained ... the core of what we now call 'citizenship,' indeed, consists of multiple bargains hammered out by rulers and ruled in the course of their struggles over the means of state action, especially the making of war" (Tilly 1990: 101–02). For example, authoritarian leaders responsed to external threats by raising taxes and expanding the fiscal base, and by conceding democracy and allowing popular rule. As Acemoglu and Robinson (p. 80) put it, "Kings needed resources, particularly taxes, to fight wars. To induce elites to pay taxes, kings had to make concessions, one form of which was the creation of representative institutions. In this account, democracy emerges as a quid pro quo between kings and elites, in which elites are granted representation in exchange for taxes." More generally, "Relatively broad, equal, protected, and mutual binding consultation at national scales resulted from national dynamics of struggle" (Tilly, pp. 192, 193) and "the main forms of democratic national states actually emerged from the very processes by which these states acquired their means of rule – how they produced military forces, how they collected taxes, how they beat down their domestic rivals, and how they negotiated with power holders they could not beat down." In sum, the politics of collective violence (Tilly 2003) involves bargaining between claim makers and their targets: "*RULERS AND CITIZENS bargain out a set of understandings concerning possible and effective means of making collective claims within the regime,*" and "*The 'BARGAINING' often involves vigorous, violent struggle, especially in*"

nondemocratic regimes" (Tilly 2006: 213, emphasis in
original). Offering a typology that addresses some of
Wedeen's constructivist concerns, Tilly suggests that citizens fashion three types of claims: identity, or claims that
the actor exists; standing, or claims that an actor belongs to
a category; and program, or claims actors make about
policy (Tilly and Tarrow 2007: 81–82). Bargaining is therefore the crucial collective choice process by which claims
are adjudicated, thereby explaining "how claims produce
effects" (Tilly and Tarrow 2007: 85). For example, to
increase their bargaining power, social movements build
up their WUNC (Worthiness, Unity, Numbers, and
Commitment; Tilly 2004). For another example, trust networks are involved in bargaining processes, producing
interactions of regimes and repertoires (Tilly 2005; 2006).

5. In the bargaining over citizen-controlled resources, negotiations between would-be state builders and ordinary
people follow a common pattern: "Across a wide range
of state transformation, for example, a robust process
recurrently shapes state-citizen relations: the extraction-
resistance-settlement cycle. In that process:

- Some authority tries to extract resources (e.g., military
  manpower) to support its own activities from populations living under its jurisdiction.
- Those resources (e.g., young men's labor) are already
  committed to competing activities that matter to the subordinate population's survival.
- Local people resist agents of the authority (e.g., press
  gangs) who arrive to seize the demanded resources.
- Struggle ensues.
- A settlement ends the struggle."

He continues: "In all cases the settlement casts a significant shadow toward the next encounter between citizens
and authorities. The settlement mechanism alters relations
between citizens and authorities, locking those relations
into place for a time. Over several centuries of European

state transformation, authorities commonly won the battle for conscripts, taxes, food, and means of transportation. Yet the settlement of the local struggle implicitly or explicitly sealed a bargain concerning the terms under which the next round of extraction could begin" (Tilly 2006: 423). Similarly to Wedeen, Tilly thus sees the construction of interests, identities, and ideas as endogenous to political struggles between regimes and citizens.

6. Regime-opposition bargaining is influenced by within-state relationships. Formal political institutions (e.g., executive-legislative relations) and informal political society (e.g., political party networks) matter. Most important, competing political elites, different electoral aristocracies, and contesting patronage/governing machines offer political opportunities for dissidents to construct claims against the state. While Acemoglu and Robinson understand "the move from partial to full democracy as not the result of intra-elite competition" but rather as a consequence of "the threat of revolution from the disenfranchised poor" (pp. 270–71), Tilly, tapping into the democratic tradition of Montesquieu and the U.S. Founding Fathers, emphasizes how power-counterpower struggles among governing elites sire mass rebellions.

7. As states bargain over their rules and their rule "a recurrent set of alterations in power configurations" both within states and outside of them produces changes in relations among states, citizens, and public politics" (Tilly, Figure 6.2 on p. 138). As political struggles create continuous interactions of popular mobilization and state response, state activities expand and thereby enlarge the reach of public policies. Building states thus also builds democracy: the integration of trust networks into public politics, the insulation of public politics from categorical inequalities, and the subordination of autonomous power centers to public politics.

8. Taxation, administration, and conscription consequently become formalized in representative assemblies that then fashion systems of social provision and economic

redistribution. While he often uses the terms regime-citizen "struggles" or "contention," the passages cited earlier demonstrate that Tilly means that bargaining results in "mutually binding consultation" or "protected binding consultation" (Tilly and Tarrow 2007: 202) – consensual agreements between citizens and the state. Continuous struggles over the rights and obligations of citizens toward states constitute the compacts behind contentious or adversarial democracy.

In sum, Tilly's core problem situation involves popular contention over state building. He traces the origins of contentious democracy to political cycles – mobilization → repression → state-citizen bargaining – that both increase state capacity and subject states to public politics. In his view, state building is a necessary condition for popular influence over public policy, or for democracy.

Tilly's contentious politics differs from the contention studied by Acemoglu and Robinson and by Wedeen. First, while Acemoglu and Robinson recognize the political struggles behind democratization, they analyze the *threats* of mobilization, violence, and revolution during coercive bargaining and negotiation. And while Wedeen (pp. 36–37) also recognizes that political struggles are behind nation and democracy, she too remains distant from actual armed conflict. Focusing on "political processes of community making" (Wedeen, p. 214), she emphasizes the construction of national identity groups through communication and agreement, cooperation and consensus, and convergence and commonality. She is thus concerned with the "sense of membership coherent and powerful enough to tie people's political loyalties to the state" (Wedeen, p. 1). Her principal questions are "Why does Yemen hold together to the extent that it does?" (p. 2) and "What makes a Yemeni a Yemeni?" (p. 212). The imaginings and consciousness of unity emerge from local and transnational piety groups, tribes, regions, and castes. Note how Tilly moves beyond Acemoglu and Robinson's "effective threat of revolution" and Wedeen's "national identity" to explore the coercive political capacity of dissident civil society. In contrast to Acemoglu and

Robinson and Wedeen, Tilly explores how pluralism, diversity, and difference produce disputation – popular claim making and state response – that involve armed and unarmed, violent and nonviolent, struggle.

Second, Acemoglu and Robinson couple democracy to class, or to the long-term macro structure of the political economy. Equilibrium coercive bargaining is about the consequences of political institutions for economic well-being. Procedural democracies are thus minimalist states: concerned only with internal war and income levels, to prevent redistribution through violence they redistribute income through taxation. Tilly recognizes the multiplicity of challengers contesting the government's claims to represent the people. Rather than viewing the macro structure of political economy as the critical environment of democratization, he studies the meso structure of political sociology. Put otherwise, struggles over the state are not just class struggles but rather consist of contention emanating from the many intermediate groups, organizations, and institutions of civil society. Tilly thus focuses on the bargaining between state-building elites and the many peoples they aim to control.

Third, Acemoglu and Robinson understand political order as a top-down process, that is, as an elite-driven grand bargain struck at the center of the polity. Tilly (p. 12) describes such a model as follows: "If only existing holders of power agree on how they want a regime to operate they can decide on democracy as a more attractive – or less disagreeable – alternative to existing political arrangements. In this view, workers, peasants, minorities, and other citizens might cause enough trouble to make concessions to representation and inclusion less costly to elites than continuing repression, but the citizenry at large only plays a marginal role in the actual fashioning of democratic politics." While he recognizes that democratization "depends fundamentally on the assent, however grudging, of people currently in power," and he understands that "democracy does by definition entail a degree of elite assent in the long run," Tilly insists that "elite assent is not a precondition for democratization"(Tilly, p. 139). In his view, popular politics – contentious struggles and political processes between rulers and ruled – is the key to democratization.

Wedeen also explicitly rejects Acemoglu and Robinson's view that elites are the critical agents behind regime change. Offering the Tillyesque argument that "Yemeni citizens take advantage of opportunities presented by the regime and by the absence of effective state institutions, but they also create those opportunities through their activism" (Wedeen, p. 125), she moves even further away from the study of elites. Her interests lay in local communities, not in national dynamics of struggle, and she studies the quotidian daily lifeworlds of ordinary people, especially their performances (or as Tilly would say, their repertoires) in everyday episodes and events. Yet Tilly agrees with Wedeen that local democratic government need not eventuate in national democracy. He too doubts that multiple local assemblies can become interdependent and interlocking bridges that create a national democracy. Nevertheless, his principal point is that the causality is reversed: the state building that results from local mobilization begets national democracy through the agency of national social-justice movements. Tilly's contentious politics thus again offers a middle ground between Wedeen and Acemoglu and Robinson.

6.3. COMPLEX CONTINGENT DYNAMIC PROCESSES

Because causality refers to invisible worlds – distant origins, unseen counterfactuals, and hidden connections – Tilly uses his explanatory framework to generate observable implications. And because dynamic mechanisms and processes, just like causal hypotheses, suffer from invisibility problems, they also require carefully delimited research strategies (Lichbach 2008).

One strategy Tilly adopts is similar to Acemoglu and Robinson: convert the general environment surrounding state building and popular contention into concrete causal contexts. Tilly thus argues that democratization and state building are driven by the exogenous shocks of revolution, conquest, confrontation, and colonization. He also points to underlying political-economy structures of coercion, capital, and commitment. Like Kohli, Tilly argues that types of states derive from types of negotiated settlements, or from state-class pacts. The capital-intensive state is thus based on the state's capacity to coerce (e.g., tax). Tilly also speculates that rulers without internal resources like oil, or without external resources like those supplied by cold-war patrons (United States or USSR), were most often involved in the state-citizen bargaining that produced adversarial democracy. Acemoglu and Robinson (p. 80) identify a related context: "In Africa [Herbst 2000], the lack of democracy is a consequence of the particular process of pre- and postcolonial state formation, which meant that political elites never had to make concessions to citizens in exchange for taxes to fight wars." Acemoglu and Robinson then widen Tilly by generalizing his argument: "The more elastic is the tax base, the more difficult it is for authoritarian rulers to raise taxes without agreement, and the greater the likelihood of concessions – here democracy" (Acemoglu and Robinson, p. 80).

Yet Tilly expresses reservations about Acemoglu and Robinson's science of comparative politics. Their causal methodology, he believes, has led comparativists to focus on a small number of input variables that drive a small number of outcome variables. When political, economic, social, and cultural environments are said to produce regime outcomes, analysts are using simplistic cause-and-effect thinking. The problem is that such supposedly exogenous variables are often poor substitutes and shallow stand-ins for the causal mechanisms that account for the dynamics, relations, and innovations that give contention over democracy and struggles over state construction their most interesting and important features. As an alternative, Tilly stresses the explanatory depth of mechanisms and processes operating across multiple levels in multiple domains. To elaborate on what others black-box, he develops such explanatory concepts or conceptual tools as brokerage, mobilization, certification, and scale shift.

Tilly is therefore less interested in determining which variables matter in a comparative-static exercise or in a regression equation than in exploring how constructive social processes operate; less interested in thin dyadic bargaining, expressed in a highly abstract and very general etiology, than in thick contentious bargaining, expressed as the empirics of interaction fields forged by actors with identities who couple interests to strategies; and less interested in the long-run origins or fateful consequences of great social change – paths of state construction and democratization as a whole – than in the short- and intermediate-term dynamics of contention. Yet Tilly studies, as indicated earlier, many exogenous factors that drive contention. Blending Acemoglu and Robinson's exogenous comparative-static regression experiments with Wedeen's endogenous agent-created dynamics, Tilly's causal theories display four notable characteristics.

First, while Acemoglu and Robinson see regimes as built by political actors, Tilly sees regimes as building politics. Political regimes are institutions that construct agents; fashion the interests and identities that become preferences; forge the opportunities that define choices and alternatives; and embody the resource constraints that create costs, assign incentives, manufacture beliefs, and support values. In other words, political institutions are structures with causal powers. Their capabilities and capacities are responsible for the mechanisms and processes that ultimately influence the behaviors of citizens and governments. Tilly thus focuses on how political opportunities, mobilizing structures, and cultural frames cause or construct contentious politics – or how institutions enable, shape, constrain, influence, guide, direct, magnify, and inhibit outcomes (McAdam, Tarrow, and Tilly 2001). Tilly's methodological focus on the political opportunities inherent in state-citizen interactions parallel Wedeen's interests in self-fashioning conditions of possibility.

Second, Tilly sees mechanisms as wheels within wheels and grillworks of gears that simultaneously move upstream and downstream: "Everywhere reduction or governmental containment of privately controlled armed force hindered the translation of categorical inequality into public politics and . . . everywhere creation of external guarantees for governmental commitments promoted integration of trust networks into public politics," subjecting the state to popular influences, which increased the breadth, equality, and protection of mutually binding citizen-state consultations (Tilly 2004: 254). Popular-contention mechanisms thus seamlessly meld into state-construction mechanisms, which seamlessly meld into democratization mechanisms, which seamlessly meld into popular-contention mechanisms, and so on and so on. Tilly's methodology thus parallels Wedeen's interest in endogenous self-creating causality, or in inherent rather than contingent outcomes.

Third, Tilly offers no simple story of freedom and liberation obtained by proreformist dissidents who construct counter-hegemonic states. He demonstrates that rebellious actions – revolutions and counterrevolutions – were not conscious products made by carriers of programs for historical change. Historical actors, as collective subjects and agents of history, were not social forces that formed classes and parties with ideas and visions, ideologies and ideals, and goals and agendas. Revolutionary and counterrevolutionary outcomes were typically the unintended consequences of the interactions of people who were pursuing localist agendas. Intended and unintended political transformations thus took the form of half-conscious gambles to remake existing local social orders. Innovations, surprises, and experiments – radically new forms of political power and models of state construction – resulted: "In watching democratization, we witness an erratic, improvisational, struggle-ridden process in which continuities and cumulative effects arise more from constraints set by widely shared but implicit understandings and existing social relations than from any clairvoyant vision of the future" (Tilly 2004: 26). Here is Tilly's principle of Uncertain Democratization: rather than the intended result of bargaining, democracy is often the unintended – and often unwanted and unexpected – consequence of political struggle; and because it emerges contingently from ongoing contention, democracy is often incoherent and unstable, and hence prone to dedemocratization. While Tilly's arguments about bargaining should sound familiar to students trained in the rational choice tradition, he therefore specifically rejects many of the ideas about bargaining during internal wars found in this literature. Returning to his early opposition to models of state building featuring intentional historical actors, Tilly offers a powerful critique of the rationalist perspective on bargaining.

Finally, Tilly's democracy is richly democratic yet social-scientifically operational. Unlike Acemoglu and Robinson, Tilly studies a democracy that is wider and deeper than its elections. He uses quantitative Freedom-House indices to tap issues of broad, equal, protected, and mutually binding commitments between states and citizens. These imperfect measurements of democracy can trace their origins to Dahl's (1971) and Gurr's (1974) concepts and operationalizations that aimed to go beyond Schumpeter's (1950) minimalist democracy. Consistent with Wedeen's rich vision of democracy as discourses and performances, Tilly (2008) also operationalizes the discourses involved in "contentious performances."

Tilly therefore deepens Acemoglu and Robinson. As indicated previously, Acemoglu and Robinson limit their empirics to comparative-statics explorations of the exogenous causal contexts of bargaining. Actual bargaining processes remain invisible and unobserved. For example, in contemporary work on coercive bargaining theory, analysts typically divide each episode of bargaining into three stages – initiating negotiations, reaching a bargain, and implementing the outcome – and then *abstractly* investigate the processes occurring in each phase. Consistent with this approach, Tilly turns Acemoglu and Robinson's Britain into *empirically* defined units of analysis – that is, units containing observable mechanisms of bargaining and visible processes of contention, some of which yielded political reform.

Toward these ends, Tilly presents capacity-democracy diagrams that innovatively isolate over-time movements on both dimensions. The diagrams allow him to trace zigzag paths of contention over building states and to connect them with episodic struggles over constructing democracies. Country trajectories are thus analyzed as multiple episodes of coercive bargaining between regimes and oppositions.

By collecting three pieces of information about these episodes of contentious bargaining, Tilly is able to turn abstract mechanisms and processes, and their endogenous self-creating dynamics, into concrete observations. First, citizen-state interactions and struggles involve the construction of publicly visible claims by citizens and publicly visible demands of states. The mechanisms and processes involved in negotiating consent over state-sustaining resources entail the popular mobilization of claims often manifested as collective violence. Tilly, of course, is one of the founders of quantitative conflict studies. Second, building state capacity affects state-citizen relations of trust, inequality, and power. His book offers many suggestions for gauging these mechanisms and processes of group construction. He thus offers visible "signs of trust networks's integration into public politics" (Box 4–2, p. 90), visible "mechanisms insulating public politics from categorical inequality" (Box 5–2, p. 119), and visible "mechanisms subjecting states to public politics and/or facilitating popular influence over public politics" (Box 6–1, p. 141). Finally, aiming to deepen Acemoglu and Robinson's procedural democracy, Tilly suggests that democratization and dedemocratization involve broad, equal, protected, and mutually binding commitments between states and citizens. While offering several "principles for description of democracy, democratization, and dedemocratization" (Box 3–1, p. 60), for operational purposes he uses Freedom-House indexes to assess contentious democracy.

In sum, Charles Tilly argues that contentious political struggles produce contentious democracy's accountability of rulers to the ruled. Though constrained by many of the exogenous or preexisting forces that concern Acemoglu and Robinson, contentious politics and adversarial democracy are also driven by many of the endogenous self-creating dynamics that interest Wedeen. The multiple ties and relationships within and between state and society are thereby continually reproduced. Put otherwise, transactions and interactions are reconstituted as the group interests and identities, and ideas and resources, constitutive of contentious democratic politics.

Because Acemoglu and Robinson focus on exogenous causality, they do not systematically study actual bargaining processes. Because Wedeen focuses on endogenous self-creating dynamics, she does not systematically study conditions of possibility. Tilly's methodological innovation is to use dynamic mechanisms and processes to encompass Acemoglu and Robinson's comparative statics of exogenous causality and Wedeen's constructivism of endogenous causality. He combines broad social-structure causality with the narrative creativity of agents coming and going, being and becoming. Tilly thus uses multiple dynamic mechanisms and processes, in interrelated and independent as well as in institutionalized and noninstitutionalized domains, to trace out the consequences of concrete social relations. Using a middle-range set of causal mechanisms and processes, he thereby reconciles endogenous, self-creating freedom with exogenous, externally limiting power.

Tilly's social relations and structural arrangements are thus differentiated and complex. His contentious politics consists of historically specific statistical aggregates, a mixture of interacting distributions rather than a single distribution with one mean, variance, and shape. And his democracy is time-path dependent, geographic-space contingent, and social-relation derivative.

Nevertheless, Tilly is the endlessly creative quantifier. He demonstrates how Wedeen's performances and discourses can be measured and modeled. Advancing operational models of mechanisms of contention that turn constructivist insights into research hypotheses, causal accounts, and study designs, Tilly offers a positivist constructivism – a third way between positivist correlationalism and humanist constructivism (Lichbach 2010). Tilly also shows how Acemoglu and Robinson's bargaining processes can be assessed empirically. Advancing measurement models that turn rationalist insights operational, Tilly offers positivist gaming – a third way between positivist comparative statics and humanist constructivism. As comparativists apply his trust networks to Wedeen and his bargaining mechanisms to Acemoglu and Robinson, Tilly's insights can deepen the study of concrete cases.

6.4. ONE WESTERN REALITY: FIT DEMOCRACY

In Acemoglu and Robinson's thin democracy, thinness rules. The environment poses so many obstacles and imposes so many blockages that collective agency in a "free and rational society," manifested as the popular sovereignty of an energetic and vital citizenry, is weak. In Wedeen's thick democracy, democracy rules. A malleable environment allows human creativity to flourish. Thick democracy thus lacks thin democracy's embeddedness: constraints that discipline freedom.

Tilly's adversarial democracy balances thin and thick democracy. On the one hand, Tilly explores the environmental causes of democracy: the exogenous shocks of revolution, conquest, confrontation, and colonialization, as well as the underlying political-economy structures of coercion, capital, and commitment. Tilly thus understands how the environment limits, constrains, and thus causes democracy. The thing itself – democracy – cannot secure its own existence. If X is necessary or sufficient for democracy, then X is needed for democracy to come forth. Because enabling conditions are required, democracy does not have to exist, and is in fact contingent on something else. Democracy, though desirable, could have been otherwise. Counterfactually, if something else had existed, something other than democracy would have been. In short, democracy, not being self-sufficient, is incomplete.

Just as he recognizes that democracies are not merely passive collective actors, Tilly also appreciates that environments are not impervious external foundations. Humans, with joyous appetites, worldly desires, and bold ambitions, have a will to power. They rethink givens as openings. The situation of the world thus offers citizens opportunities, and they become empowered. Alert to their environment, citizens respond to environmental shocks, crises, and challenges by adapting to contingencies and adjusting to situations. Current human constructions, subject to revision, are thus error-correcting and self-improving. By experimental problem solving – the collective intelligence of learning and discovering, inventing and creating – democracies thrive in changing and threatening environmental conditions. In sum, fit democracies, reflexively learning from experience, secure their survival by monitoring their performance.

Tilly therefore explores the consequences of democracy. As state building proceeds, states adapt to their environments, demanding taxes and labor from their citizens. Citizens then mobilize and demand political institutions that will provide them with the public policies and social services, for example public education and public health, they seek. In this bargaining game, organized state power is reciprocally related to organized citizen counterpower. Democracy thereby restructures its environment: democratization reshapes trust networks, categorical inequalities, and autonomous power centers. Tilly's adversarial democracy thus turns environmental contingencies into institutional outcomes, social conditions into political results, and exogenous determinants into endogenous inputs. Put otherwise, fit democracy draws building blocks – energy and nutrients – from its environment and attempts to remake and thereby sustain itself. As creative popular action deconstructs old structures, agents use parts of the old order to fashion new institutions. Democratization therefore involves a new organization of possibilities, a new arrangement of probabilities, and a new conception of what is permissible. Environmental constraints matter, but politics is always about the good and bad choices entailed in deconstructing institutions and rebuilding them.

The key to adversarial democracy is that citizens evaluate results. They judge what adaptations perform best under which environmental conditions, or which acclimations are the most effective under which structural settings. In the abstract, democracy offers an endless supply of good things: participation, deliberation, rationality, accountability, legitimacy, representation, justice, equity, and efficiency. Peace and prosperity, freedom and liberty, and stability and security are promised. Citizens acting in concrete circumstances determine whether their performance criteria – the qualities of life that they believe assure healthy democracy – are indeed satisfied. As democratic institutions produce policies; as the outputs of democracy affect outcomes; and as democratic performance shapes democracy itself, democracy persists and changes.

Tilly therefore demonstrates the environmental limits to thick democracy: the thing itself – democracy – cannot secure its own sustenance. If democracy is sufficient for performance criteria Y, and if Y is needed for democracy to endure, then something more than democracy is required for democracy to continue to exist. To survive and become self-sustaining, to persist and to become resilient, democracy needs Y. Because democracy cannot exist for very long without Y, Y has instrumental value for democracy. Not self-sufficient, democracy is incomplete without Y. A minimum pragmatic defense of democracy thus must include a defense of democratic performance criteria Y.

In sum, Tilly's fit adversarial democracy joins thin democracy's notion – X → democracy – with thick democracy's premise – democracy → Y – thereby offering a reciprocal relationship – (X + Y) ↔ democracy. Without initial conditions X (e.g., war, revolution) democracy is unachievable. Without subsequent outcomes Y (e.g., social services, civil liberties) democracy is unsustainable. Fit democracies take account of their environmental causes and their political consequences and hence are reachable and stable. Theorizing about the normative desirability of democracy is therefore wrapped up with its etiology and its pragmatic virtues.

So here is the basic principle of fit democracy: instead of adapting to its environment, as the rationalists say, or adapting its environments to itself, as the constructivists say, democracy and its environs coconstruct and thereby coevolve. In Tilly's view, democracy and environment are mutually constitutive. The persistence and change of democracies involves environment/organization coadaptation. In a fit democracy, the state adjusts to its environment, and in so doing alters it. Social circumstances, especially the world-historical conditions of state building, produce the comparative dynamics of democracy. Democracy, in turn, (re)produces those historical conditions. As constrained choices shape capacities, capacities in turn shape constraints. The mutual causality of environment and democracy, rooted in the dynamics of state building, is responsible for democratic stability.

Fit democracy thus combines freedom and constraint. Freedom is about the power to transform contingencies in a way that balances external environmental challenges and internal adaptive agency. Evolution occurs in the midst of things. A fit democracy, as revealed in Tilly's democracy-capacity diagrams, thus looks like a series of punctuated equilibria: as crises, contradictions, and tensions occur, short-run equilibrium institutions follow one another. During critical junctures, enabling circumstances and opportunity structures allow democracy to build state capacity. Public claim making offers different responses to the environment. Alternative state-building strategies are proposed and various paths of development advanced. Plans are implemented differentially. Variability results: adaptations are variables, not constants. Different democracies, different adaptations. While the losers die out, the success stories proliferate. Democracies thus display multiple paths to fitness.

Historical, dynamic, and transformative trajectories of democracy and state building thus turn out to be evolutionary developments. Its underlying evolutionary roots allows Tilly's adversarial democracy to combine structure and action, product and process. His contentious-politics approach thereby offers a compromise solution, a middle-ground synthesis, to the classic puzzles of how a system persists and changes, and how it reproduces itself and reforms its institutions.

"A biologist trying to explain the adaptive behavior of an organism by studying only what it did while totally ignoring its environment would not get very far," writes Shapiro (1990: 35). Evolutionary thinking is thus a valuable social-scientific heuristic: "Although later events are shown as evolving causally from earlier ones, and in that sense being determined by them, there is no necessary sense in which they *had* so to evolve. If some critical events had been different they might have evolved differently. Biology offers good examples of this: evolutionary biologists regularly employ teleological explanations as heuristic devices, yet this requires no questioning of their assumption that biological evolution depends critically on random events, or that organisms might have evolved differently than they have. The nature of the organism, its need for survival, and the nature of its environment all place limits on the possibilities of adaptive change available to the relevant organisms, but these are contingent limits that will vary with both organisms and circumstance" (Shapiro 1986: 301).

Ideas about evolution can also address a key problem raised by Wedeen. Unger (1987: 200) writes that we should "imagine ourselves more fully as the context-bound yet context-resistant and context-revising agents we really are." Shapiro (2002: 250) similarly notes that "[h]uman beings are shaped by context and circumstance, but they are also constrained by their inherited constitutions. These constitutions may themselves evolve, but at a given time and place they limit the possibilities of social reconstruction. Human psychology is always malleable but never infinitely so, and certain ways of shaping it are likely to be more effective than others in any given situation. The interesting questions concern what the limits of this malleability are and which forms of social reconstruction are likely to be more satisfying and effective than others." Shapiro then adduces the policy implications for Wedeen: "Identities are fixed to some – usually unknown – degree, but they also adapt to circumstances, incentives, and institutional rules. The goal should be to reshape such constraints, where possible, so that at the margins identities evolve in ways that are more, rather than less, hospitable to democratic politics."

If environmental determinism is a variable, the relative weight of exogenous determinants and of collective human agency in various circumstances is an empirical question unsuited to armchair speculation. And Tilly is no armchair theorist. As his political theories are joined to his causal methodologies, he addresses the Barrington Moore Problem: reconciling the causal claim of "no bourgeoisie, no democracy" with the normative "dream of a free and rational society." The final chapter draws on his insights to offer comparativists suggestions for moving forward.

PART III

CONCLUSIONS: THREE CHAPTERS, FIVE THEMES, AND TWELVE THESES

Daron Acemoglu and James A. Robinson, Lisa Wedeen, Atul Kohli, and Charles Tilly write from within Barrington Moore's Problem situation: in the competitive international environment facing developing countries, which alternative modernities challenge democratic liberalism? How do social forces contend, democratic states arise, and policy regimes matter? And what are the origins, operations, and outcomes of state institutions? In addressing these questions, these comparativists confront the Barrington Moore Problem: the elective affinities of normative ideas about democracy and empirical conceptions of causality. An author's normative democratic theory bears a strong relationship to his or her empirical causal methodology.

Moving forward, offering solutions and not only characterizing problems, Part III's three chapters advance five constructive themes elaborated into twelve theses. While the texts examined here have strengths and weaknesses that can serve as complements and substitutes, Chapter 7 urges comparativists to begin with Tilly's contentious-politics approach. The best way to advance democratization studies is to use Tilly as the springboard and the others as sounding boards to study the causal agency of individuals (Thesis 1), groups (Thesis 2), and democracies (Thesis 3). The chapter then advocates pairing the three types of collective agency with an exploration of three corresponding moral dilemmas: ought/ is (Thesis 4), freedom/power (Thesis 5), and democracy/causality

(Thesis 6). Chapter 8 argues that the recent focus on causal analysis should not push big-P Paradigms and big-M Methodology from the center of comparative politics. Theory (Thesis 7) and method (Thesis 8) offer creative heuristics that can stimulate studies of democratization. Because normative and empirical ideas coming from a research school indeed bear a family resemblance (Thesis 9), the chapter also suggests that recognizing the elective affinities of theory and method leads to their undoing (Thesis 10). Comparativists who play with the schools can creatively combine prescriptive and descriptive approaches to democratization. As comparative politics becomes a mixed-theory and mixed-method field, democratic theorists and causal methodologists become allies rather than adversaries. Finally, Chapter 9 argues that as comparativists develop the observable implications of different methods and theories, the play of paradigms for creativity's sake must be constrained by the empirics of regime fitness. Because democracies operate in the midst of environmental constraints, comparativists should study pragmatic questions about political power (Thesis 11) and democratic performance (Thesis 12): in building a democratic state, which democracy under which conditions is best, and how might it be achieved? In returning to this core concern of the 1960s, today's comparative politics can renew its past and strengthen its future. As comparativists address Barrington Moore's ought/is dilemma of causal collective human agency in democratization, they come to understand how alternative modernities challenge liberalism, how state building occurs amid contentious world politics, and how institutions arise, persist, and change.

7

Agency

Taking its cue from the contentious politics approach, Section 7.1 urges comparativists to study the causal agency of individuals (Thesis 1), groups (Thesis 2), and democracies (Thesis 3). Section 7.2 suggests that the three types of collective agency be examined in conjunction with three corresponding moral dilemmas: ought/is (Thesis 4), freedom/power (Thesis 5), and democracy/causality (Thesis 6).

7.1. CAUSAL AGENCY

People have causal agency with respect to democratization. This section begins by urging comparativists to explore how causal mechanisms and processes operate at the level of the individual.

Thesis 1. Individual and Agency. Adopt an internal perspective on the self-understandings of agents struggling for democracy: individuals hold values and beliefs, are moved by intentions and motives, and make strong evaluations and political judgments.

Slighting the importance of values and beliefs, intentions and motives, and evaluations and judgments, Moore (1966: 421–22, 485–87) famously focused on material structure. Rejecting theories explaining how culture intervenes between structure and action, he offered a thin theory of human agency. The texts examined here also avoid this important piece of the causal puzzle behind democracy's origins.

Recall that Acemoglu and Robinson make assumptions about political actors facing a particular problem situation. When choosing a regime, actors have preexisting preferences that they can articulate publicly. With their values in hand, they attempt to achieve their goals, matching their political strategies to their preferred results. Dynamic interactions during a political struggle then aggregate everyone's ends and means into collective outcomes. Hence, the authors's central claim: a contract or bargain among political-economic protagonists generates a political regime.

Acemoglu and Robinson thus view procedural democracy as an equilibrium system based on spontaneously self-reinforcing compliance. Self-interested elites abandon their aim of preventing or toppling a democratic regime that might subject them to electoral defeat. Hoping to prevail in an election, or at least expecting to restrict the victors's redistributive policies, elites calculate that they are better off losing the vote than risking revolution. Similarly, the majority abandons its aim of violent revolution. Expecting to prevail electorally, nonelites calculate that they can turn their electoral power into political outcomes.

If self-interest guarantees democracy, then democracy does not require agents to hold any particular values. As Shapiro (2002: 257) puts it, "trying to induce normative commitments to democracy in elites is a waste of time. In the circumstances where they are needed to prevent breakdown they will probably not produce that result, and where breakdown does not threaten, they are redundant. Just as incentives matter more than constraints in this scheme, they also matter more than culture and beliefs." Preferring to focus on the structural conditions that "ultimately" determine political outcomes, Acemoglu and Robinson's brief narratives never explore complex patterns of thinking and believing manifested in concrete regime-choice situations. Their empirics leave the content of political discourse unexamined. And their evidence never penetrates to the depths of specific contentious interactions. While Schmittean ideological polarization is central to their story, and while clashing transcendent understandings of democracy operate as the backdrop to their tale, social identities and political ideologies are add-ons to a fundamentally structural-strategic analysis (Acemoglu and Robinson, pp. 109–13). Put otherwise, the players in Acemoglu and Robinson's regime-choice game manifest a very thin form of human agency.

For Tilly, even minimal intentionality is too much intentionality. Reminding comparativists that political actors do not necessarily espouse programs for democracy or autocracy, he (2004: 9) observes that "few if any of the participants [in political revolutions] were self-consciously trying to create democratic institutions." Citizens in autocratic regimes do not necessarily demand democracy and then mobilize behind their demands. Moreover, blocs of people do not always espouse regime-building programs and then bargain with one another over political institutions. Democratization sometimes even occurs "at the initiative of power holders, in efforts to maintain their power" (Tilly, p. 139). Because contending parties need not reach formal or informal agreements about political order, understanding a regime as a stable equilibrium of interactions among protagonists, or interpreting a state as a steady balance of power among historical forces, belies complex and dynamic real-world relationships. In addition to the problem of actors without the requisite intentions, Tilly reminds us that Acemoglu and Robinson's approach confronts the problem of intentional actors who produce unintended consequences. A regime built for one set of purposes can take on a life of its own. Given that effects can run contrary to the designers's goals, the original intent of constitutions often become perverted. Because problems of the sorcerer's apprentice, Pandora's box, and Frankenstein's monster arise eventually, Acemoglu and Robinson's social-contract approach to regime construction is myopic. The deep problems of political contractualism lead Tilly (2004: 9) to conclude that social scientists should not "look for [subordinate classes and groups] having democratic intentions, seeking to discover how and when they get chances to realize those intentions" during their struggles against autocratic elites. Understanding claim making as complex, he (p. 193) concludes that "only in tendentious retrospect can we imagine that self-conscious democratizers put these institutions in place."

Wedeen also rejects the idea of focusing on intentional actors. Wondering whether we can "get into people's heads" (Wedeen, p. 218), she questions attempts to penetrate inner psychological lives in an effort to discern true motives and real beliefs. Public articulations of political convictions, she maintains, are not necessarily believable evidence about emotional attachments to those convictions: "stated commitments of national loyalty do not mean that people actually experience this allegiance, although they might. Feelings of national solidarity, moreover, in no way imply a consensual understanding of what 'the nation' means or whose policies best represent the interests of an abstract national citizenry" (Wedeen, p. 155).

More concerned with performance than agency, Wedeen (p. 17) prefers to study intelligibility rather than intentionality: "If, in interpreting actions in this way, I privilege intelligibility over deep-seated meanings, I do so for the following reason: Intelligibility does not presuppose grasping an inner essence or getting into the heads of informants understood as captive minds of a system, but rather is centered on the ways in which people attempt to make apparent, observable sense of their worlds – to themselves and to each other – in emotional and cognitive terms. In stark contrast to grasping an inner essence, this conceptualization of meaning requires us to discover what in fact we know (that children are saluting a flag or ballots are being checked and counted, for example) and what we need to know (what work this flag salute or ballot tallying is doing in the context in which it is happening)." In a statement (p. 17) that Acemoglu and Robinson could readily endorse, Wedeen stresses the scientific utility of her positivist constructivism: "Such an inquiry then prompts us to ask questions about the conditions under which specific material and semiotic activities emerge, the contexts in which they find public expression, the consequences they have in the world, and the irregularities they generate in the process of reproduction. By focusing on the logics of a discourse and its political effects in material practices, we can specify how ideas relate to institutions; how group identities are summoned into existence; and how publics – national, deliberative, pious, and transnational – get made." In Wedeen's operationalized constructivism, interpretable actions thus takes a back seat to causal questions about how performances are shaped, how they vary among locales, and how they change over time. Questions about temporalization and historicization, social context and power relations, and networks and diffusion animate her work. As she puts it, "identifying democrats has less to do with specifying the values inhering in particular groups and more to do with recognizing the kind of work" that democratic performances accomplish (Wedeen, p. 146).

Her book therefore offers few concrete descriptions of intimate experiences – everyday discourses and local practices – as Wedeen hears them, records them, and ultimately understands them. Unlike readers of James Scott's (1985) anthropological fieldwork in Malaysia, Wedeen's readers never really get to know anyone in Yemen. Aiming to impose her own authorial vision, she filters messy and unruly observations into general points and universal themes. Because the reader comes away from her book with little local texture, her pairing with Acemoglu and Robinson is eerily appropriate. An important part of Wedeen's interests in Yemen, as theirs in Britain, lay in a whole social object suitable for broad comparative analysis.

Just as Wedeen's constructivism never allows her readers to learn about people and their principles, her discursive democracy never commits any of its citizens to any of its principles. Disliking democratic proceduralism, she nevertheless fails to supply content to democratic deliberation. Exalting imaginative will and the indeterminacy of choice, her romantic relativism avoids a battle of ideas about the content of discourse. Forgetting Kurt Vonnegut's (1966: v) words, "We are what we pretend to be, so we must be careful about what we pretend to be," Wedeen ignores the notion that real power is getting what you need and not what you say you want. She forgets that constructivism, like Freudian psychology, is at its best when it encourages people to look at themselves and examine their ideas.

Dunn (1999: 133) reflects on the moral ambiguity of political theories that are agnostic on the question of political values:

"Fatalist political pathologies are genuinely politically alarming; but *ex ante* indeterminacy is simply the price of freedom. It is absurd to presume both that we truly are free to choose in politics and that we are also bound to choose benignly or intelligently." Benhabib (1996: 8) poses the necessary empirical questions: "How can we be so sure that the agon of episodic politics, or the contest of pluralisms that cannot be adjudicated at the highest levels, will all be instances of good and just democratic politics as opposed to being instances of fascisms, xenophobic nationalism, right-wing populism? Are the people always wise? Are their decisions always just? Is the will that guides them always worthy of respect?" She adds: "Radical visions of agonistic politics are subject to the kinds of objections which liberal-constitutional theory articulates so well: the democratic *demos* may be unjust, racist, fickle, and capricious. How can theorists of agonistic democracy safeguard freedom and justice, respect for the rights of citizens as equal and free beings, if they are unwilling to place some constraints that bind, trump, limit, and otherwise confine the will of the sovereign people?"

For example, qāt chews could fortify attachments to tight-knit kins, small religious enclaves, and ethnic heritages. Instead of overcoming membership in localist communal associations, qāt chews might reinforce the prejudices found in the bad parts of civil society. Social conformism could reproduce combative provincialism, and mob psychology might stifle individual judgments. By exalting human power, Wedeen's positivist constructivism can be used to justify violence, the reductionist ad absurdum of a will-to-power that is often irrationally self-destructive and mutually catastrophic. The democratic beliefs and preferences of participants in qāt chews – indeed whether they are "democratic" at all – therefore bears investigation. What do the members of a qāt chew want? How well informed or enlightened is the group? Are members civil and mannerly or uncivil and disruptive? Do the participants express trust in one another? What range of views are accommodated and which set of ideas excluded? Are diverse viewpoints expressed with adversarial verve? If someone challenges the group consensus, is their voice drowned out by unequal power relations? Are conversations ruled by passion and emotions, performances based on eloquence and rhetoric, or do reason and logic rule, with inference and evidence carrying the day? Are the values of equity or efficiency espoused? Do participants articulate cosmopolitan or parochial viewpoints? Is the talk dogmatic or tolerant? Is it moderate or fanatical? Are the participants engaging in anti-modern or anti-American discourse? If so, for what stated purpose? After participants leave the qāt chew, do their private commitments to the group differ from their public ones? For example, after meetings do the participants turn into violent militias, organized crime families, and fanatical fundamentalists, or do they become participatory democrats engaged in communal affairs? The point, of course, is that such questions are as important as they are endless. By avoiding blame or praise, Wedeen also sidesteps addressing significant issues. By eschewing evaluation, she cannot offer a satisfying theory of human agency. And by not discriminating among discourses, she is powerless to engage a meaningful concept of freedom.

Because Wedeen observes conversations but does not evaluate them, she never excites us about the participants in qāt chews. If we never really care about Wedeen's citizens, why should we value their performing discursive democracy any more than we should support Acemoglu and Robinson's players gaming procedural democracy? In her own way, Wedeen is as bloodless a social scientist as Acemoglu and Robinson. Neither text examines the moral foundations of democracy. By not examining the content of people's conceptions of the public good, the authors fashion regimes that no comparativist could wholeheartedly endorse. Without investigating the individual human agency behind democratization, the authors depict regimes that comparativists could never wholly approve.

Certain social-scientific orientations – materialism, economism, naturalism, utilitarianism, hedonism, behavioralism, Darwinianism, and Machiavellianism – emphasize the technical assessment of the external conditions that enable and constrain human agency. Rather than accepting the agent's point of view, these research programs bypass it. The authors examined here do not go quite so far.

Normativity slips into their rational choice-, social constructivist-, state/society-, and contentious-politics approaches. In Acemoglu and Robinson's analysis, working classes are assumed to actively seek procedural democracy. Since class trumps nationalism and wealth trumps religion, values are relevant – albeit understood as preferences and beliefs. Kohli attributes normative agency to state politicians seeking economic development. And Tilly assumes that parts of civil society – its social movements – aim to redress their grievances.

Intentionality often seeps into Wedeen's work. She implicitly assumes that communities value and thus share in discursive democracy. While she does not study "the material, emotional, and spiritual incentives such group identifications afford" (Wedeen, p. 180), Wedeen (pp. 191–92) allows that "consideration of economic motivations must thus be complimented by an analysis that takes seriously the discursive content and political-affective impulses underpinning Islamic projects." And recognizing that democratic subjectivity should be scrutinized, she notes that "[w]e may have to acknowledge that we cannot know how profoundly most actors believe or feel, although we can offer grounded speculation about their political motivations. We can also make intelligent guesses about the intensity of affect, if not its nature, at least on issues about which people are prepared to die" (Wedeen, p. 183). Apparently death is a universal experience that allows researchers to infer internal preference intensity from external observable behavior. One recalls Trotsky ([1932] 1980: 93): "To a tickle, people react differently, but to a red-hot iron, alike."

By adopting methodologies committed to readily observable descriptions, the four texts never deepen our understanding of individuals' values and beliefs about democracy. Because neither the external causality of comparative statics, nor the intersubjectivity of constructivism, nor the structural capacity of state-society relations, nor the endogenous dynamics of mechanisms and processes satisfactorily explain the human agency behind the democratic state, the approaches examined here need to be supplemented by richer perspectives that unpack intentional actors. The bargains, discussions, coalitions, and struggles undergirding democracy engage cognitively and normatively alive people. Comparativists want to know how their agency operates. Do people want democracy? If so, what sort of democracy do they seek and why? When people struggle to achieve democracy, how do they understand their strategies and tactics? Methodological positivism leads the authors examined here to mostly ignore such questions. Viewing intentions as causes, other comparativists explore preferences and beliefs as part of the etiology of democracy. Their work thus addresses important causal questions about how values and perceptions influence democracy. In *Mandates and Democracy: Neoliberalism by Surprise in Latin America*, Susan C. Stokes (2001) attributes causal agency to the politicians in an electoral democracy. *When Ways of Life Collide* by Paul M. Sniderman and Louk Hagendoorn (2007) emphasizes the causal significance of liberal values in a democratic electorate. In *Democracy and the Culture of Skepticism: Political Trust in Argentina and Mexico*, Matthew R. Cleary and Susan C. Stokes (2006) show how structural conditions bring about causally consequential mass and elite values in a voting public. And *Modernization, Cultural Change, and Democracy: The Human Development Sequence* by Ronald Ingelhart and Christian Welzel explores the causal linkages between deep-rooted cultural orientations and democracy. These comparativists are skeptical that a content-less democracy could come into being and operate effectively enough to persist in the long run. Four causal propositions are relevant.

No democrats, no democracy. Many nondemocratic cultures are held responsible for nondemocratic regimes. Asian values are said to emphasize order over conflict, community over liberty, family over pluralism, and deference to leaders over skeptical participation. Catholic values in Latin American are supposedly absolutist, elitist, hierarchical, and corporate. Islamic values are often taken to emphasize Sharia Law, which encourages the ideological dogmatism believed to work against democratic tolerance, pragmatism, and compromise. African values emphasizing the Big Man, it is also alleged, restrain the individual freedom that prevents regime authoritarianism. If led by strategically influential, militarily powerful, and/or economically successful states, such nondemocratic zeitgeists can cross national boundaries and spread autocracy. Germany in 1930s and the Soviet Union in 1950s are the key historical examples of dictatorships that served as exemplary states in the global order.

If democrats, then democracy. Comparativists have also explored the democratic values behind the choice of a democratic regime. They have investigated orientations toward the rule of law and order; property rights and human rights; liberty and freedom; justice and fairness; noninterference and restraint; popular sovereignty and regime accountability; tolerance of diversity and openness to opinion; trust and good will; dialogue and persuasion; creativity and inventiveness; political compromise and coalition building; and centrist politics and pragmatic flexibility. Such values and orientations matter.

No democrats, no stable democracy. Many comparativists recognize that states are not the only violators of human rights. Civil society also plays a role as guarantor of personal liberties. Such comparativists appreciate that ordinary people are not necessarily democrats and that democracy does not necessarily house liberals. Citizens can join nondemocratic movements against democracies and dedemocratization need not occur top-down through elite coups. Moreover, compared to citizens in a communal or contentious democracy, citizens in a procedural or class-coalition democracy might think of themselves as relatively powerlessness. If they are cynical and distrustful skeptics, their apathy and alienation could undermine democratic institutions. Alternatively, citizens of a procedural democracy might be nihilistic and relativistic, which could also undermine democracy. Blasé conformity to political norms is another threat to a certain type of democratic political system.

If democrats, stable democracy. In addition to popular opposition to democracy, popular support behind democracy has also been investigated. Wedeen's discursive democracy or Tilly's contentious democracy could build the political capital needed to sustain itself through challenging times. Encouraging the public use of reason and buttressing the importance of civil associations in political society, such democracies might promote social trust, national solidarity, and cooperative decision making. As civic spirit and citizen virtue flourish, democratic institutions arguably gain the political legitimacy to persevere through crises.

Can a democracy be created and sustained without its democrats espousing democratic values? Acemoglu and Robinson argue that the political process can lead to compromise about democracy – in other words, a dynamic strategic situation can result in a constitutional pact. Perhaps political actors then need not have clear-cut and foundational political commitments. Maybe they could, following Wedeen, simply perform democracy, or maybe they could, following Tilly, use democracy as a forum to contend politically. Suppose these comparativists are right and that actors are indeed contingent democrats – democrats depending on conditions. If so, comparativists should still want to investigate whether the hypothesized conditions actually induce democratic preferences and beliefs. After all, they could have the causality backward: rather than political orientations causing governing regimes perhaps governing regimes cause political orientations. If so, comparativists would want to evaluate a political system by judging the quality of the political agency it encourages. Rather than asking what kind of character democracy requires, comparativists would ask what kind of character democracy fosters.

More generally, many comparativists recognize that the world is not only objective but also subjective, not only material but also intersubjective. They appreciate that neither naturally nor artificially constructed groupings fully explain why agents with complex dispositions are motivated to address the problem situations in which they find themselves. Their work thus explores the rationally and socially constructed moralities that cause people to act on their perceived interests and identities.

Individuals and their strivings therefore command the attention of many comparativists. People and the ways they understand their problem situations fascinate. We care about how people, pursuing moral beliefs and making rational choices, cope with contingency and uncertainty. We are enthralled by people who are frustrated by the unintended and unwanted, unpredicted and unexpected, and unstable and incoherent consequences of their interactions with others. Tragedy and comedy, irony and pathos, thus stimulate our interest in the political predicaments of regime choice. The French revolutionaries who were conscious of themselves as revolutionaries – ready to act on a moral-political project and confident that reason could change their lifeworld – intrigue comparativists. Other bourgeoisie revolutionaries – the Dutch, English, and Americans who became aware of themselves as revolutionaries only after their revolutions began – also spellbind us.

Many comparativists therefore recognize that causal human agency requires the critical spirit needed to distinguish good and evil and to invent new ideals supporting moral judgments. After all, human beings are not natural relativists. Postmodern relativism, just like all understandings, is socially constructed. Agents generally care about the kinds of beings they are and commonly attempt to live up to their sense of self. Motivated by abstractions, people gain fulfillment, meaning, integrity, dignity, self-respect, honor, nobility, and virtue through their commitments to principles of right and wrong. As humans acquire social obligations and righteous causes that extend beyond the self, they join morality to ethics. In other words, they tie what is right to do to with what is good to be, or link rules about other-regarding actions to the self-fulfillment experienced through performing other-regarding actions. Imperatives such as democracy, freedom, and prosperity are thus fashioned through the moral deliberation that builds ethical sensibility. The oughts coming from a transcendent God, natural human mind, or social community come to be understood as laws freely imposed on the self.

While Jon Elster (2007) accepts Acemoglu and Robinson's view that desires + beliefs → actions, Charles Taylor (1985) thus stresses the importance of second-order reflections about preferences and cognitions. Emphasizing the background evaluative frameworks that provide horizons of meaning and significance, he suggests that humans make strong evaluations. Put otherwise, people value hypergoods. Recognizing the difference between base and noble, and between deep and shallow, people single out certain objects as especially elevated, noble, virtuous, and deserving, Making qualitative distinctions among goods, they choose bundles of goods ranked higher and worthier. These ideal images give meaning to life. Serious commitment and passionate choice can generate fervor in political action. Enhancing motivation, building courage, inducing the willingness to take risks, causal moral agency can also underwrite political order. Ideals become sacralized blueprints, prescriptive outlooks, and normative standpoints for political programs to conserve regimes, reform government, and revolutionize politics.

Afraid to fully anthropomorphize people, the authors under examination here underwrite thin theories of human action. Acemoglu and Robinson, Wedeen, Kohli, and Tilly do not examine how people value democracy and understand causality, the twin roots of Moore's Problem. Nevertheless, a rich causality of individual human agency is a prerequisite to a thick understanding of democracy. Comparativists should therefore reject challenges to intentionality and defend the rational agency of values and beliefs. The last best hope of achieving democracy, a rich causality of human agency also offers the best avenue for explaining democracy.

Thesis 2. Collectivity and Agency. Demonstrate how collective human agency, or the freedom and power of actors in the face of complexity and ambiguity, results from the unintended and unwanted, unpredicted and unexpected, and unstable and incoherent consequences of their interactions.

Two common perspectives on democratization should be avoided. Cultural extremists draw upon Montesquieu's (1989) spirit of the laws, Durkheim's ([1893] 1933) collective consciousness, Parsons's (1951) functionalism, and Wittgenstein's (2009) forms of life. The extremists make many valid points: culture matters by constituting, and not only reflecting, reality; culture is a nonreductive public realm of meaning that enables human agency; values are embedded, instantiated, reproduced, transmitted, and popularized in ways of life and in performances of doing things; ideologies and

perspectives are potential ideas-in-action that in concrete contexts
become real practices; language consists of discursive speech acts,
events that create meanings and shape understandings; and texts
are objects in the world with real causal impact. While it is true that
agents are causally empty without culture, it is also true that culture
is causally impotent without agents. A group is more than a
language-based construction of ideas giving a discursive performance of its values. More than a flux of textual relationships,
culture has sturdier ontological roots.

Comparativists should also avoid a second type of extremism.
While rationalists are right to place the individual at the core of
social theory, as methodological individualists they fail to recognize that a group is more than an aggregated collectivity lacking
real existence. Because a group is more than the sum of its parts, it
has a firmer ontological basis.

In sum, culturalist reductionists and rationalist reductionists
view collectivities as abstract entities without definite being, or as
ideal formations lacking boundedness. Groups are consequently
depicted as superficial realities, mere appearances contingent on
deeper processes. Democratization studies should steer toward a
more concrete social ontology. Our four texts indeed offer the
intellectual resources needed to study more causally efficacious
collective agency.

To study the rich causality of collective agency, comparativists can begin with the world-historical perspective that Kohli
takes from Moore: the timing of industrialization. To industri-
alize, early developers like England needed a powerful state.
Following Moore, such a state was acquired through a revolution in state-society relations that helped fashioned the collective
agents that brought about change. To catch up, middle developers like Japan needed an even more powerful state, which was
again achieved by collective actors who revolutionized states and
societies. Late developers like China acquired an ever more
powerful state through collective action by self-conscious agents
of revolution. Finally, when late-late developers like Nigeria
avoided revolution, their nexus of collective agents stalemated
economic development.

To move the actors in this world-historical drama, comparativists can turn to Acemoglu and Robinson. In England, coercive bargaining – threats and promises backed by force – produced grand struggles over paths of development. Working classes, engaged in mobilization and violence, warned of revolution. As their unrest challenged the regime, the state offered short-term political concessions. Credible commitment problems, however, undid the state's strategy. The state also tried short-term political repression, but high costs doomed these efforts too. Where revolution was avoided, regime and opposition settled on a grand bargain: long-term enfranchisement of the working classes coupled with the retention of the institutions (e.g., House of Lords) that allowed elites to keep their special powers ensuring them against the redistribution of wealth. Exogenous structural factors created the class preferences, beliefs, and powers behind collective agency; if those factors had been different, regime outcomes would also have been different. Acemoglu and Robinson thus probe research areas opened up by Kohli, and then move in entirely new directions.

Tilly's explanation sketch contains mechanisms and processes that allow comparativists to dig deeply into Acemoglu and Robinson's coercive-bargaining game. How did various types of social actors actually bargain over a regime? Behind the grand coercive bargaining of the protagonists of civil society lay the meso-level dynamics of the contentious politics in political society that resulted in unwanted internal wars, unexpected peace agreements, and unstable governing arrangements. Coercive bargaining over regimes involved political struggles over state-sustaining resources (e.g., taxes, conscripts, food, means of transportation). As state demands encountered collective resistance, both sides organized for a fight. As regimes built state strength, social movements fashioned what Tilly called their WUNC (Worthiness, Unity, Numbers, and Commitment). When dissidents took advantage of their political opportunities, state demands on society were least effective. For example, when intraelite competition split governing elites, dissidents developed creative response strategies. Actual bargaining was shaped by, and ultimately reshaped, a rich set of state-citizen-policy relationships. Tilly theorizes about the integration of trust networks into public politics, the isolation of public politics from categorical inequalities, and the subordination of alternative power centers to public politics. He suggests that bargaining between regime and opposition can ultimately produce broad, equal, protected, mutual agreements – in short, democracy. If so, regimes can be based on the consent of the governed and on the commitments of the governors. There are many observable consequences of Tilly's elaboration of Acemoglu and Robinson's coercive-bargaining game: democratization is neither gradual, nor deliberate, nor irreversible; dedemocratization is more rapid and more violent than democratization; state capacity is reciprocally related to democratization; and violent struggles bring about the democracy which ultimately turns struggles less violent. Tilly's big dependent variables are affected by equally big exogenous forces – revolution, conquest, colonization – and by the just-as-big structures of political economy – coercion, capital, commitment. In sum, for Acemoglu and Robinson, coercive bargaining between elites produces equilibrium institutions as grand bargains; for Tilly, coercive bargaining between states and citizens produces punctuated equilibria as temporary solutions to state building. Tilly thus probes research areas opened by Acemoglu and Robinson, and then moves in entirely new directions.

Turning to Wedeen allows comparativists to dig deeply into the collective agency behind Tilly's contentious politics: how do contending actors arise? Once they are constructed, how do their interests and identities spread among a population? After their messages diffuse, how are groups organized? As they institutionalize, how do groups contend internally among themselves? And as regime-opposition disagreements evolve, how does contention transform groups? To address these questions, constructivists study a group's everyday quotidian discourse. In their public deliberations, discussions, and debates, constructivists see the dissemination of practices and performances. Appreciating how markers such as custom and dress discipline agents, constructivists note how groups become operational via language. Symbol, as expressed in theatre and spectacle, and meaning, as expressed in ritual and routine, enter collective consciousness. Wedeen's constructivism also allows comparativists to appreciate the relational character of the groups involved in contentious politics. Categorical differentiation – conceptual categories – create the artificial borders and boundaries that make groups thinkable and desirable, and paradoxically natural. Political subjects with interests, identities, and ideas, as well as mutual understandings of solidarity and strategy, are (re)produced by power structures. Regimes and elites, organizations and institutions, forge the conceptual categories that sustain themselves and build their futures. While political agents are also influenced by shocks, the effects of catastrophic national events are always felt through their impacts on category construction. In sum, Wedeen probes research areas opened by Tilly, and then moves in entirely new directions.

Turning back to Acemoglu and Robinson and channeling Wedeen can also allow comparativists to dig deeply into regime bargaining. Discourse is an audible and visible manifestation of the concepts and ideas central to grand bargains. When the ruled in a discourse community seek to influence the rulers and the rules, they define their problem situation, articulate moral principles and priorities, and create strategies to engage in political struggles. Elites, on the other hand, articulate beliefs about how authority is constructed, offer legitimations and justifications of their power, and develop strategies for maintaining the status quo. How are grand paths of development discussed by the actors engaged in contentious politics? What do these dialogues reveal about their beliefs and constraints, aims and goals, and strategies and tactics? How do cognitions and understandings harden into the ideologies and dogmas that actors bring to coercive bargaining? And how does a national discourse over grand strategies emerge from and reflect back on local conversations? Wedeen thus probes research areas opened by Acemoglu and Robinson, and then moves in entirely new directions.

This synthesis of the texts began top-down, with Kohli's world-historical context, moved to Acemoglu and Robinson's grand bargaining over regimes, worked toward Tilly's mesopolitical struggles, turned to Wedeen's local dialogues, and then returned to Acemoglu and Robinson's regime structures. In fact, the

142 Conclusions

authors offer four starting points for comparative inquiry into collective agency. Comparativists could also begin with Tilly. The study of mesocontentious political struggles between rulers and ruled would then pivot toward an examination of grand state-building struggles over democracy, probe the creation of state capacity, and finally engage local debates about regimes. Or one could begin bottom-up with Wedeen's discourse. Speeches, writings, and other recorded utterances of citizens and leaders would then lead comparativists to address mesopolitical struggles. Researchers could then analyze macrocoercive bargaining over regimes and states in particular world-historical eras.

While the best strategy for examining collective agency is to begin in the midst of concrete political struggles, in other words with Tilly's pragmatic theoretical and methodological compromises, here is the point: to raise new questions, discover new problems, find new puzzles, and create new research opportunities about collective agency, comparativists can take Kohli, Tilly, and Wedeen to Britain and study coalitions, struggles, and dialogues over grand bargains; take Kohli, Acemoglu and Robinson, and Wedeen to France and study grand bargaining over coalitions and the dialogic bases of contentious political struggles; take Kohli, Acemoglu and Robinson, and Tilly to Yemen and study how coalitions, grand bargains, and mesostruggles emerge amid local and national discourses; and take Acemoglu and Robinson, Tilly, and Wedeen to India and study grand bargaining, political struggles, and discourses about state building.

More generally: no collective causal powers, no democratization. Because inventive collectivities are the generative powers that transform governance structures, comparativists should study collective human agency as the causal capacities, competences, and capabilities that drive democratization. Following Wedeen, there are no natural, biological, or environmental limits on democratization. The current world is a human construction, and collective human action can construct something better. As human collectivities exert collective control, they can bring about democratization. Acemoglu and Robinson also offer room for optimism. Bad things are avoidable not inevitable, and even antagonistic groups can forge creative (i.e., Pareto-optimal) solutions to problems of governance. Following Tilly, democracy without a political society is impossible, because democracy requires such action-oriented collectivities as interest groups, social movements, and political parties. Tilly thus also leads comparativists to an optimistic vision of collective agency in which the agents of social change include both the instant democracy of mobs and crowds and the organizational democracy of parties and unions. Kohli, of course, offers a more pessimistic take on collective agency and democratization. When agency adheres in state actors whose causal powers derive from their relationships with societal actors, political democratization occurs at the cost of economic development.

Even more generally: belonging to groups is a condition of human existence. Self-realization occurs as a function of the social life into which one is born. It is also a function of the lifeworld in which one remains. The texts examined here demonstrate the logical consequence for democratization: social causation flows from social relationships. While individual human capital is important, the social capital that inheres in networks of coordination and associations of cooperation produce the structural relationships that define social life and create political order.

As comparativists place the causal collective agency of groups at the core of democratization studies, they should locate real social entities and identify their precise range of referents. Midsize or intermediate bodies in civil society, such as nongovernmental organizations, collective associations, and voluntary collectivities, transmit popular will and thereby bring about democratization. To explore the collective human agency of the "carrying classes" of democratization, comparativists should ask a series of questions.

1. What are the particular types of social entities that constitute the objects of concern in democratization studies? Moore (2001: 691) writes that "It is necessary to look at society as a working whole and especially at the fault lines reflecting domestic conflicts." His theme,

    economic origins → social organizations → political outcomes, places class, status, and power groups at the core of comparative inquiry. Driving outcomes, they are the starting points of any study of democratization.

2. What bounds the key social entities? Tilly reminds us that groups are not necessarily coterminous with national societies. While nowadays states have well-defined perimeters, societies do not. Cross-cutting social structures, overlapping social systems, and intersecting social orders are important features of today's social entities.

3. How are the parts structured so as to produce, in nonlinear fashion, the whole emergent social entity? The relations and networks among subgroups yield the connections and interdependences that result in the communications and interactions that forge organized social entities.

4. How does a coordinated social entity come into existence, or how does it emerge from its parts? Comparativists should explain higher-level social phenomena in terms of lower-level parts and their dynamic relations, showing how upward causation yields emergence. How is the group bound together to produce an organized social entity? Given that processes of endogenous composition create boundary problems, how does the group deal with overlapping and intersecting memberships? Put otherwise, how does a group solve its collective action problem? Rebels seeking democratization must address a Rebel's Dilemma. Solutions to collective-action problems entail creative collective problem solving. Social dilemmas can be solved in four basic ways (Lichbach 1995). The four types of solutions, or morphogenic causes that bring collectivities into existence – market, community, contract, and hierarchy – stand for the unrealized possibilities, or the counterfactual alternatives, to uncoordinated social entities.

5. How does a social entity persist and adapt? Aiming to preserve itself, groups are concerned with their survival. Compositional consistency and stable configurations are important group goals. If structures are to be reproduced, breakdown must be avoided. An inert equilibrium has

difficulty preserving parts and relations that are in tension with one another. In a dynamic steady-state equilibrium, groups can change and adapt. For example, once formed an equilibrium can persist by replacing incumbents with agents filling similar structural roles. As the parts are renewed, groups resist deconstruction and the whole is kept together. In addition to being the origin of groups, solutions to collective-action problems are thus morphostatic causes that sustain collectivities. Solutions to the collective-action problem therefore also involve downward causation: the causal impact of the whole on the parts, or the group's conditioning of the individual agency of its members. In other words, the social group acts as an external force. Its patterns of interaction exert causal powers that influence the preferences and beliefs, projects and identities, knowledge and information, and actions and practices of its members. Agents are thus controlled by the endorsement and enforcement, and interpretation and implementation, of their commitments to the group. As individual human agents become part of collective agents, their causal agency is channeled.

6. What are the causal powers and properties that emerge and then flow from group structure? Groups have collective agency – the capacity or potential to exert efficacious power. In other words, social objects are causally effective social entities. Causal machines with causal capabilities and causal capacities, they coordinate and pool the productivity of their members. The collective causal power of the group is therefore greater than the sum of the causal powers of their individual parts. Comparativists must study how the organizational structure of the group exerts causal powers through its agents acting collectively. They also must explore how the emergence and persistence of a group – how its collective action problems are solved – give rise to the specific causal mechanisms and processes that allow the parts and their relationships to produce the emergent causal powers of the whole.

7. Finally, how do social entities, with their causal properties and powers, jointly cause the democratization events that comparativists ultimately hope to explain? The causal powers of social groups are merely propensities. Liabilities and tendencies, they are only potentially generative of democracy. Once formed, interacting groups affect their environment by generating democratization events as outcomes. The intersecting social groups exert their separate causal powers and thereby bring about democratization. Put otherwise, while the possession of causal powers is internal to social entities, the realization of those powers depends on context. External interactions with other such entities bring about democratization. While causal collective agency affects the choice of regime, the consequences of group actions are therefore unintended and unwanted, unpredicted and unexpected, and unstable and incoherent. Such effects bear especially close scrutiny.

"The big battalions of the state, of capitalist relations in agriculture, and of demography itself are arrayed against them," says James Scott in *Weapons of the Weak*. So he wonders "[w]hy are we here, in a village of no particular significance, examining the struggle of a handful of history's losers?" He answers that "[t]he justification for such an enterprise must lie precisely in its banality – in the fact that these circumstances are the *normal* context in which class conflict has historically occurred" (Scott 1985: 27, emphasis in original). If it is to have value, comparative politics must connect the global constraints on nation, state, regime, and policy construction to the local creative possibilities that inhere in everyday life. By working global and local inquiries through meso-level contentious struggles over state capacity, comparative politics can unearth the collective agency that offers the kind of causal understanding sought by Scott.

Tilly also reminds us that authority patterns, power structures, organizational forms, and patterns of rule are forever challenged. The problem of agency in politics is indeed how to become a principal. In the face of a social division of labor, pattern of economic resource allocation, and form of cultural exchange, authoritative governance, including democratic legitimacy, sometimes emerges. The four texts examined here prod comparativists to explore how social relations become the agential political relationships that cause democratization.

Thesis 3. Democracy and Agency. Defend contentious democracy as the last best hope for a free and rational society, because it encourages pragmatic critical reason, creative problem solving, and political adaptability.

"Treating categories as if they were substantial entities prompts scholars to take for granted, indeed to contribute to, the very phenomenon of group making in need of explanation" (Wedeen, p. 157). By suggesting that academic discourse helps construct the political world in which academics live, Wedeen comes closest to posing Barrington Moore's Problem of the connections between academic scholarship's empirical findings and its normative goals. Repeating her charge that "[s]ocial scientists invoking categories in this way naturalize a set of identifiable attributes, reproducing the very classifications they claim to interrogate" (Wedeen, p. 181), she again claims that "social scientists contribute to the very phenomena they seek to describe" (Wedeen, p. 181). Wedeen's critical-theory instincts are particularly animated by the real-world influence of academic advocates of procedural democracy: "Przeworski et al.'s discussion of democracy ... contributes to a political project that has significant effects in the world. Przeworski et al.'s studies tend to be user friendly for international agencies, in a situation in which the labeling of a country as 'democratic' or 'authoritarian' can have far-reaching and sometimes devastating consequences for international funding or for relations among states. The authors' claims to value-free science also obscure important ideological commitments – ones that anchor democracy in a minimalist conception of electoral competition, disqualifying other understandings of the term and effectively rending them impractical" (Wedeen, p. 106). She adds that "ideological convictions trouble claims of impartiality, enabling the minimalist definition to coalesce with a defense of U.S. liberalism" (Wedeen, p. 110).

What exactly is wrong with academics contributing to projects that aid the IMF and the World Bank? Because she recognizes that scholarship is not value-free, one would expect Wedeen to tell us why she believes that U.S. liberalism, and especially U.S. foreign policy, is morally and/or practically flawed. One would also expect her to offer an alternative vision of global governance and to explain why that following her path would be better for America and for the world. Of course her book is not about the pros and cons of current policy issues. Its stated purpose is to critically evaluate academics's causal theories of democracy and to propose an alternative that helps them understand Yemen. As indicated earlier, however, Wedeen's focus on democratic performances left her unable to pass normative judgment on the policies and institutions that concern her. If Wedeen's goal is to deconstruct the causal claims of others, her positivist constructivism allows her to mask her own value commitments. If democracy "is" its performances, why, we might ask, are the performances more valuable than performance art?

Wedeen demurs from such questions, repeatedly arguing that individual values and beliefs are unobservable. She disputes the value commitments of others, but never offers a hierarchical ranking of good-to-bad or best-to-worst values with which to evaluate and judge discursive democracy in Yemen. Her positivist constructivism, as value-free and impartial as rationalist comparative-statics, is thus deeply ironic: if permanent commitments are not possible, enduring characters never fixed, essential identities never determined, stable values always suspect, and set beliefs inevitably a fiction, then humans must commit every day, everywhere, and in every way. Choice, reason, justification, and reflection become critically important. Even more than the rationalists who can always fall back on simple cost-benefit analyses of constraints, constructivists must offer a rational defense of their commitments.

Though their relatively value-free forms of social science hide their normative underpinnings, Moore tells us that academic theories hold consequences for the world. The rationalist *is* means incentive-compatible equilibrium institutions that are conflict resolving; the constructivist *is* means emergent social constructions that confer identity and fashion boundaries; the capacity *is* means linking state and society to achieve development; and the contentious politics *is* means joining structure and action to achieve democratic responsiveness. Paradigms of politics thus inevitably couple academic theories to political agendas. As comparativists study "free and rational" societies empirically, they necessarily investigate the normative oughts of good government. As they explore rational choice theory, social constructivism, state capacity, and contentious politics, our authors thus address the core policy question raised by Moore: what is the best development strategy for the global south? Because the texts's political commitments are underdeveloped, I am forced to speculate. And because my aim is to draw sharp contrasts, I will have some fun with shorthand slogans.

Acemoglu and Robinson are modern, liberal, and bourgeois. Satisfied that procedural democracy delivers material goods and social peace, they expect that citizens aim to enjoy safety and prosperity. Looked at counterfactually, Acemoglu and Robinson aim for a minimalist democracy, or one that protects citizens from the worst things: the cruelty of government oppression and the riots of civil-society hooligans, as well as the famines associated with poverty (Shklar 1984). While the market is efficient – the key to economic success – it is also inequitable – the door to social unrest. Nevertheless, the market's distributional problems can be solved by the social contracts that fashion procedural democracy. Constitutional government, especially its free and fair elections, allow voluntary political-economic associations to form. Representative national institutions can balance the various interests. Markets and democracy are thus the cause and consequence of prosperity, but a prosperity that can be coupled to domestic peace. And peace and prosperity are what the global south requires from a path of development.

Acemoglu and Robinson's game of procedural democracy thus turns power politics into legitimate authority. To see how, recognize that politics is about power, and that politics and power are everywhere and in everything about collective life – or so one might glean from a reading of Plato (1974) and Aristotle (1981), Hobbes ([1651] 1988) and Marx ([1869] 1963), and Mosca (1939), Michels ([1919] 1962), and Pareto ([1920] 1980). Lasswell's (1950) definition, "who gets what when and where," focuses on politics as agonistic. Shapiro (2002: 239) summarizes the post-Foucaultian, poststructuralist and postcolonialist perspective as "collective life remains power and domination all the way down" and that "power relations suffuse virtually all human interactions." Different types of power relations, or different types of mechanisms, processes, and institutions, manage power differently. Collective power is manifested in markets (e.g., property rights), communities (e.g., norms of fairness), contracts (e.g., legally enforceable bargains), and hierarchies (e.g., state violence). Politics involves struggles over power relations, or control over collective decision making. Politics also involves struggles over the creation and distribution of scarce private and public goods: A gets what, where, and when because of his or her power relations and situational interactions with B. In addition, politics is about compromise and bargaining under threats and promises. And politics involves conflict over questions of identity and difference: disagreements over values and conflicts of interests.

Nevertheless, political science cannot only be a science of conflict. It must also ask: how do people achieve collective goods, reach social norms, and manifest common purposes? In public settings, why does anyone obey a collectivity? How do states acquire the legitimate public authority needed to express collective meanings and common purpose? Easton's (1953) definition of politics, "the authoritative allocation of values," and Weber's (1946a) definition of politics, "authoritative coercion," focus on politics as the legitimate exercise of power. By legitimizing the results of the struggle for power, power becomes authority and organization becomes identity.

Political science is thus the study of the endless cycles between conflict and consensus, the study of how the struggles over power create the institutionalized and legitimized exercise of power, and the study of how these centers of power beget new struggles over power. Almond and Verba's (1963) empirical theory of democracy stressed normative integration and stability. It indicated how legitimation and consensus emerged from affective, cognitive, and evaluative processes. Political theorists such as Arendt (1958), Barber (1988), and Wolin (1996) see democratic politics as creating the collective power to will and to do. In a democracy, the mechanisms of debate, processes of deliberation, and procedures of decision turn the battle over individual intentions into legitimate collective outcomes. Wolin (1996: 31, emphasis in original) thus distinguishes "politics" as the struggle over power from the "political" as the authoritative exercise of power: "I shall take the *political* to be an expression of the idea that a free society composed of diversities can nonetheless enjoy moments of commonality when, through public deliberations, collective power is used to promote or protect the well-being of the collectivity. *Politics* refers to the legitimized and public contestation, primarily by organized and unequal social powers, over access to the resources available to the public authorities of the collectivity. Politics is continuous, ceaseless, and endless. In contrast, the political is episodic, rare." Democracy turns politics into the political, which explains why authority relations are constitutive of democracy. As Barber (1988: 115) puts it, "the political task is not to wish power away but to make it legitimate." He concludes that "the significant political question is thus always how to render coercion less illegitimate, force less blind, power less arbitrary" (Barber 1988: 115).

This idea also follows from Arrow's (1951) problem: given unlimited domain, independence of irrelevant alternatives, and Pareto optimality, collectivities trade transitivity for dictatorship. Thick democracy, too relativist and unconstrained, wanders anywhere. Because a regulative order that limits individual rights and freedoms is required, any complete theory of democracy must include a conception of coercive power (Mansbridge 1996). To be workable, that coercive power must be authoritative to its citizens.

All theories of governance therefore must address politics and the political. Is there then nothing special about the way democracies secure agreement on collective action, legitimize policy outcomes, and institutionalize political structures? Is democracy, no more than dictatorship, an irrelevant epiphenomena of deeper structures of power? Does democracy, more than any other regime, make politics meaningful for its citizens? Arendt, Barber, and Wolin argue that democracy legitimizes politics, turning it into the political. Via institutions of conflict resolution, Acemoglu and Robinson's procedural democracy indeed turns power politics into political authority. Minimizing the pain and suffering of political violence and economic insecurity, they could claim, is a desirable goal for the global south.

Turning to Wedeen, it is useful to begin with a different slogan. Wedeen is a postmodern communal activist with left-leaning, radical-democrat inclinations. She distrusts power and discipline, motives and goal-directed behavior, and leadership and organization. Valuing multiple identities, she is forever wary of the hierarchical implications of any status quo that temporarily emerges from the ebb and flow of politics. Preferring endlessly consultative democracy, she wants to maximize collective freedom so that creative solutions to collective problems can emerge. An active civil society, she believes, creates its own democratic possibilities through popular mobilization. Her populist innovatism is highly decentralized. Placing her faith in small groups situated in local communities, she lodges civic responsibility in village-level action. As communities are compounded into a nation, nationalism buttresses the sort of state sought by the global south.

Wedeen thus sees democracy as a problem-solving institution that endogenously generates creative solutions to public issues. Dunn (1999: 137–39) explains how democracy unleashes the potential of causal collective human agency:

In a democracy political structure *ex hypothesi* gives no guidance whatever on the deliberative content of its politics. It is that deliberative content, however politically implemented (however the game-theoretical problems of coalition formation and commitment are solved within it), which gives the outcome of democratic political choice. It cannot be validly explained from the outside (as it were, from underneath, something more fundamental) or from what came before (historically). It can only be explained from within the deliberative sequence itself. Democracy, on this understanding, is, stipulatively, a system in which a miscellany of free agents deliberate freely with one another and choose interactively what is to be done through the apparatus of public choice and what must be left severely to one another outside that apparatus. . . . Under democracy it is not pregiven interests that determine political outcomes. Rather, democracy itself, deliberatively and heuristically, defines the content of interests.

Wolin (1996: 43–44) explains how discursive self-government encourages human flourishing and development:

[O}rdinary individuals are capable of creating new cultural patterns of commonality at any moment. Individuals who concert their powers for low income housing, worker ownership of factories, better schools, better health care, safer water, controls over toxic waste disposals, and a thousand other common concerns of ordinary lives are experiencing a democratic moment and contributing to the discovery, care, and tending of a commonality of shared concerns. Without necessarily intending it, they are renewing the political by contesting the forms of unequal power that democratic liberty and equality have made possible and that democracy can eliminate only by betraying its own values.

Wedeen's democracy – in which ordinary citizens, operating in a buffered community independent of a controlling environment, can take advantage of their capacity to construct creative solutions to political problems – is something that Dunn and Wolin could endorse.

An apt slogan to describe Kohli is "postcolonial socialist." In the wake of the flotsam and jetsam produced by disintegrating empires, he believes that the best, perhaps the only, way out for late-late developers is to sacrifice political democracy on the altar of state-led economic development. Kohli's state is consequently Weberian: centralized, it exerts military control over its urban and rural territories; capitalist, it provides security for property rights; authoritarian, it allies with capital to control labor; directive, it plans national goals; bureaucratic, its mandarins are a professional civil service that efficiently implement development strategies; managerial, it directs the economy with the latest scientific principles; modernizing, it allows late-late developers to compete in today's world; and benevolent, it produces efficient and positive economic results for the nation. The global south needs such strong states.

Kohli thus reminds comparativists that organisms are selected for their causal agency under competitive conditions. Because they can make advantageous adaptations to their circumstantial constraints, the survivors of competition dominate their environment. To survive politically, states thus adopt innovative political-economy responses to changing global conditions. Learning from their competitors, they adapt old strategies of development and innovate new ones. The states that survive are thus flexible and malleable. States that are rigid, or states that let their settings dominate, are selected out of the highly competitive arena of world politics.

Finally, Tilly is best described as a democratic socialist concerned with social justice. Arguing that the scales have tipped too far against democracy and toward market, his preferred development strategy is a high-capacity democratic state. Such a redistributive government would offer exactly what so many in the global south seek: the integration of trust networks into the state, the mitigation of categorical inequalities, and the control of autonomous centers of military power. Like Moore, Tilly is a realist who does not shy away from political violence. Recognizing that revolution often accompanies development, indeed expecting political change to mostly occur through violent political struggle, his contentious democracy pits the victims of state building against their victimizers. And the global south has no shortage of oppressors who oppress the oppressed.

Comparativists need explicit value commitments that can be probed carefully. Our authors' background assumptions about democracy are tacit and unacknowledged, and hence undertheorized. By focusing on questions of democracy and agency, their analyses can become more reflective and their political projects brought to the light of day. Methodological positivism (modernism) and methodological constructivism (postmodernism) need not turn into value relativism and political nihilism, leaving democracy helpless against various authoritarianisms. Because I believe that it encourages the pragmatic critical reason and creative problem solving that supports political adaptability (Sect. 6.4), I would defend contentious democracy as the last best hope for a free and rational society. Nevertheless, its actual value-in-use is an empirical question. Thesis 12 addresses the issue of democratic performance.

7.2. CAUSAL AGENCY AND NORMATIVE THEORY

Looking back on his career, Moore (2007: 102) wrote that "for the most part, my work is not driven by normative concerns in the service of trying to make a better world. I am trying to get better answers to problems. I've always been highly skeptical of do-gooders, from Marxism to Christianity. Explicit and intellectually sloppy do-goodism get on my nerves." Some comparativists indeed see themselves as pure intellectuals. Detached and restrained, they treasure objectivity and honesty. Careful and circumspect, they adopt value-neutral strategies in the name of truth. Using general concepts to elaborate abstract theoretical structures, they avoid real-world policy problems. Employing ponderous study designs to parse a seamless and senseless reality, they study causal methodology's "is" for the pure joy of satisfying their curiosity.

Other comparativists, equally neutral toward politics, study democratic theory's "ought" for the intrinsic pleasure of pondering human ideals. Many place democratic theories in the context of concrete empirical battles and then reflect on the metaphysical domains where democracy resides. Arguing that the purpose of social science is to investigate moral claims, they use the great discoveries of the science of democracy – its models and arguments, methods and procedures, and findings and laws – to revisit and rethink, revise and reshape, and ultimately redefine and reformulate the fundamentals of democratic theory.

Pure intellectuals, goes the complaint, join inbred academic communities who produce dead-end and useless – narrow and sterile, lifeless and ultimately irrelevant – results. Because social-scientific problems concern people, still other comparativists aim for value relevance and engage the major controversies of their times. Aiming to address vital normative issues, they examine a problem's applied side. Believing that as authors they have political agency, these comparativists confront issues of public policy. Feeling a responsibility to influence the human condition, they move from contemplation to action. Reformists and revolutionaries seeking the best-performing regime and the most-just social order, they want their theories to contribute to a better world: "Heretofore the philosophers have only interpreted the world, in various ways, the point, however, is to change it" (Marx [1845] 1998). Another vision of the comparativist is therefore the action intellectual. Such comparativists operate in the public sphere as political journalists, popular essayists, contentious polemicists, and combative muckrakers. Aware of the ideological underpinnings of their work, they turn their ethical assumptions into well-elaborated normative arguments. Combining philosophical reflection with empirical social science, these scholar-practitioners are politically engaged, public spirited, and civic minded. They model themselves on public intellectuals who have produced important scholarly work: Adam Smith, Edmund Burke, Alexis de Tocqueville, Hannah Arendt, Václav Havel, Leo Strauss, Isaiah Berlin, Raymond Aron, Henry Kissinger, and Pat Moynihan. If organized into transnational advocacy networks, they can mix the two worlds of academic science and policy advocacy.

The three causal agencies identified herein – individuals, collectivities, and democracy – generate three normative dilemmas for the latter group of comparativists. This section first discusses the ought/is binary: how can comparativists reconcile normative value commitments with factual causal claims? It then turns to the freedom/power dichotomy: how can comparativists reconcile internal group agency with external social structure? Finally, the section explores the democracy/causality dual: how can comparativists reconcile democratic theory with causal methodology?

Thesis 4. Ought and Is. Reconcile normative commitments with causal claims.

Is "ought/is" an unyielding "ought" coupled with an inflexible "is"? Alternatively, is "is" not also "ought" and "ought" not also "is," and thus should "is" also be "ought" and "ought" also be "is"?

Weber (1946c: 350–51, emphasis in original) accepts Hume's guillotine on which the prescriptive "ought" and the descriptive "is" never meet: "whenever rational, empirical knowledge has consistently worked through to the disenchantment of the world and its transformation into a causal mechanism ... science encounters the claims of the ethical postulate that the world is a God-ordained, and hence somewhat *meaningfully* and ethically oriented, cosmos. In principle, the empirical as well as the mathematically oriented view of the world develops refutations of every intellectual approach which in any way asks for a 'meaning' of inner-worldly occurrences." In other words, while values are a priori metaphysical principles, universal ultimates capturing the significance and meaning of reality, facts are a posteriori concrete particulars, empirical observables grasping surface realities. Irreconcilably split, "ought" and "is" never coincide. To collapse one into the other, or to reduce one to the other, degrades both. Weber's positivism assumes that there is no objective or demonstrable validity to values, and hence fashions an unbridgeable chasm between values and science. Positivists thus stress value neutrality: in inquiry, scholarly detachment creates the distance that intellectual freedom requires. In undertaking pure science, or science for science's sake, questions of values must bear no relationship to questions of fact. Given any set of facts, comparativists are therefore free to adopt any number of values; before any set of values, they are free to entertain any number of facts.

To think otherwise is to commit the naturalistic or historicist fallacy of confusing the real with the rational. It is a category mistake to hold that if something "is," it "ought" to be. Put otherwise, one cannot derive an "ought" from an "is": "Henri Poincaré, who once remarked to Durkheim that from the scientific proposition 'A toadstool is a poisonous mushroom' one cannot derive the proposition 'Don't eat toadstools'" (Lukes 1985: 500). The world is therefore always out of balance. Things are never what they should be. Everything is what it is and not something else, and surely not what it should be. Counterfactually, everything should be what it should be, and not what it is. Things consequently never make complete sense: benevolence can bring about evil; bad things happen to good people; suffering does not only inflict the sinful; crime does not always fit the punishment; virtue is not necessarily happiness; and so on.

On the one hand, the absence of value commitments holds instrumental value for research: if the variability of the world implies moral indeterminacy, comparativists can proceed with science. They can develop descriptive generalizations about a particular group's standards that hold at a particular time, in a particular place, and under particular circumstances. Comparativists can also develop explanatory generalizations about how their descriptive generalizations came to be (origins) and how they matter (consequences). On the other hand, comparativists limited to describing and explaining values cannot demonstrate that one value is superior to another. And when values are impervious to facts, the facts ultimately eat the values. Empirical single-mindedness screens out normative judgment. Without value commitments, all values are equal, and by not seeking to understand the good of a thing, all forms of human life become equivalently desirable. When knowledge of the facts of existence becomes inquiry's sole concern, moral equivocation, masked as skepticism and cynicism, results. Comparativists then face three sets of problems.

First, a scientific positivism blind to the rational justification of ethics fools itself. Because value relativists and moral neutralists claim that they have something to say about ethos – that all standards are relative – their claim is self-refuting. Positivists in fact share values. They hold dear the norms of a philosophy of science that emphasizes research design and statistics. Values are also part of their science because they advocate theories based on epistemological desiderata of parsimony, coherence, simplicity, beauty, naturalness, and past predictive success. Moreover, "facts" have many of the same weaknesses in scientific inquiry as "values" have in normative justification. "Facts" are theory laden, changeable, and contextually relevant. As for values, so it is for facts: scientists offer reasons for facts being facts.

Second, even if science is not called upon to justify ethics, the pragmatic question – So what? – is significant. What do comparativists do with the facts once they find them? The "fact situation," or the "pure facts," is an insufficient basis for a scientist's problem situation. Facts without values are fatuous – trivial and sterile, pointless and useless. A cognitive interest in objective facts is an inadequate basis for a comparative science of democracy because it ignores important questions about the good life. If comparativists study the causal agency of individuals and collectivities seeking human emancipation, they must show how values ultimately confront facts.

Finally, even if rational criticism of an ethos is not possible, political choices are made anyway. Stability and order become favored over reform and revolution. When democracy lacks moral foundations or ethical justifications, tradition, faith, habit, and necessity dictate political order. Where democratic values are purely subjective, realpolitik and force become the arbiters of human affairs. And if positivistic science ignores questions of the highest good and most complete goodness, interest shifts to the lowest common denominator: private satisfaction of bodily needs resulting from the material wealth and economic prosperity guaranteed by the peace and security available from a state that exercises minimal interference in lifeworlds.

Comparativists therefore should recognize that "ought" implies "is" for several reasons. First, an empirical "ought" often becomes an empirical "is." While they come to understand the structural logic of a given situation, people begin to appreciate the false necessity of inevitability. Only stoical slaves see appearances as unyielding and inexorable. Many come to realize that a given problem is not the final problem situation. Moreover, humans can scrutinize the order behind perception and, following Marx, recognize that order as someone else's order, not a God-given order. Rousseau thus wanted to "take men as they are, and laws as they might be." The difference between the world as it is – evil, unjust, and corrupt – and the world as it should be – good, virtuous, and moral – motivates people to perfect the world, to turn the Rational into the Real, Ought into Is, and this-world corruption into other-world idealism. "All historical experience confirms the truth – that man would not have attained the possible unless time and again he reached out for the impossible." Hence, as George Bernard Shaw ([1903] 2010) quipped, "The reasonable man adapts himself to the world: the unreasonable one persists to adapt the world to himself. Therefore all progress depends on the unreasonable man." Neiman (2009: 15) puts the paradox as follows: "Of course the ideas of reason conflict with the claims of experience. That's what ideas are meant to do. Ideals are not measured by whether they conform to reality; reality is judged by whether it lives up to ideals. Reason's task is to deny that the claims of experience are final – and to push us to widen the horizons of experience by providing ideas that experience ought to obey." Put otherwise, humans desire to realize their goals, and to turn moral inquiry into political activity. Moderns dream of changing the world, of reshaping reality to realize their hopes, and of living their dreams. Rather than resigning themselves to someone else's grim and fixed reality, to taking the world at face value, moderns question experience, imagine that things could be better, and aim to change a piece of creation. By making goodness and truth coincide, they attempt to begin the world anew.

Praxis thus involves turning an "ought" into an "is," or making ideals real. Practical reason, refusing to abandon the world to the facts, can change the facts. When the facts of the world are not what they should be, if the facts go wrong and the world does not make sense, people ask why and wonder why not. In Robert F. Kennedy's phrase, "There are those who look at things and ask why? I dream of things that never were and ask why not." Put otherwise, a "should question" yields a "why not question" which is the counterfactual of a "why question."

"Ought" also implies "is," secondly, when sentences that express norms imply that emotions motivate action: I really *should* do this and not do that. Third, "ought" implies "is" when norms generate social facts due to the compulsion of threats and promises: You really *should* do this and not do that. Finally, "ought" implies "is" when "ought" implies "can." To say that someone should or must do something is to assume that he or she can do it. Otherwise, the injunction lacks moral force: "If it is not possible for me to do something then it cannot be the case that I morally ought to do it" (Hardin 1995: 43). Normative theories are thus conditional upon empirical propositions about preferences and beliefs, resources and capabilities, contexts and institutions, and actions and behaviors.

Because "ought" implies "is" in several ways, inductive methods can evaluate norms. The science of morals thus investigates the empirical concomitants of ethical activism. For example,

Weber ([1924] 1968) argued that normative ideas have consequences, but not without the agency of subjective interests behind
them. His claim could be tested with data on the moral judgments
behind political action. The science of morals could also investigate beliefs about the empirical world. Gross (1997: 18) thus
examined the philosophical principles and contextual understandings that cause people to act on behalf of others. The results
were surprising: "The case studies of social activism described
earlier ... suggest that enlightened moral judgment is of little
consequence for successful action. Activism is not driven by
moral maturity as Rawls, Habermas, and Mill suggest. Instead,
parochialism and convention are the dominant forces behind
ethical activism. This leads us, perhaps somewhat reluctantly,
toward a weak model of political morality and democratic per-
sonality characterized by political efficacy rather than moral wisdom, a minimal rather than full understanding of objective moral
norms, and attenuated but not full autonomy." In other words,
"the most politically competent individuals are, most often, the
least morally competent. Enlightened political actors, on the other
hand, are often long on moral indignation but short on political
action" (Gross 1997: 11).

Turning the ought/is problem around, description leads to
explanation which leads to prescription. For example, it is easy
to see how two empirical "is's" can determine a logical "ought."

Is (fact) Number 1: If I punch the police officer, I will go to jail.
Is (fact) Number 2: I do not want to go to jail.
Conclusion: I ought not punch the police officer.

Moreover, rather than necessarily being neutral, descriptive terms
are often evaluatively loaded. Comparativists indeed find it is
impossible to avoid the judgmental words and concepts that
shape the possibilities of experience. Terms such as violence, revolution, alienation, law, development, crime, citizenship, repression,
and, yes, democracy cross the fact/value dichotomy. The language
used in comparative politics thus includes ethically colored ideas
that mark out the morally relevant features of a situation. Their
nomenclature allow comparativists to investigate moral principles

and thus to offer reasoned judgments about how people seek to
maximize pleasure and maintain human dignity. As Taylor (1985:
90) notes, moral sophistication requires the ability to wield a complex and sensitive moral vocabulary: "A given explanatory framework secretes a notion of good, and a set of valuations, which
cannot be done away with. . . . For establishing a given framework
restricts the range of value positions which can be defensibly
adopted. . . . The framework can be said to distribute the onus of
argument in a certain way. It is thus not neutral." Moreover, "The
only way to avoid this while doing political science would be to
stick to the narrow-gauge discoveries which, because they are,
taken alone, compatible with a great number of political frameworks, can bathe in an atmosphere of value neutrality. That
Catholics in Detroit tend to vote Democrat can consort with almost
anyone's conceptual scheme, and thus with almost anyone's set of
political values. But to the extent that political science cannot
dispense with theory, with the search for a framework, to that
extent it cannot stop developing normative theory."

Assessing when "is" implies "ought" means abandoning a
deontological view of ethics. If an ethical "ought" is intrinsic,
commitment to a democratic theory is then a duty, an end-in-itself
or idealistic calling that is the right thing to do in all circumstances. In other words, "ought" dominates "is" because faith in
a higher moral obligation trumps any consequences of morality.
However, the transcendental illusion of a privileged access to the
right reifies the unconditional. Scholastic metaphysics, absolutist
speculation, and fanatic idolatry follow. Absent the power of a
transcendental deduction, humans lack objective knowledge of
the moral law. Possessing only incomplete knowledge of the right,
people must find practical ways to attain their ends. In a teleological view of ethics, "is" thus generates "ought" through the
utilitarian or practical consequences of "is." Rather than the
speculative metaphysics of God or nature, the origin of values is
experience and the ground of norms is consequences. Value commitments can thus be based on factual consequences: in situation
X, the net benefits of option A are greater than the net benefits of
option B. In the marketplace of values, commitments are therefore

selected or rejected on the basis of their fruitfulness. Because values are amenable to empirical investigation, there is a rational and objective basis for deciding right and wrong. The rational assessment of consequences turns values into a kind of moral fact. Institutions, for example, marriage, property, and language are constitutive rules or norms that everyone ought follow (Hardin 1995: 44) because it is practically useful to follow such conventions (i.e., driving on right side of road).

As people create ideals that cannot be fulfilled, they confront their lofty principles with mundane reality, and deal with the bittersweet tensions between truth, beauty, and justice. Notwithstanding the difficulties of learning from facts, norms of knight errantry that prove to be quixotic are often changed. Despite the capacity for error and self-deception, utopian fantasies are often abandoned. As the empirical implications of valueless values are worked out, new and more realistic ones are created. Put otherwise, after some empirical testing, people adjust their ideals. As people turn "ought" into "is," attempting to make the "ought" work, they turn the thinkable into the possible, and then iterate. An "ought" that lead to an "is" often means a revised "ought."

Hence, "is" implies "ought" and "ought" implies "is" because of cycles of is-ought-is and ought-is-ought. As people act according to their fictions, ideal stories turn into empirical facts. And as people adjust their expectations they create new stories that turn empirical facts into fictions. Political engineering or praxis thus involves a perpetual swinging back-and-forth, a cyclical dynamic between "is" and "ought." The dynamic involves prediction and testing, conjecture and refutation, criticism and creation, evaluation and selection. As people measure realities by ideals and ideals by realities, norms and facts, theories and practices, regulative ideas and concrete experiences become intertwined. Instantiated in the real world, the ought/is dichotomy is elaborated by reason and evidence.

Rawls (1971) thus writes of a reflective equilibrium between the claims of theory and the evidence from practice. A realistic utopia, such a pragmatic equilibrium results from mutual adjustment. When their intended and unintended consequences are taken into account, normative principles are feasible, implementable and thus desirable.

Pragmatism thus aims for the unity of theory and practice. Pragmatic research on norms and empirics is a dialectical and dialogical tool that synthesizes in the midst of things. Based on reason and deliberation, it reconciles facts with values through learning and updating. Revisions of commitment unite the world-that-ought-to-be with the world-that-is.

Barrington Moore's concluding reflections adopt this perspective on is-ought cycles. He implies that people do not always draw deterministic conclusions about causal necessities and historical forces. They often question where they came from and where they are going. As agents struggle with and against others, battling their environment in an attempt to transform it, their ideas free them from bondage to the local empirical world. Motivating them, their ideas give their agency momentum.

Moore's Problem thus assumes that the social scientific search for universal and systematic empirical regularities should not deter normative investigations into human freedom and social justice. Comparativists should recognize people's capacity to change and transform, and to bring about something new. Human creativity is rooted in the symbolic capacity of human beings: cognitive representations of the rules and operations of language allow the abstract thinking that fuels the imagination. As people visualize alternative futures, picturing counterfactual scenarios gives actors the causal agency they need to realize their general values and particular goals. Practical reason – how to do things – emerges in lifeworld situations in which people ponder possibilities that are always wider than they currently think. In short, the causal agency behind democracy involves creative processes. Operating in the midst of problem situations, citizens try to find solutions to problems.

People thus attempt to discover the possibilities that adhere in particular times and places to liberate themselves from finality and to enrich the human potentialities of the here and now. In doing so, they become aware of the external world as genuinely external. To have free will, to be more than "I am what I am" and "I do what I will do," agents must be able to push that external reality around. Put otherwise, free will entails recognizing real external constraints on agency. Human power is thus parasitic on situational factors because agents take advantage of conditions and seize the opportunities offered by context.

Is-ought cycles thus result from reflexivity, or the experience of recognizing ourselves, understanding how we live our lives, situating ourselves in the world, and appreciating our significance for the social construction of political events. What we do is influenced by whom we think we are and what we think we are doing. Because thought is linked to action, self-interpretation affects behavior. How we come to see our existence, how our consciousness operates, and how we talk about ourselves shape our agency. Our forethought in selecting goals, making plans, deliberating about expected outcomes, and regulating our actions entails self-awareness, self-reflection, and self-examination.

Moreover, self-understanding is a variable that can be criticized, corrected, and improved by empirical inquiry. If we come to see our self-understandings as mistaken and wrong, inadequate and misleading, they can be jettisoned for alternative interpretations. Adjustment comes from an internal hermeneutic dialogue. Reasoned reflection and refined judgments are made about preferences and beliefs, goals and knowledge, identity and cognitions, commitments and information, morals and understandings, practices and performances, emotions and sentiments, memories and expectations, capabilities and resources, and decisions and calculations.

Reflexivity thus requires learning, and learning requires objective inquiry into the facts of a situation. One distances oneself from oneself and puts oneself in different positions. As one tries on different shoes, reflexivity entails engaged impartiality: the distance from the real that is needed to judge or evaluate. Weber (1946b: 129) thus begins with the conditions of the external world: the historical facts and forces dictating necessity, and the social context and conditions determining inevitability. Only after the historical narrative unfolds does he turn his attention to internal meanings and the agency of the actors.

Combining a study of the heart – the moralist duty, calling, mission, or obsession – with a study of the head – the cognitive beliefs and understandings of the how and why – Weber fashions a study of the stomach – the practical, the utilitarian, and the instrumental.

Reflexivity increases our causal capacity because it allows humans to be self-organizing, self-regulating, and self-constituting. Through proactive intentionality, we develop the competence and skills that build causal agency. Explanations of democratization therefore must ultimately include self-understandings of actors, or how actors explain themselves to themselves.

In sum, "ought" and "is" have permeable boundaries because norms and empirics are two ways of understanding one concrete reality. Constituted by both, the whole is composed by the two approaches. Ideals and practices are thus a mutually supporting system. In the context of some environment, they provide the opportunities and constraints of choice.

Comparativists, Weber taught, must combine an ethics of conviction with an ethics of responsibility, or value rationality with instrumental rationality. If there is too much "ought," hope trumps analysis. The utopian revolutionary, too optimistic, ignores constraints and thereby lacks the patience needed for success. If there is too much "is," analysis trumps hope. The passive conservative, too pessimistic, fetishizes limitations and thereby lacks the creative agency needed for action. Whitehead (cited in Fung 2007: 443) comments that "The tragedy of the world is that those who are imaginative have but slight experience, and those who are experienced have feeble imaginations. Fools act on imagination without knowledge, and pedants act on knowledge without imagination."

Barrington Moore believed that science could address questions of value. He thought that comparativists could pursue a moral project within causal parameters. He wanted comparativists to reflect critically on both ends and means in order to clarify and critique, judge and evaluate, and ultimately restrict and limit, choice. Research in this vein becomes an untidy mixture of deep passion and cool analysis, speculation and facticity, principles and predictions, and moral thought and analytic history. Its theories are at once practical and scientific.

Thesis 5. Freedom and Power. Reconcile group agency with causal social structure.

Causal laws are scientific regularities that impose regulative restrictions on human behavior. If empirical laws operating in democracy limit the range of implementable normative ideals, citizens must work within these laws. Are the people then truly free? Can they still decide the values under which they will live? If positive theories of democracy constrain freedom, can collectivities response to challenging new problem situations by fashioning creative new political constructions, or must democrats succumb to the dictates of exogenously determined realities? Put otherwise, must citizens operate under heteronomously imposed causality, or can a free people fashion their own causal laws?

Shapiro (2003: 17) outlines the freedom-determinism problem: "The allure of science and the commitment to individual rights are both basic to the political consciousness of the Enlightenment." However, "Science is a deterministic enterprise, concerned with discovering the laws that govern the universe. In the social and political realms this point has obvious potential for conflict with an ethic that emphasizes individual freedom: if human actions are law-governed, how can there be the freedom of action that gives the commitment to individual rights its meaning and point?" (Shapiro 2003: 16). Hence the question: "If there are unassailable right answers about political legitimacy that any clearheaded person must affirm, in what sense do people really have the right to decide this for themselves? But if they are free to reject what science reveals on the basis of their own convictions, then what is left of science's claim to priority over other modes of engaging with the world?" (Shapiro 2003: 17).

Behavioralists offer one response to the question of whether environments determine or if people decide. Behavioralist explanations are outside-in theories of contextual contingency. Experience then responds like a passive mirror to an objective world. While individual preferences and beliefs might be causes

(Thesis 2), these causes are in turn caused by habitat. Structured habitats possess exogenous causal capacities that exercise external causal powers over an agent's thoughts and deliberations, emotions and intentions, and strategies and commitments. Carrotted and sticked, rewarded and punished, action is coerced by conditions. People are thus pawns of mechanical causality. Human fate is to live a factual existence, subject to setting and subordinate to surroundings. When humans are objects acted upon by collisions with their neighborhoods, a fatalistic naturalism results: nature bounds human activities. Exogenous factors, which trump all else, are the forces that people can neither go behind nor around, neither below nor atop.

Most important, as input leads to output, throughput is ignored. If comparativists attribute necessity to decisive environmental causes, preferences and beliefs are reduced to epiphenomena. When environmental independent variables affect subjective dependent variables without a mechanism that selects and decides, motivates and judges, adapts and adjusts, and regulates and executes, choice is dependent on a deeper reality that is outside of choice itself. If environmental causes are inevitable and decisive, if the blind forces of fate are unresponsive to human agency, futility results: people are objects, not subjects, and their voices irrelevant. Without wiggle room for decision making, all people can do is endure the pleasures and pains conferred by their situation.

Chomsky (1959) offers a powerful criticism of input-output or stimulus-response behavioralism: our verbal repertoire is far greater than repeating the sentences that we learn in early childhood. In other words, behavioralism ignores people's inborn creative cognitive powers. If the mind has the capacity to invent new sentences, externalism is a cheap reductionism that cannot explain the complexity of human thought.

Reflectivist theories argue similarly: humans are more than cogs in the wheel of some group mind or collective consciousness, greater than pawns of some managerial elite or ruling class, and stronger than prisoners in some iron cage of a bureaucratic hierarchy or structural system. Born into a world they did not make, people can take a stand for or against that world. Humans are thus free moral agents guided by their own chosen values and beliefs who can act strategically to devise ways that implement their goals. Inside-out or interior-to-exterior theories thus emphasize creative and experimental responses to the environment. Human agents are in fact enabled by structures: their roles or place in the social system confers agential power that allows them to be more than passive reactors to causal mechanisms and structures. Withstanding conditions and circumventing constraints, agents use trial-and-error procedures and adapt to changing environments. Agents also adapt by shaping their environment. Finally, agents adapt by selecting their environment, that is, by moving from one environment to another. Dunn (1999: 133) characterizes voluntaristic humanism as follows: "All polities allocate and constrain agency: the raw causal capacity to act and bring about effects by such actions. ... None eliminates agency. Agency, until proven otherwise, simply is free and mind-dependent." Challenging factual experience with counterfactual imagination is the best guarantor of human flourishing.

Environmentalist and reflectivist perspectives can be combined. Barrington Moore recognized that theories of society influence social reality by creating expectations that motivate action to change the world. While pessimism about the environment might lead people to see situations realistically and thus to offer no solutions to their problems, optimism about the environment could lead to greater creativity. For example, Moore believed different periods of revolution yield different levels of agency. In the prerevolutionary era, the old regime has an aura of inevitability. In the midst of the revolution, everything seems to be within easy reach of a new regime that encourages unlimited human aspirations for social engineering. After the revolution, pragmatism – or if you prefer, cynicism – emerges, as people stop to think about whether they have actually made things different and better. Expectations thus become either self-fulfilling prophecies or self-denying auguries. Hence the key questions: how do people come to understand the causes of their misery as political and social constructions of unjust fates? Where do their causal understandings of the world come from? Moreover, under what conditions do people believe that their ideas are efficacious forces for change? And given their understandings of what can be done, how do they come to know what ought to be done? In sum, what are the reasons for the political conceptions and perceptions, thoughts and beliefs, feelings and emotions that define their problem situation? Other comparativists claim that time frame affects agency: as historical time increases, human agency decreases. Rational-choice institutionalists thus assume that the short run involves choice and decision making. While institutions are intentionally designed to produce particular outcomes, agency produces unintended consequences that cannot easily be resolved. Sociological institutionalists thus assume that norms and practices grow organically over time and eventually come to exert power over people. Finally, compared to the here-and-now and to the being-and-becoming, in the long durée structure dominates. Historical institutionalists thus assume that the long run involves limits and constraints. In short, the long run is determinative, the medium run developmental, and the short run situational.

As part of the causal structure of the world, human agency thus contributes to the course of human events. Intended consequences matter. Creating opportunities rather than waiting for them, humans manage history to produce the outcomes they prefer. Unintended consequences also matter. Not leaving destiny to chance, humans also create chaos. The result is a refined form of reflexivity known as Hegel's "cunning of history": unintentional consequences are structured along an inevitable path in a certain direction.

Moore (1978: 461) entered the debate between behavioralists and reflectivists with some wise words: "In human affairs, it requires tremendous effort to produce the inevitable." He (1978: 377) continued: "By asking to whom the necessity applies and who gets what out of its application, it is possible to avoid the pitfalls and retain the kernel of anti-utopian truth: not everything is possible all the time." Moore (1978: 377, emphasis in original) therefore theorized about potentiality. The world-historical situation facing collective agents consists of open paths and suppressed alternatives: "A big part of any empirical investigation would be to determine the extent to which any given situation actually *was* open; more precisely what facts limited the range of options to those men and women whose behavior strongly influenced the course of events." To show that the present is neither inevitable nor permanent, Moore explored how things were and how they could have been different. Explaining potentialities requires a study of who gains and who loses, or an examination of concrete interests at play. Moore thus developed genetic tales of options foreclosed at the beginning, historical causal stories behind lost possibilities, and genealogical plots of might-have-beens that never happened.

Moore's exploration of historical factuals and counterfactuals are the basis of his causal methodology: "History may often contain suppressed possibilities and alternatives obscured or obligated by the deceptive wisdom of hindsight" (Moore 1978: 376). Hence, "the aim is to show in some concrete historical situation just what was possible and why" (Moore 1978: 376). Moore thus tried to explain variations in the leverage of collective causal moral agency: which actions were possible and why? His questions became: where does causal leverage come from? What conditions enable agency? What influences the capacity to make choices that matter? When are purposes, chosen by humans, taken on by themselves rather than imposed by society? Must free will always succumb to the requirements of natural law, or is there "freedom to comprehend natural law by one's own lights" (Shapiro 2003: 16)? And most important, when are humans liberated enough to create a free and rational society?

In short, Moore tried to establish the parameters of the possible. He saw the research problem as combining causal human agency with social causation, and human freedom with social structure. Rather than agency or environment being the independent variable, the prime or unmoved mover, he theorized about their coevolution, dynamic interaction, reciprocal causation, duality, bidirectionality, and feedback. Rather than seeing the normative and empirical realms as conflated, inseparable, nonreducible, and nondifferentiable, he explored a mutually constitutive analytic dualism. Moore thus saw a stratified reality consisting of the mutual interplay of two autonomous and separate causal powers, each capable of independent variation, where the two can be out of phase with one another, and where emergent codetermination rules. Humans are thus producers and products of their environment, authors of and authored by past conditions and future states. Humans transform their environment as the environment transforms them. Existing structures constrain action and limit voluntarism at the same time that they are the enablers making action possible. The environment offers constraining contexts and permissive conditions. Rejecting a social science that insists that the causal arrow must be set one way and not the other, Moore followed Marx's ([1869] 1963) famous words in the 18th *Brumaire*: "Men make history, but they do not make it just as they please. They do not make it under circumstances chosen by themselves, but under circumstances directly encountered, given and transmitted from the past."

Given that both human agency and historical structures matter, Moore (1978: 473) believed that emancipatory politics had to be based on a solid understanding of how the political world works: "Circumstances are what human beings respond to, but the way they respond makes a difference, sometimes a very big difference. From this standpoint political will and political intelligence can make a powerful difference in the outcome even if, as pointed out earlier, this degree of leverage has its own set of causes. An accurate understanding of these causes can contribute to the effectiveness of political will and intelligence in the future, while an inaccurate one can perpetuate and even increase stultification." To predict which changes will have what consequences, and therefore to evaluate alternative normative courses of action, causal explanations are required. With a correct causal explanation in place, Moore believed that people can be better assured of progress rather than retrogression.

And this leads to a normative task. When they can make a difference, humans have a responsibility to make a difference. Hence, they must take "moral responsibility for missed opportunities [and] to create a less cruel and repressive social order" (Moore

1978: 376). Nevertheless, Moore (2007: 103) indicated that his great book "has a rather ambivalent attitude about doing good." Worried that utopias become disutopias, Moore (1978: xiii) thought that it was hard to do the right thing. Aware of the irony of unintended consequences, he was not preachy: "Historical and social analysis can provide powerful insights into what kinds of morality are probable and feasible under specific circumstances. Such analysis can also tell us about the cost in human suffering of different types of morality and who bears the costs. This knowledge is indispensable for informed moral judgment. But it is no guarantee by itself of correct moral judgment" (Moore 1978: 434).

Moore's central theme was therefore the linkage between the internal social structure of states and their external circumstances. Focusing on the timing under which premodern institutions either broke down or adapted themselves to industrialization, he tried to explain the origins of Western democracy. Nowadays, some comparativists wonder whether human societies have exhausted the possibilities within liberalism. They claim that globalization produces a neoliberalism with neither choice nor capacity. Have we reached nonagency, a complex world spinning out of control? Other comparativists claim that globalization produces agents of change with new choices and novel capacities. A weakening state, for example, could offer transnational groups opportunities to exercise agency. Decentralized teams, for instance, can work together in scattered locations across time, space, and situation.

Kohli and Acemoglu and Robinson fall on the behavioralist side of the group agency-social structure question, Tilly and Wedeen on the reflectivist side. Accepting the agency of nonstate actors, the latter believe that there are no uniform causes of democracy, no necessary preconditions of democratization. Tilly and Wedeen resolve the contradiction between the causal necessity of the world and the freedom of spontaneous human capacity by attributing practical reasoning and problem solving to collectivities. On the other hand, Kohli and Acemoglu and Robinson love reality as it is and for itself: *amor fati*. Neither cynical, skeptical, nor disillusioned, their social science sees people adjusting to existing circumstances.

Thesis 6. Democracy and Causality. Reconcile democratic theory with causal methodology.

Political philosophy traditionally addressed the universal bases of politics. In its idealism, it sought political reasons and principles, philosophical truths and verities. When pursuing metaphysical grand syntheses and sweeping philosophical systems, it aimed at the high science of invisible realities. Faulting its armchair speculations supported by ad hoc collections of illustrative stories, empirical realists charged that political philosophy theorized about a generic human nature. Empiricists therefore criticized its abstract foundations as cosmological axioms and empty formalisms. Empirical democratic theory, priding itself on being down-to-earth, would overcome these flaws and describe how democracy actually works. Democracy, in fact, was not what it was supposed to be, in theory. The empiricists thus advanced what they thought to be the scientific method: concrete investigations of the connections between theory and evidence. In their view, studying ought/is dilemmas offered the best opening into the causal forces behind and within democracy. When empirical facts confronted normative theory, the empiricists believed, the facts of democratic practices would lead to a revision of the norms of democratic theory.

Empiricist critiques of democratic theory thus have a lengthy history. While Madison (Madison, Hamilton, and Jay [1788] 1987) feared that religious and class conflicts would produce factions – intermediate associations, clubs, unions, and parties – Weber (1946b) worried about bureaucratic rationalism deadening democracy. Many were skeptical of populism and majoritarianism. While Tocqueville feared a tyranny of the majority, Mosca (1939), Michels ([1919] 1962), and Pareto ([1920] 1980] feared the opposite: elite dominance. Mosca thus wrote of a ruling class, Pareto of the circulation of elites, and Michels of the iron law of oligarchy.

In the 1960s, normative theorists confronted the upstart empiricists. Theory-empiric dialogues examined several ought/is dilemmas involving, for example, polyarchy and power. The comparative politics of the 1960s was a key battleground. Traumatized by the rise of democracy in 1920s and the fall of democracies in 1930s, the 1960s saw the growth of comparative theorizing about democratic stability.

Rational choice theorists, in particular, challenged existing normative theories. They investigated social welfare functions that seemed to be the foundation of the good polity or the proper realm of good government. Schumpeter (1950) focused on competition among elites. Arrow (1951) investigated the general imperfections of social choice rules. Downs (1957) and Olson (1965) suggested that ignorance and nonparticipation could be rational. May (1952) studied the conditions under which majority rule is normatively desirable. In comparative politics, Dahl was probably the most influential critic of democracy. In 1956, his *A Preface to Democratic Theory* focused on pluralism and its implementing procedures. Influenced by Arrow (1951), his work was a precursor to Acemoglu and Robinson's text. Dahl (preceded by Dahl and Lindbloom 1953: chs. 10 and 11 and later refined in Dahl 1971 and repeatedly since) focused on "the preconditions and characteristics of polyarchy" (1956: 135). Offering (pp. 67–71, 84) eight definitional characteristics of polyarchy, Dahl (p. 63) indicated the "necessary and sufficient conditions for social organizations possessing these characteristics." He (pp. 75–81) then suggested nine hypotheses about institutional requirements or guarantees for democracy.

A new breed of culturalists also challenged classical normative theories. Gabriel A. Almond and Sidney Verba's (1963) *The Civic Culture: Political Attitudes and Democracy in Five Nations* was a breakthrough book. Almond and Verba (1963: ix) wrote that "We are concerned in this book with a number of classic themes of political science: with what the Greeks called 'civic virtue' and its consequences for the effectiveness and stability of the democratic polity; and with the kind of community life, social organization, and upbringing of children that fosters civic virtue." Arguing that democratic stability was rooted in political legitimacy, Almond and Verba's seminal exploration of political culture and stable democracy was a precursor to Wedeen's constructivism and dialogic democracy. Focusing on civic culture, they asked, what is democracy, and what are its causes and consequences? Almond and Verba (1965: x) thus wrote that "[t]his is a study of the political culture of democracy and of the social structures and processes that sustain it." Harry Eckstein's (1966) *A Theory of Stable Democracy* offered another culturalist challenge that combined innovative theory with inventive method.

Structural challenges to normative theories of democracy came in many flavors. While Deutsch's (1966) systems analysis was too abstract for most comparativists, Almond and Powell's (1966) structural-functionalism attracted a great deal of attention. More concrete versions of structuralism received even greater interest. Lipset's (1963) *Political Man* appealed to comparative political sociologists. Samuel Huntington's (1968) institutionalist *Political Order in Changing Societies*, a precursor to Kohli and Tilly, focused on state building and political order. Lipset and Rokkan's (1967) *Party Systems and Voter Alignments*, Bendix's (1969) *Nation Building and Citizenship*, and de Schweinitz's (1964) *Industrialization and Democracy* attracted considerable attention among historically minded comparativists.

In sum, the 1960s was a time of great turbulence in academic comparative politics. Moore's neo-Marxist *Social Origins* was only one of several paradigm-defining books that set the tone for challenging received normative democratic theories with new empirical causal methodologies. As rationalist, culturalist, and structuralist paradigms offered new methods tied to new theories, the field's problem situation shifted toward a battle of the paradigms. The next chapter demonstrates how research schools help comparativists understand the nexus of democratic theory and empirical causality. It also demonstrates how big-M Methodology helps fashion "look and see" democratic theorists. Using paradigms and methodologies to creatively confront democratic theories with causal methods allows the comparative politics of today to reinvent its past and draw strength for its future.

8

Research Schools

Comparativists (LaPalombara 1970) did not like their battle of the paradigms in the 1960s and comparativists (Laitin 2007: 642–43) do not like the battle now. Intellectual contention among methodologies is also seen as an academic vice that holds no scholarly virtue. The critics suggest that paradigmatic and methodological discourses kill scientific inquiry. Studying philosophy of science means not doing actual science; exploring abstract methodology means not addressing concrete problems.

This book disagrees. Comparativists work with paradigms in the midst of things, and methodological reflection is part of their working life. Comparativists who dislike philosophy of science are commonly in the grips of an old philosophy of science; and hostility to social theory often masks support of one's favorite social theory. As Eagleton (2008: xi–xii) put it, "Keynes once remarked that those economists who disliked theory, or claimed to get along better without it, were simply in the grip of an older theory. . . . Hostility to theory usually means an opposition to other people's theories and an oblivion of one's own." Without some philosophy of science, comparativists cannot distinguish good from bad science; and without some social theory, comparativists cannot distinguish good from bad theory. Comparing comparativists' paradigms thus offers valuable distance from actual scientific practices. Comparativists can then reflect on the routinely accepted methodologies behind their working structures of problem solving.

Examining paradigms and methodologies therefore does not deter or destroy substantive work; their examination indeed clarifies and stimulates creative comparative analyses. Causal analysis thus should not push big-P Paradigms and big-M Methodology from the center of comparative politics. Section 8.1 argues that paradigm (Thesis 7) and method (Thesis 8) helps comparative politics understand and explain the affinities of democratic theories and causal methodologies, thereby stimulating the growth of the mixed theories and mixed methods that many now agree creatively advance studies of democratization. While normative and empirical ideas coming from a research school bear a family resemblance (Thesis 9), Section 8.2 suggests that recognizing how the elective affinities of democratic theory and causal methodology are rooted in big-P Paradigms and big-M Methodology leads to their undoing (Thesis 10). Comparativists who play with research schools can turn the elective affinities of prescriptive and descriptive approaches to democratization into creative tensions.

8.1. PARADIGMS AND METHODOLOGY

If my central claim is true, if there is indeed an elective affinity between democratic theory and causal methodology, what explains the connection? Is the Moore Curve accidental or causal? If causal, do causal methodologies function as antecedents, concomitants, or consequences of normative theories? What are the mechanisms and processes generating the Curve?

Thesis 7. Big-P Paradigms and Comparative Politics. Use paradigms as creative heuristics.

One hypothesis: given his or her favored causal methodology, a comparativist will adopt a corresponding version of democracy. The hypothesis derives from the law of the methodological hammer: if one favors a method, one prefers the theory that best suits the method. The tool used to study democracy therefore becomes the justification for the type of democracy studied. Hence: if a comparativist employs comparative statics, he or she will study something akin to procedural democracy; if a comparativist adopts social constructivism, he or she will investigate a social object like discursive democracy; if a comparativist employs structural capacity, he or she will examine a rendering of multi-class democracy; and if a comparativist applies mechanisms and processes, he or she will analyze a variant of contentious democracy. More generally, the rise of liberal democracy has been explained by the rise of causal positivism (Barber 1988). Perhaps individualistic democracy has an elective affinity with logical atomism; the state of nature with mechanistic reductionism; psychological hedonism with physical mechanisms; and ambivalence about political power with ambivalence about true knowledge. In short, theory is derivative of method, and is quite helpless against it.

A second hypothesis: given his or her preferences about democracy, a comparativist will practice a corresponding causal methodology. Procedural democrats gravitate to comparative statics, discursive democrats to social constructivism, multiclass democrats to structural capacity, and contentious democrats to dynamic mechanisms. In short, method derives from theory, not the other way around.

Or, perhaps a third variable is producing the connections. Something else might ground causal methodologies and democratic theories. Perhaps both have unexamined philosophical premises or deep underpinnings that are revealed when they are juxtaposed. For example, Thesis 11 argues that democracy and causality are about freedom and power. More generally, the interplays working together and the complementarities yielding interfaces constitute paradigms for the study of politics. In other words, questions of democracy and of causality are related because both are components of larger structures of knowledge. Because such paradigm thinking has been attacked as detrimental to the field (LaPalombara 1970, Laitin 2007: 642–43), consider the critics's arguments.

After peaking at the statistical analyses produced by the comparative politics of the 1960s, Eckstein (1980: 138) remarked that "positive and negative factors ran amok." His observations were reaffirmed by Przeworski et al.'s (2000) killer finding of the 1990s:

while rich democracies endure forever, wealth does not explain the origins of democracy – but neither does anything else. In the etiology of democracy, positive and negative factors apparently run amok.

Over the last four decades, two solutions to this methodological dead end, one statistical and the other theoretical, have been offered (see p. 67). Drawing on advances in econometrics, today's comparativists have better statistical techniques than the comparativists of the 1960s. Comparative politics is in a statistical moment. After King, Keohane, and Verba (1994) and their followers put qualitative methods through a statistical crash course, attention turned to causality. If science is all about isolating variables and drawing causal inferences, there can be only one gold standard of causal methodology: randomized controlled trials (RCT). On the theoretical side, social science has come to be seen as all about getting the right underpinnings of explanatory theories. And if science is all about the microfoundations of macropropositions, there can be only one gold standard here too: rational choice theory (RCT). Modern comparative politics is therefore rational-choice theory coupled with causal-statistical methodology: RCT*RCT, or $(RCT)^2$, a single narrative that disciplines comparative politics.

If comparativists could execute this vision, they would have no need to embed theory and method in larger structures of knowledge. Research paradigms and theoretical programs would hold no added value because, after all, the end of inquiry is a single unified rational-choice theory of some phenomenon that is scrutinized in randomized-control situations. As they turn away from paradigms, comparativists could be problem driven. Finding out what causes what, where and when, how and why, would occupy their time.

It is a great idea. In fact, it is so great an idea that similar notions have been tried before. Positivism in the 1800s, logical positivism in 1930s, and behavioralism in the 1960s offered versions of $(RCT)^2$. Is the current unified social science superior to its predecessors? Can the vision of a paradigm-free social science work this time around? After all, there is no doubt that social science now has better theories, better methods, and better ways to align the two.

Nevertheless, two of the most prominent founders of modern comparative politics have expressed doubts about the two gold standards of contemporary comparative inquiry. In his review of statistical approaches to exogenous (preexisting) causality, Adam Przeworski (2007) asks "Is The Science of Comparative Politics Possible?" And in his study of the nuts and bolts of endogenous (self-creating) causality, Jon Elster (2007) asks "Is Social Science Possible?" Here is Przeworski's (2010: xv) answer: "I do not believe that history is driven by any 'primary causes' or 'ultimate instances,' whether ideas, forces of production, or institutions – but that means that everything is endogenous. If it is, then identifying causes is hard, if not impossible. Hence, often I can say only that some aspects of ideational, economic, and political life evolved together, without ever trying to detect which were the causes and which the effects." After discussing the "pathologies of hard obscurantism," Elster's (2007: 462) presents his answer: "[W]hat rational-choice practitioners do is often so removed from reality that it is hard to take seriously their claims that they are engaged with the world."

While their judgments may seem harsh, this book has also expressed reservations about one-dimensional causal explanations tied to one-dimensional causal strategies. Rather than two gold standards, today's comparativists employ different types of theories and exploit different types of causality. As democratic theorists, comparativists include those analyzing constrained coercive bargaining over procedural democracy and those studying creative group-defining practices of discursive democracy. As causal methodologists, comparativists employ group-constraining comparative statics and group-defining social constructivism. While rational choice theorists couple procedural democracy with comparative statics, constructivists join discursive democracy to constructivism.

Wedeen's social construction of multiple performances entails multiple possibilities, a dramatic contrast to Acemoglu and Robinson's comparative statics. Rather than exploring the exogenous preexisting forces that drive essentialist groups to make collective choices, Wedeen uses constructivism to examine the endogenous self-creating dynamics behind group formation and category reproduction. Her democracy is all about the discourse that creatively constructs its own political possibilities – a democracy that can be realized in many different ways. Institutions, such as elections, the rule of law, constitutionalism, and separation of powers are not the vigorous parts of her democracy. Indeed, they could well be drags on history, obstacles to the reconstruction and refashioning of politics and society. Because creative practices and generative performances are driven by the power of ideas and words, discursive democracy is relatively free from the exogenously binding causality that occupy Acemoglu and Robinson. Conditions of possibility – for example, economic, political, social and other limits on qāt chews – are duly minimized.

While Acemoglu and Robinson and Wedeen offer dramatic contrasts, other paradigmatic differences are equally revealing. As the four authors undertake comparative studies of procedural, discursive, coalitional, and contentious democracy, they elaborate their causal frameworks. Table 3 summarizes how the authors explain origins, or how democracy comes about; understand operations, or how democracy functions; and account for outcomes, or how democracy persists and changes. With respect to democracy's origins, Acemoglu and Robinson believe that procedural democracy results from the natural givens of a class-based political economy. Wedeen thinks that discursive democracy is open-endedly tied to nation formation. Kohli believes that fragmented multiclass democracy derives from colonialism and state-class relations. And Tilly suggests that contentious democracy comes from a mixture of exogenous structures and endogenous mechanisms and processes of state construction. With respect to democracy's operations, Acemoglu and Robinson believe that median-voter redistribution and coercive bargaining result from such exogenous forces as the class structure of the political economy. Wedeen again sees open-endedness in discursive democracy's categories, practices, and performances. Kohli believes that state-citizen relations produce state capacity. And Tilly, again striking a compromise, argues that contentious democracy

TABLE 3. *Democracy-Causality Connections*

	Acemoglu and Robinson	Weden	Kohli	Tilly
Origins	Class-based political economy	Open-ended nation building	Colonialism	Exogenous structures and endogenous processes of state building
Operations	Class-based median-voter redistribution rooted in coercive bargaining	Discursive categories, practices, and performances	State-society relations	State-citizen relations of trust, inequality, power and state-citizen consultations that are broad, equal, protected, mutually binding
Outcomes	Class-based enfranchisement	Open-ended	Economic development	Cycles of state capacity and political democracy, and political repression and social mobilization

Conclusions

derives from a mixture of exogenous structures and several endogenous mechanisms and processes: state-citizen relations of trust, inequality, and power, and state-citizen consultations of a broad, equal, protected, and mutually binding character. Finally, with respect to democracy's outcomes, Acemoglu and Robinson hold that enfranchisement results from class-based determinants. Wedeen maintains that discursive democracy can produce multiple identities and outcomes. Kohli suggests that economic development derives from state capacity. And Tilly sees contentious democracy as part of cycles of state capacity and political democracy, and political repression and social mobilization.

Note what happens as we move methodologically from Kohli, to Acemoglu and Robinson, to Tilly, and finally to Wedeen: we begin with deep world-historical structures, consider the exogenous causality of comparative statics, shift to the endogenous causality of dynamic mechanisms and processes tied to exogenous structures, and finally turn to the constitutive causality of endogenous social construction. Concomitantly, theories of the origins, operations, and outcomes of democracy become increasingly fluid and open-ended, provisional and transient. In other words, democracy becomes increasingly about "possibilities" rather than "probabilities." Kohli thus stresses the determinism of structural causes producing state capacity. Acemoglu and Robinson emphasize the "always" of cause-and-effect regularities and historical schemas that are tied to democracy's game-theoretic equilibria and comparative statics. Tilly recognizes the "often" of historical legacies and path dependencies that are connected to the practical problems of recognizing patterns in comparative-historical narratives of democracy. And Wedeen sees the "sometimes" of flexible repetitions of democracy's complex and historically constructed practices and performances – not much of a guide for prediction, but then again, many things are permitted to creative communities engaged in democratic discourse.

Put otherwise, Acemoglu and Robinson are principled hedgehogs. According to them, the external circumstances of procedural democracy and political economy structure diverse agents and complex realities in a forever repeated game. Wedeen is a principled fox. Rather than permanent patterns, she sees democratic agency creating replayable but not unvarying local performances, repeatable but not constant immediate experiences, and recurring but not unalterable everyday practices. Tilly is the pragmatist tormented by his principled colleagues. Holding out the hope of discovering a few big truths, he is all-too cognizant of how the multiple ebbs and flows of interacting dynamic causal mechanisms are pushed by external circumstances and pulled by endogenous constructions into all-too-few repeatable historical paths and generalizable national trajectories. And Kohli is the empiricist tormented by his principled and pragmatic colleagues. Also holding out the hope of discovering a few big truths, he is all-too aware of how the circumstances of time and place move certain types of states to fashion certain types of outcomes.

Four paradigmatic approaches to democracy and causality thus define the problem situations that comparativists face. As implied by the discussion of actor agency earlier (Thesis 2), explanation sketches can then be used as heuristic idea-generating machines. Comparing and contrasting the research schools can yield inventive claims about democracy.

Tilly and Wedeen thus respond to Acemoglu and Robinson and Kohli, who are quite aware of contentious politics and discourse alternatives. Indeed, Wedeen writes a book of foils. If falsifying or deconstructing theories is the measure of science, Wedeen is clearly the best scientist of the bunch. In contrast, Acemoglu and Robinson write a book of models. Starting simple, they build a unified theory world. Alternative mathematizations produce an aesthetically appealing set of hypotheses. Tilly positions himself pragmatically between postmodernist and modernist tendencies. Comparing and contrasting alternative ideas and evidence, taking wisdom where he finds it, devising new ideas and inventing novel techniques when he thinks it necessary, Tilly measures and explains empirical phenomena. Kohli is mostly concerned with getting his historical narratives of South Korea, Brazil, India, and Nigeria correct. With these rich and detailed comparative analytical histories in place, Kohli (p. 417) believes that he can begin to understand the different patterns of industrialization and the divergent economic growth rates of late-late developers: "It is difficult to isolate the relative significance of a number of causal variables via comparative analysis of a few cases. Immersion in the details reveals at best a feel for what might be the most significant causal dynamics at work. I claim no more."

Good work in comparative politics indeed depends on strong models and sturdy foils that serve as reliable touchstones for inquiry. Comparing and contrasting research paradigms therefore has great heuristic value. Comparativists who juxtapose approaches can generate creative insights about democracy. Mixing and matching theory and method offers comparativists critical perspectives on current theoretical and methodological work, and suggests inventive new possibilities for research. Modeling and foiling, bouncing ideas off one another, reinvigorate and reenergize old problem situations. Because paradigms raise causal questions about structure/action and power/freedom, comparativists can also call upon big-P Paradigms to deepen their political commitments. The paradigm wars in comparative politics are therefore no mere philosopher's dispute. They are of world-historical significance.

The four books under examination here thus offer four visions of democratic agency in post-Moore paths to state, nation, regime, and policy building. However, Acemoglu and Robinson, Wedeen, Kohli, and Tilly are too sophisticated to be satisfied with an emotional commitment to a theory of democracy. Because affective attachment to a particular democratic theory is child's play, the authors buttress their political views with carefully chosen methodological strategies. And behind the theoretical and methodological controversies about grand strategies of development in the global south one finds formidable social scientific apparatuses. By studying how comparativists employ both democratic theory and causal methodology, we discover how the foundations and justifications of theory and method are connected. Behind the assumptions made by democratic theorists and causal methodologists lay complex structures whose internal grammars and rules of discourse yield intelligible talk, core meanings, and justifiable assertions. The affinities between theory and method emerge from common roots: research paradigms – communities with traditions, schools with languages, approaches with programs, and frameworks with procedures – in which democratic theories and causal methodologies are reinforcing parts of a greater whole of inquiry.

Thesis 8. Big-M Methodology and Comparative Politics. Use methods as creative heuristics.

In their *Oxford Handbook of Political Methodology*, Janet M. Box-Steffensmeier, Henry E. Brady, and David Collier (2008) identify three core values of the newly emerging field of political methodology:

> "*Utility for understanding politics* – Techniques should be servants of improved data collection, measurement, and conceptualization and of better understanding of meanings and enhanced identification of causal relationships . . .
> "*Pluralism of approaches* – There are many different ways that these tasks can be undertaken in the social sciences . . .
> "*Cutting across boundaries* – Techniques can and should cut across boundaries and should be useful for many different kinds of researchers."
> (p. 29)

The growth of "causal thinking," they also suggest, has helped unite different types of political scientists – those doing qualitative case studies and those doing quantitative statistical analyses – around these core values. After decades of neglect and avoidance, causation has become the preeminent methodological heuristic of the discipline.

Causal thinkers band together because all must address two core invisibility problems: counterfactuals are unobservable and a factual's cause producing its effect is similarly unobservable. Suppose a comparativist suggests that a high level of economic development causes democracy. Because a country with high GNP is also one that does not have low GNP, he or she cannot observe the counterfactual, which is the fundamental problem of causal inference (Holland 1986). The comparativist also cannot observe the country's high GNP "causing" – the hidden strings connecting to and generative of – the country's democratic regime. In other words, he or she cannot record the traces of differences or the tracks of distances of input variable X producing differences and distances of output variable Y (Stinchcombe 2005). Because comparativists favor their own normative/positive visions of how democracy should/does operate, it is consequently easier to proliferate their theories rather than eliminate plausible rival hypotheses. Problems situations in comparative politics thus usually result from ad hoc inductivism, or the accumulation of many partially true causal claims.

Science begins with the discovery of correlations between observables. It then moves toward an explanation of why the linkages occur. All sciences possess languages, representations, and models of a reality they presume is causal. Because investigators do not have direct access to invisible causation, they deploy research designs to increase their knowledge of the world, the observational power of their theories, and the empirical content of their arguments. Research design is thus all about the pragmatics of seeking observable implications, or about the practices of operationalizing causality. Put otherwise, analysts invent methods for inferring unobservable causality from visible observations. For example, to address the invisibility of counterfactual causality, methodologists construct relevant counterfactual instances; and to address the invisibility of factual causality, methodologists trace processes between causes and effects. While political scientists vigorously disagree about the worth of the causal theories under investigation, methodologists seemingly more often agree on the best practices of causal empirical inquiry. Methods thus apparently guarantee conclusions because they insulate investigators from the conflicts and compromises of parties holding different theoretical commitments and alternative conceptual identities. Disinterested and dispassionate comparativists can therefore employ a universal and transferable scientific toolbox to judge the results of causal inquiry.

A second strategy for addressing causality's invisible worlds is to embed observable implications in deep explanatory theories. This strategy follows from five contributions to Box-Steffensmeier,

Brady, and Collier's volume. The editors write "that 'causal think-ing' is not the only approach to political science discourse" (p. 11) and recognize that their "volume does not encompass all of method-ology" (p. 29). For further discussion of "interpretive and construc-tivist methods, along with broader issues of situating alternative analytical tools in relation to an understanding of culture" (p. 30), they refer their readers to a companion volume, the *Oxford Handbook of Contextual Political Analysis*, coedited by Charles Tilly (Goodin and Tilly 2006). Second, Brady (2008) discusses several alternative approaches to causal analysis: neo-Humean regularity, counterfactuals, manipulation, and mechanisms/capa-cities. As the field of political methodology develops methods for investigating different types of causality embedded in different types of theoretical explanations, methodologists explore nonmainstream conceptions of causality rooted in heterodox explanatory frame-works. Third, Collier and Elman (2008: 780) appreciate the hetero-geneity of the field of political methodology and thereby distinguish "mainstream qualitative methods" from "interpretive and con-structivist methods." They question whether different methods are complements, to be subsumed within a conventional social-science toolbox, or substitutes, distinct alternative "others."

Fourth, because grounding causal theories in empirical data is a necessary concomitant of causal thinking, efforts have been made to bring formal or mathematical modelers into the field of political methodology. The movement for Empirical Implications of Theoretical Methods (EITM) arose to repair the disjuncture between deductive and inductive reasoning, or as John H. Aldrich, James E. Alt, and Arthur Lupia put it, place "causal inference in the service of causal reasoning." In other words, EITM emerged when inferential testing – regression equations – proved to inadequately probe the causal linkages derived from comparative-static exercises. Once researchers realized that causal theories held implications for research design and data analysis, they backtracked to the applied formal models whose empirical implications were the estimating equations. Aldrich, Alt, and Lupia (2008: 839–940) thus recognize that theory-data connec-tions are quite expansive: "Theory is broader than game theory and methods are broader than inference from statistical models and controlled experiments. In addition to game theory, formal models include differential equation dynamic models, simple decision theory, complicated behavioral decision-making models, and computational models. The empirical tool kit should include not only statistical inference and experiments but also focused and analytically-based case studies and computational models."

The rise of causal thinking has thus led the field of political methodology to backtrack from estimating equations to causal hypotheses, from such propositions to the applied models that generate them, and finally from the applied models to the different explanatory frameworks and theoretical approaches that are the origins of our ideas about causality. Moving forward, political methodologists can start with a research program, develop an applied model, work out causal claims, and then generate research designs suitable for inferential testing. A generalization of EITM – call the field EITE or the Empirical Implications of Theoretical Explanations – would connect various forms of causal theorizing to empirical tools. Such a field would not only unite quantitative and qualitative empiricists, but also formal mathematical modelers and discursively oriented theorists.

Finally, after weighing these issues Mark Bevir calls for a critical philosophy of social science that reflects on current practices of explanation and causality. Reminding us of the connection between different types of causality and alternative research traditions, he (2008: 69) warns against taking the volume's topic, political methodology, too far: "Today we might worry about hypermethodologism – the application of methodological techniques without proper philosophical reflection." Bevir (2008: 68) also maintains that "political science is too often committed to forms of empiricism, realism, and formal explanation that increasingly lack philosophical plausibility." By suggesting that another set of philosophical assumptions is more plausible, hence, presumably more legitimate and respectable, than mainstream presumptions, Bevir is telling political scientists that they need a newer and better philosophy of social science. Turning the claim of "progress" in political methodology on its head, he argues that the "best practices" to discern explanatory and causal relations in the empirical world must be rooted in the "best practices" of the philosophy of social science. To many political methodologists, Bevir opens a can of worms. While a comparison of the different causal methodologies housed within alternative explanatory theories could unite methodologists around fundamental insights into research choices, a discussion of the metamethodologies behind explanatory programs could also turn into a battle of the paradigms that divides methodologists. Most would accept Randall Collins's (1998) distinction between Big Problem Philosophy and Rapid Discovery Science: while philosophers engage in endless debates about enduring problems, scientists advance pragmatically, moving cooperatively from discovery to discovery. Put otherwise, political methodology unites scientists and facilitates progress; philosophy of science divides investigators and impedes inquiry. If philosophy of social science encourages paradigmatic battles that make transparadigmatic comparisons impossible, the goal of political methodology – to make transparadigmatic investigations possible – is subverted. Moreover, political science is an empirically oriented discipline that is typically more interested in investigating its empirical questions than in uncovering its metaphysical commitments. Suspicious that political philosophers and social theorists thin inquiry and turn analysis abstract, many political scientists are skeptical of grand explanatory programs.

Social science has once again misread natural science. Many in the "hard" sciences are philosopher-scientists and scientific-philosophers. Using the tools of natural science, these scholars reflect on the nature of space, time, quantity, matter, reality, order, and determinism. Holding that methods presuppose philosophical underpinnings, background commitments, metaphysical intuitions, and speculative themata, these scholars demonstrate how such imagined principles hold real-world implications for understanding and explanation.

Believing that philosophical concepts have misled empirical inquiry, many great comparativists, including Robert Dahl, Harry Eckstein, and Gabriel Almond (1988), also turned to methodology. For example, David Easton's critique in the 1950s of the hyperfactualism of social science – the brute empiricism of coding schemes and the theoretical eclecticism of proposition inventories – once haunted the discipline. Once upon a time, political scientists heeded Easton and entertained grand explanatory programs that could undergird isolated causal claims. Two classics from the 1960s, Anatol Rapoport's (1960) *Fights, Games, and Debates* and Brian Barry's (1970) *Sociologists, Economists, and Democracy*, compared the emerging rational choice theory to then currently available theoretical alternatives.

This book has demonstrated that today's contractual, discursive, structural, and contentious comparativists employ four types of explanatory frameworks for understanding democracy and the state, and that the frameworks are linked to four types of methodologies for causal inquiry. The study of coercive bargaining leads students of rational choice to investigate the institutional equilibrium of procedural democracy. The study of discourse leads students of constructivism to investigate the performances and practices of national citizenship and discursive democracy. The study of structures leads students of state-society relations to explore the capacity of cohesive-capitalist states. And the study of struggles over state building leads students of contentious politics to explore the dynamic mechanisms and processes behind state capacity and adversarial democracy. Through bargaining, discussing, coalescing, and fighting people sort out their power relations and go about building states, constructing nations, forming regimes, and adopting policies.

In studying these processes, comparativists rely on explanatory programs that they hope will demonstrate their value by producing solid empirical work. When faithful supporters retreat into aesthetically pleasing but abstractly invisible foundations, comparativists are not impressed. While Acemoglu and Robinson, Wedeen, Kohli, and Tilly begin with different paradigms and ultimately produce explanatory claims about different parts of the world, as comparativists they move from research programs to descriptive and causal claims, turn to the observable implications of sensitizing concepts and speculative hypotheses, and then go on to data and evidence. By refining invisible causal patterns into core problems, explanatory theories, and observable evidence, the authors move beyond a preoccupation with first principles and do more than defend the artistry of their approaches.

Rather than taking research toward the abstract metaphysics of a priori invisible worlds, the authors use epistemological and ontological assumptions as heuristic models and foils to address concrete problem situations, causal mechanisms, units of analysis, contexts, and test implications. In their hands, abstract principles of political order thus become heuristic research methods for scientific discovery, generating interesting and important problems; for scientific explanation, yielding reflexive conceptualizations and fruitful theories; and for scientific evidence, producing systematic observation and severe testing of empirical statements. In short, since the texts demonstrate that deep explanatory theories hold observable implications, they connect the two ways of addressing causality's twin invisibility problems.

Answers to the Barrington Moore Problem therefore lead comparativists to study world-historical battles over paths of development in the context of academic struggles over paradigms. Because paradigms may be used to discover the underlying affinities behind normative commitments and research strategies, this is good news. By moving from small-m methodology to big-M Methodology, comparativists can also come to appreciate Moore's centrality to contemporary studies of democratization.

While comparativists are both democratic theorists and causal methodologists, democratic theory and causal methodology remain compartmentalized research traditions. The literatures do not speak to one another. The standard treatments of democracy and causality do not even mention one another. However, their juxtaposition in comparative inquiry leads one to suspect that causality and democracy are not distinct topics. The separation of the two research traditions is not a profitable scholarly division of labor.

Big-P Paradigms and big-M Methodology can help bridge the two halves of democracy studies. By showing how questions of democracy and causality have developed out of Barrington Moore's analysis, this volume has demonstrated why the different big-P Paradigms in comparative politics will not be absorbed by small-m methodologies: plausible rival research programs contain plausible rival conceptions of theory and of causality. Different paradigms produced different forms of research in the 1960s. As the paradigms changed, additional differences emerged. In a field where "positive and negative factors run amok," perspectives and points of view inevitably turn up different kinds of normative and empirical truths about phenomena. Used creatively, different strategies of explanation and stratagems of evidence can generate discovery in the midst of things.

Comparative politics has thus stubbornly remained a mixed-theory and mixed-method field. Rather than pushing big-P Paradigms and big-M Methodology from its center, recent causal analyses have reaffirmed their importance to comparative inquiry. Comparativists who appreciate the Barrington Moore Problem, and thereby recognize how different explanatory approaches join theoretical and normative visions to empirical and causal frameworks, can creatively capture the regularities and repetitions – laws and constructions – of politics, especially post-Moore paths of development in the global south.

8.2. ELECTIVE AFFINITIES AND CREATIVE TENSIONS

While reflecting on big-P Paradigms and big-M Methodology reveals that normative and empirical ideas coming from a research school bear a family resemblance, recognizing the elective affinities of theory and method lead to their undoing. Comparativists can play with the schools, creatively combining prescriptive and descriptive approaches to democratization.

Thesis 9. Research Schools and Elective Affinities. Recognize that the ostensibly different ideas coming from a research school bear a family resemblance, thereby appreciating the elective affinity between democratic theories and causal methodologies: the more external the causal methodology, the thinner the democratic theory (The Moore Curve).

What causes democracy? It depends on what "democracy" means and what "cause" means. If "democracy" involves normative questions and "cause" entails empirical ones, how are democratic theories and causal methodologies related? In other words, what is the relationship between moral and philosophical ideas of democracy and scientific and evidentiary notions of causality? To address these questions, I conducted an empirical study of how four texts written by comparativists – Acemoglu and Robinson, Wedeen, Kohli, and Tilly – connected democracy and causality.

What is this thing called "democracy"? Where is "democracy" to be found and how does it work? Comparativists as democratic theorists investigate abstract and ideal conceptions of good government. Many types of democratic theories – procedural, discursive, statist, and contentious – have been developed. Acemoglu and Robinson are concerned with procedural democracy as an aggregate grand bargain among market interests. Wedeen cares about discursive democracy as a performative local consensus, an enactment of social agreement tied to a national identity. Compared to cohesive-capitalist states, Kohli believes that fragmented multiclass democracies are ineffective governing coalitions. And Tilly is interested in contentious democracy as multiple consultations among the many interest and identity claims resulting from state construction.

Democracy is therefore a complex multidimensional phenomenon. While it cannot be reduced to a single concept, it can be decomposed in several isomorphic ways. The authors examined here therefore offer four complementary understandings of the challenges of governing the democratic state in the global south. From least to most demanding: Kohli, who aims for development, claims that democracy does not work and thus finds it to be a predicament; Acemoglu and Robinson, who seek peace and prosperity, argue that democracy works only procedurally and thus find it to be a puzzle; Tilly, who seeks social justice, believes that democracy works contentiously and thus finds it to be a struggle; and Wedeen, who longs for community, thinks that democracy works discursively and thus finds it to be a spectacle. Moreover, while Tilly sees conflict as the lifeblood of democracy, the others seek solutions to the problems of value pluralism. They offer three ways to resolve difference, manage conflict, and find the public good. Acemoglu and Robinson stress institutional procedures to manage conflict procedurally. Kohli emphasizes an overlapping consensus of elites engaged in economic management. And Wedeen highlights membership in a civic community that encourages the debate and deliberation that constructs national interests, identities, and ideas. In sum, democracy is a rich concept that should be understood by individually incomplete yet collectively congruous perspectives.

What is this thing called "cause"? Where is "causality" to be found and how does it work? Aiming to find the contexts and conditions of possibility, thereby revealing open and closed historical paths, causal methodologists study the real-world concomitants of democracy. Several causal methodologies – comparative statics, constructivism, structural capacity, and mechanisms and processes – have been developed. Acemoglu and Robinson study the comparative statics of exogenous shifts in causal forces that disturb equilibrium. Wedeen examines the endogenous causal construction of social phenomena. Kohli investigates the causal structural capacity of class coalitions and the state. And Tilly explores the complex – contingent and dynamic – mechanisms and processes that underlay causal relations. Hence, we have four representations of "X causes Y." In comparative statics, we have "X acts on Y," or X increases the probability of Y. In social construction, we have "X is Y," or X and Y are mutually constitutive of the possibility of X and Y; in structural capacity, we have "Y of X," or X has the power to affect Y; and in mechanisms and processes, we have "X into Y," or X becomes Y.

Comparativists as causal methodologists thus investigate the tough social-scientific question of turning invisible principles of political order into observable research methodologies. In addition to operationalizing causality (Thesis 8), comparativists conceptualize causality. One possibility is strong causality: in situation S, X is the cause of all causes of Y. In other words, some comparativists seek a hierarchical or rank-ordered causality, a systematic or unifying etiology that aims at one final causal representation that is true and deep.

The field of comparative politics as a whole evidently pursues a causal pluralism in which the diverse aims of inquiry yield different kinds of causal systems. Moreover, cultures – popular and scientific – experience causality differently. Causality is thus complex and multifaceted. There are many ways in which something may be said to cause something else. If no one thing counts as causality but rather many things count, "the" logic of causal inference does not exist. Comparativists need to understand the different types of causality. Once they appreciate each causality's ontology, epistemology, and methodology, they can recognize its practical uses in inquiry. The comparative strengths and weaknesses of the approaches for a particular problem situation can then be evaluated. What does a commitment to each type of causality entail? What are its best practices? To fashion a research design aimed at investigating the observable implications of a theory, multimethod approaches should address these questions.

In sum, "democracy" is evidently not a single type of politics with one underlying type of "causal" structure. Though some now claim that there is only one way to remain a democracy – high wealth – there is little doubt that there is no one path to democracy, no one manner in which all democracies operate, and no one set of outcomes all produce. The democracies studied by comparativists are therefore highly variable social objects. They range from thin to thick, from minimalist to maximalist, from formalist to informalist, and from idealistic to realistic. Different conceptions of democracy are associated with different causalities of democracy – its origins, operations, and outcomes. The causes, concomitants, and consequences of procedural democracy are different than the causes, concomitants, and consequences of deliberative democracy. Because different democracies manifest different causal powers, the different kinds of democracy invite investigation with different kinds of causal methods. Different democracies, different causalities.

Democratic theorists do not write about causal methodology and causal methodologists do not write about democratic theory.

This is unfortunate because the practice of comparative politics inevitably connects theory and method. Democratic theories and causal methodologies work in tandem and are balanced in use. Rooted in research schools, their analytical properties, conceptual structures, and component logics hold striking parallels. Students of procedural democracy gravitate toward a causal methodology that suits it. The standards elucidated for justifying political commitments to procedural democracy are connected to the standards for investigating causal arguments about procedural democracy. The same holds for other forms of democracy.

Working with big-P Paradigms and big-M Methodology has therefore revealed a clear empirical relationship between democratic theory and causal methodology: as the level of external causal determinism increases, the thickness of democracy decreases. Put otherwise: as causal methodology becomes exogenously structural, democratic theory loses its endogenous agency. Acemoglu and Robinson's democracy is procedural, their state weak, and their causality external. Wedeen's democracy is deliberative, her state weak, and her causality endogenous. Kohli is more structural and less agential than Acemoglu and Robinson, and his state is strong. Tilly is more structural and less agential than Wedeen, and his state is also strong (Table 4).

TABLE 4. *Democratic Theories and Causal Methodologies*

		State	
		Weak	**Strong**
Democracy	**Thick**	Wedeen's Constructivism discursive democracy + social constructivism	Tilly's Contentious Politics contentious democracy + contingent process
	Thin	Acemoglu-Robinson's Rational Choice procedural democracy + comparative statics	Kohli's State-Society multiclass democracy + structural capacity

The stylized facts uncovered herein thus point to the elective affinity of democratic theory and causal methodology. The Moore Curve – the more external the causal methodology, the thinner the democratic theory – governs democratization studies.

Thesis 10. Research Schools and Creative Tensions. Recognize that the ostensibly different ideas coming from a research school contain creative tensions between democratic theory and causal methodology that can be used as heuristics to energize comparative politics.

The world is constituted by norms that comparativists examine empirically. What are the barriers to mutually productive collaboration between democratic theorists and causal methodologists? How can empirical studies of democracy be made more relevant to political theories? And how can political theories speak more effectively to empirical studies of democracy? To address these questions about the organization of inquiry, the book used the results of its empirical study to reflect on what ought to be the connections between philosophical ideas of democracy and scientific notions of causality. It demonstrated that a combination can be productive in two important ways.

First, the combination serves critical aims. Causal methodologies allow comparativists to reflect on democratic theories. Normative theories of democracy must be consistent with three sets of empirical facts. The first is origins: how can such a democracy be brought about? The second is operations: can its institutions implement its principles? The third is outcomes: do the norms and institutions produce intended and unintended consequences that stabilize democracy and allow it to flourish? In other words, comparativists face the world as it is, pragmatically taking account of the empirical causes, concomitants, and consequences of democracy. As empirical research reveals the conditions that realize their theories, comparativists can flush out the ideas and show the internal contradictions and external suitabilities.

The empirical inspection of democratic ideals can play the critical function of challenging conservative biases. Comparativists could critique those who ignore fruitful counterfactuals and thereby take advantage of a particular status quo. Empirical scrutiny of democratic norms can also play the critical function of challenging radical hubris. Comparativists could criticize those who disdain realizable counterfactuals and thereby privilege a utopian future. Comparative politics is the ideal field to evaluate whether a particular normative vision of democracy is achievable and sustainable at all times, in all places, and under all conditions. The field, renewing a path that began in earnest during the 1960s, is now investigating the causal claims behind political theories. The authors examined here thus supplied grounds for supporting the political values they implicitly held. Wedeen defends the qāt chew, just as Kohli defends strong states. Good empiricists, they explain with origins. Good pragmatists, they justify with outcomes. In an apparent effort to address Wedeen's charges against Acemoglu and Robinson's procedural democracy, Przeworski (2010) examines current empirical work on the causes, concomitants, and consequences of electoral democracy. Tilly defends social democracy as the best possible democracy.

Nevertheless, assuming that in a certain sense a polity is a "democracy," finding out how it actually operates, and then concluding that "democratic theory" ≠ "real democracy" is not a sufficiently ambitious research agenda. Empirical research into democratic theory can accomplish much more. Alternatively, beginning with a study of a real "democracy," turning to democratic theory for analytical guidance, and again concluding that "democratic theory" ≠ actual "democracy" is also not adventurous enough. A more penetrating analysis of democracy would identify critical assumptions, problematize particular conditions, evaluate certain contexts, and then offer alternatives. Suggesting that political scientists "problematize redescriptions," Shapiro (2005: 17, 83) writes that "[p]olitical theorists have important roles to play in political science just because there is no algorithm that dictates the correct descriptive cut at the social world. Among our central tasks is to identify, criticize, and suggest plausible alternatives to the theoretical assumptions, interpretations of political conditions, and above all specifications of problems that underlie prevailing empirical accounts and research programs, and to do it in ways that can spark novel and promising problem-driven research agendas. And, especially when esoteric forms of redescription are involved, they must elucidate the links to more familiar understandings of politics."

A combination of democratic theory and causal methodology can be productive in a second way. Just as big-P Paradigms and big-M Methodology are heuristics that can stimulate comparative inquiry, the elective affinities and creative tensions of democratic theories and causal methodologies are heuristics that can energize comparative politics. While it is possible to fashion ideal-type paradigms with coherent cores and extended peripheries, research schools do not contain logical relations summing to an absolute whole that is independent and complete in itself. In other words, there are no metaphysically necessary connections between democratic theories and causal methodologies. Because democratic theories and causal methodologies inhabit a pluralistic universe, only practical elective affinities exist and only pragmatic compromises occur. Social-science constructions are thus plastic and diverse. As inquiry unfolds, the parts enter into a variety of relationships. Without regard for the phantom of coherence, comparativists can experiment with creative combinations. Assuming only loose and provisional empirical connections, researchers can mix and match, and evaluate the results afterward. New connections are indeed invented all the time. Pragmatic and experimental inquiry moves research in unexpected directions, developing new possibilities. As comparativists begin with different purposes and work out various compromises, their formulations change. After all, researchers always work in the midst of things.

In sum, the combination of democratic theories and causal methodologies serves critical and creative functions in comparative inquiry. If we privilege causal methodology, its theoretical implications will unintendedly shape the way we value the world. If we privilege democratic theory, its methodological implications will unintendedly shape how we examine the world. Which is cause and which is effect, which is the leader and which is the follower, are thus not useful chicken-and-egg questions. Because democratic theory grows naturally out of the conditions of democratic life, empirics lead back to norms, and vice versa. The examination of concrete democratic institutions, practices, and regimes thus leads to new normative theories. As interdependent parts of inquiry, democratic theory and causal methodology have always faced a binding problem. As constituent parts of inquiry, problems of theory and method have always been solved in the midst of things.

Mutually enriching, a dialectic of study and a dialogue of learning, theory and method are equal partners in critically and creatively addressing problem situations. Democratic theories that are rich and relevant relate to the empirical world; causal methodologies that are expressive and exciting connect with the normative world. Democratic theory without causal methodology is blind and unconvincing. Causal methodology without democratic theory is empty and insignificant. Intellectual history – a history of thought – by itself, without actions or deeds, is boring. Lacking drama and comedy, pathos and satire, it requires interesting empirical work to spice things up.

9

Political Power and Democratic Performance

As the paradigmatic debates of the 1960s played themselves out, comparativists came to recognize that rather than being a purely descriptive concept, "democracy" is a judgmental term. As Skinner (1974: 298) remarks, "Such terms are applicable if and only if a certain state of affairs obtains, but whenever the relevant state of affairs does obtain, then to apply the corresponding term is not only to describe the state of affairs, but also (and *eo ipso*) to perform the speech-act of commending it." In other words, while comparativists do not necessarily support something they label as "political" or "governmental," they do approve of something they call "democratic." After debating questions of "democratic stability," comparative politics thus came to recognize that the empirical study of democracy had normative significance. The early literature then turned to evaluations of "power" (Eckstein and Gurr 1975) and of "democratic performance" (Eckstein 1971; Powell 1982).

Comparativists nowadays should address the key empirical and normative questions about political power raised by Kohli (Thesis 11) and about democratic performance raised by Tilly (Thesis 12): in building a democratic state, which democracy under which conditions is best, and how might it be achieved? Section 9.1 suggests that returning to the core concern of the 1960s would allow comparativists to address Barrington Moore's ought/is dilemma of causal collective human agency in democratization. Comparative politics, Section 9.2 suggests, could then come to understand how alternative modernities challenge liberalism, how state building occurs amid contentious world politics, and how institutions arise, persist, and change.

9.1. POWER AND PERFORMANCE

Thesis 11. Democracy, Causality, and Power. Recognize how power is central to democracy and causality.

Democracy and causality are about freedom and power. Political theorists seek to understand freedom from interference and the power to fashion one's life. Empirical social scientists want to locate causes that are free from obstructions and that have the power to affect outcomes. Because both theorists and empiricists are centrally concerned with questions about freedom and power, the kinds of democracy theorized by comparativists hold elective affinities for the kinds of causality they employ.

Consider the qāt chew collectivity. The chew is free when it has the internal power to decide, act, and perform. Working in concert, its members can get things done. For example, a qāt chew could encourage the regime to provide goods and services and to "advocat[e] on behalf of the village, electoral district, or local group" (Wedeen, p. 114; also see p. 126). A qāt chew collectivity is also free when it has the power to (re)constitute itself through vivid and creative performances of democracy. Recall one of Wedeen's most penetrating remarks: "political self-fashioning" (Wedeen, pp. 114, 126) and "political subject formation ... takes place through the practice of discussion" (Wedeen, p. 140) because "the very activity of deliberating in public contributes to the formation of democratic persons" (Wedeen, p. 105). Power is thus required for, and is constitutive of, freedom because power means positive liberty: the group can become its own master and the collectivity control its own affairs (Berlin 1958). However, to have the positive liberty to make its own destiny, determine its own fate, and create its own forms of democratic life, a qāt chew's power must constitute negative liberty. The chew must have the capacity to break free of its conditions of possibility, indeed it must be able to turn its constraints into opportunities. When external conditions – the conditions of possibility – are obstacles that restrict and impede, barriers that limit and obstruct, coercions that impose and constrain, and impediments that infringe and violate, a qāt-chew collectivity lacks power.

Wedeen thus chooses to study the endogenously created enablers of qāt chews rather than their exogenously fixed constraints. Minimizing the constraining power of the qāt chew's conditions-of-possibility allows her to maximize its enabling powers and creative energies. If Acemoglu and Robinson wrote a game-theoretic model of how Yemen's qāt chews produced outcomes, their comparative statics would probably aim at the collectivity's constraints. If Tilly studied qāt chews, he would likely quantify their discourse and explore how external forces shaped their somewhat unique historical paths. And if Kohli studied Yemen's qāt chews, he would probably explore their structural capacity to produce desirable outputs under specific historical conditions. Such thought experiments can deepen comparative inquiry, a point made earlier.

More generally, when Acemoglu and Robinson's external constraints define causality, environments have power and collectivities have but negative liberty. When Wedeen's conditions-of-possibility define causality, environments lack power and collectivities enjoy positive liberty. Freedom as noninterference, or the absence of external obstacles to individual choice, is indifferent to power as long as power is neither exercised nor likely to be exercised. Freedom as the absence of active or threatened coercion misses the idea of power as a capability or potentiality – a "could" backed by "might" – and the idea of power as a process or dynamic – a mechanism generating transformation. Kohli's structural capacity goes even further than Acemoglul and Robinson in emphasizing how the powers of the environment restrict the powers of the collectivity. Tilly, the pragmatic theorist of the middle range, studies contentious political struggles that occur in the midst of things. He is therefore best able to explore how the opportunities and constraints of the environment shape the positive and negative liberty of collectivities (Berlin 1958).

TABLE 5. *Democracy, Causality, and Power*

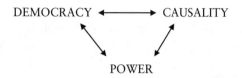

In sum, democratic theories have elective affinities for causal methodologies because both involve power. Shapiro (2003) says that theories of democracy must take account of power. In fact, democratic theories examine power in several ways: there are many faces or forms of power in democracy. Cartwright (1989) says that theories of causality must take account of power. In fact, causal methodologies examine power in several ways: there are many faces or forms of power in causality (Table 5).

The faces of power in the democracy literature therefore bear important similarities to the faces of power in the causality literature.

Democratic Theory. Do not think of freedom as autonomy in a natural world. Because individual and collective agents are always embedded in a social realm, think of freedom as a combination of positive and negative liberty: given that agent A has freedom or liberty from something B, A has the freedom or liberty to do or to not do, to become or to not become, something C; perhaps C can even eventually reshape B. (MacCullum 1967)
Causal Methodology. In causal-statistical (potential outcomes) terms, agent A is free from the causal power of something B when a change or difference in C is unaffected by a change or difference in B; perhaps C can ultimately refashion B. In other words, if manipulating the counterfactual of B has no power over what happens to C, A is free from B to do/become C; perhaps, in the limit, C can manipulate B. (Rubin 1974)

The parallels are striking. When the people in a democracy (A) are free from external constraints (B), they can exercise their freedom to create outcomes (C) and perhaps even reconfigure (B). The more positive liberty (freedom to) comparativists attribute to democracy, the more causal power they attach to its freedom. The more negative liberty (freedom from) comparativists attribute to democracy, the less causal power they attach to its external constraints.

These parallels help clarify certain ought/is issues. Neither democratic theory nor causal methodologies rest content with appearances. Causality in empirical science and evaluations in normative theory go beyond experience to investigate counterfactuals – possible worlds that begin in the imagination. Not taking "givens" as truly given, they explore things that could have been and might well, someday and somewhere, become. In other words, democratic theories and causal methodologies investigate how power may be used to manipulate counterfactuals.

Democratic ideals, after all, always conflict with causal realities. That is what they are meant to do. We measure reality by ideals. And we ask why there is a difference. "Ought" thus makes claims on "is," claims that are resolved by critical reflection. Reason thus refuses to accept a gap. We then use our freedom to challenge the empirical world. Moreover, we seek emancipation from norms. We criticize existing values, construct novel desiderata, and set new goals. Practical reason – pragmatism – thus works in the midst of perpetual dissatisfaction about norms. Life's ceaseless struggle to reconcile "is" with "ought," indeed to find the "ought" worth fighting for, gives meaning to the demands of social life. The struggle allows humans to become at home in the world, and to ensure that our lives are not arbitrary.

The comparativists studied here vary in how much they push back against naturalism. In Acemoglu and Robinson's procedural democracy, thin freedom is the freedom to choose under constraints, transactional freedom the freedom of interactions and mutual choices, and modern bourgeois freedom the freedom of the private enjoyments of the peace and security that derive from agreements among political adversaries. These types of freedoms give insufficient attention to context. Because alternatives are givens that arise outside the chooser, thin freedom bends toward necessity. Power makes existing social, economic, and political realities seem natural.

Not all forms of power assume inevitability. In Wedeen's discursive democracy, collectivities have the power to shape their
own agency. By fashioning their alternatives and choices, preferences and beliefs, subjectivity and values, interests and identities,
and ideas and ideologies, the collectivity creates its own power. By
shaping its situation, the qāt chew creates its own possibilities in
its fields of action. Wedeen thus reminds us that ancient freedoms
took account of collective agency, social power, democratic subjectivity, public citizenship, political duties, and popular participation. Thick freedom is the freedom to fashion the constraints
under which one chooses. Freedom from structure implies the
capacity to shape the conditions under which actors choose,
allowing the satisfaction that comes from disciplining necessity.

Here we confront a paradox. In classical rational choice
theory, individual preferences, beliefs, and choices are products
of exogenous environmental conditions. In social constructivism,
individuals working together achieve endogenous autonomy
and agency – capacity and power – vis-à-vis environmental
constraints. Social constructivists therefore offer people more
freedom than rational choice theorists. An old joke goes,
"economics is all about choice and sociology all about how
people have no choices to make." Here's the new joke: constructivism is all about the power of collectivities and rationalism all
about how collectivities are impotent.

Of course, the joke can be carried too far. Acemoglu and
Robinson's work is a species of rational choice institutionalism.
Their model explores how rich elites and poor dissidents bind
themselves to a mutually productive equilibrium. Binding is
needed because the protagonists find that in the state of nature,
force (aggression) and fraud (exploitation) interfere with good
outcomes. Elites and dissidents require laws – an equilibrium of
procedural democracy – that compel them not to do X (take
noncooperative actions) so that they are free to do Y (take cooperative actions). The state of nature enables nothing, and liberty is
the freedom to live under laws that create freedoms to disable the
(noncooperative) actions that decrease welfare while enabling
other (cooperative) actions that increase welfare. In other words,

procedural democracy is a stable, self-chosen, and mutually binding commitment.

Because freedom to self-bind is a social good, it is overseen and supervised by society. Individuals endogenously generate structures, norms, and rules of their own choosing. Freedom, just like democracy, is not natural but rather quite artificial. It is socially constructed, historically shaped, and politically engineered for the good of all.

Modern liberals often think of freedom as freedom *from*: independence due to the lack of connections to others. However, freedom is also freedom *to*: social connections enable cooperative outcomes. Acemoglu and Robinson and Wedeen agree on these points. They part company about a comparative-static version of causality that recognizes that individuals make their own histories, but only under circumstances, limits, and conditions that are not of their own choosing. A fixed or natural environment gets in the way of a social constructivism that sees social collectivities as free from obstructions that restrict their power. Similarly, an all-powerful collectivity gets in the way of a rational choice theory that sees actors' choices as situationally determined.

Absolute freedom kills: the absence of social constraints, interpersonal bonds, and community belongings mean the absence of meaning and, according to Durkheim ([1893] 1933), the presence of murder and suicide. More generally, constraint is good. Schwartz's (2004) paradox of choice indicates that to make better choices we need to limit our choices: by surrendering to God, nature, or the environment we impose constraints on our liberty that make us better off. In Acemoglu and Robinson's model, self-binding, accepting the apparatus of self-control imposed by a social equilibrium, is good.

In fact, absolute freedom is impossible. Freedom as choice without constraints is a chimera. Restraints always exist. One cannot abolish all limits because something without limits cannot be contained in boundaries narrower than the Whole or All. With heteronymous forces, meaning is pregnant in the world. We cultivate the latent values and meanings of things – perhaps in opposition – to a preordained order. As we discover this order, we gain the agency to create meaningful new orders.

Structures are thus essential because they control impulses and regulate passions, preventing humans from being slaves to their random impulses and passions. By creating distance from the cacophony of the world, structures also focus attention and limit stimuli. In addition, structures spur action: no constraints, no creativity. If it looks as if there is no way out, people try even harder to figure a way out.

Freedom is thus parasitic on constraints and power provides the opportunities to exercise liberty. As Fish (2011: 32–33, emphasis in the original) writes, constraints are liberating because opportunity follows form:

> A famous sonnet by William Wordsworth begins, 'Nuns fret not at their convent's narrow room; /And hermits are contented with their cells; / and students with their pensive citadels.' Wordsworth's point is that what nuns, hermits, and students do is facilitated rather than hindered by the confines of the formal structures they inhabit; because those structures constrain freedom (they remove, says Wordsworth, 'the weight of too much liberty'), they enable movements in a defined space. If the moves you can perform are prescribed and limited – if, for example every line in your poem must have ten syllables and rhyme according to a predetermined pattern – each move can carry a precise significance. If, on the other hand, there are an infinite number of moves to perform, the significance of any one of them may be difficult to discern. (This is one of the insights of information theory.) That is why Wordsworth reports himself happy 'to be bound/ Within the Sonnet's scanty plot of ground.' It is a scanty plot because it is bounded, and because it is bounded, it can be the generator of boundless meaning. This, then, is my theology: *You shall tie yourself to forms and the forms shall set you free.*

Freedom requires capabilities, capabilities derive from resources, and resources come from structures. Moreover, structures enable alternatives. Conclusion: freedom requires structure.

Democracy's freedoms, in particular, require structure. The individual right to do something that pleases oneself can only be guaranteed by a social order. Without law, there are no rights. Put differently, individual rights are social rules. Negative liberty or noninterference presupposes the existence of a political association – a legal regime that protects civil liberties. Rather than a natural condition in the state of nature, liberty is a civil condition in a political association. Menard (2001: 409) writes that "[c]oercion is natural; freedom is artificial. Freedoms are socially engineered spaces where parties engaged in specified pursuits enjoy protection from parties who would otherwise naturally seek to interfere in those pursuits. One person's freedom is therefore always another person's restriction: we would not even have the concept of freedom if the reality of coercion were not already present." The state supplies the ability to make political claims. By establishing rights, it provides the immunities needed to make the liberty of claim-making operative. Since a state without law and order is impossible, democracy without a state is equally impossible.

Menard (2001: 409) adds that "[w]e also think of rights as privileges retained by individuals against the rest of society, but rights are created not for the good of individuals, but for the good of society. Individual freedoms are manufactured to achieve group ends." The good of freedom is the good of the group. The rationale is social and not private: "We do not (on Holmes's reasoning) permit the free expression of ideas because some individual may have the right one. No individual alone can have the right one. We permit free expression because we need the resources of the whole group to get the ideas we need. Thinking is a social activity. I tolerate your thought because it is part of my thought – even when my thought defines itself in opposition to yours" (Menard 2001: 431).

Huntington's (1968) famous opening was that the function of government is to govern. Law and order are the necessary conditions of democracy. Preceding Kohli by decades, he emphasized the necessity of external constraints on democracy. The citizen-agent, the bearer of rights and responsibilities who can operate with practical reason and moral judgment, requires a state that defines citizenship rights. Because the state gives legal status to citizen-agents, freedoms to practice democracy are based on the state's capacity to maintain and enforce the legal and moral principles required of democracy. State laws guarantee the freedoms that constitute democracy. Laws sanction violations of these democratic norms. Sanctions for noncompliance are backed by administrative force. Laws thus create the actionable and enforceable social facts that enable democracy to operate. Put otherwise, the factual generation of democracy occurs via administrative enforcement that coerces people. Hence, the state is needed to define democratic agency and thereby create the norms of democratic practice and performance. Since state laws legitimize the processes and procedures of democracy, democratic agency depends on state agency, which, as Tilly might point out, is collectively fashioned but becomes external to the democratic process.

Because freedom is everywhere constrained, democracy depends on the type rather than the mere existence of constraints. Pettit (1997: 5) thus offers freedom as nondomination, or immunity from arbitrary interference, as a third way between positive and negative liberty: "Being unfree does not consist in being restrained; on the contrary, the restraint of a fair system of law – a non-arbitrary image – does not make you unfree. Being unfree consists rather in being subject to arbitrary sway: being subject to the potentially capricious will or the potentially idiosyncratic judgment of another. Freedom involves emancipation from any such subordination, liberation from any such dependency." In short, freedom requires a meaningful or legitimate structure.

Democratic theorists recognize, and some theorists aim to control, the human quest for power over others. Scientists also appreciate, and often hope to harness, the power of causes to produce effects. My analysis of Acemoglu and Robinson, Wedeen, Kohli, and Tilly has indeed unearthed a key affinity between democratic theories and causal methodologies: both address questions about power. Put differently, questions about power are at the root of the affinity between democratic theories and causal methodologies. So are questions about democratic performance.

Thesis 12. Democracy and Performance. Address the key practical problem of democratic performance: in building a democratic state, which democracy under which conditions is best, and how might it be achieved?

Given the multiple modernities he depicted, Moore recognized the many ways for a country to become a "free and rational society." Isaiah Berlin (1958) makes two related points: individuals hold many values that are potentially conflicting, and a collectivity embraces several norms that are potentially incompatible. Often irreconcilable and uncombinable, Berlin tells us, values interact and produce complex intended and unintended consequences. In other words, if there are many ways for a country to become a "free and rational society," there are also many wants behind a "free and rational society." If there is then no one cosmic plan for a "free and rational society," if humanity does not march in one democratic direction, where are democracies up to their environmental challenges? Put differently, when does a democracy perform well?

The comparativists examined here offer different visions of the possibilities for democracy. Some say that democracies in today's global south cannot deal with the challenges of neoliberal capitalism and a hegemonic state system. Democratic states that are late-late developers cannot be effective states. In today's global south, a "rational" society cannot also be a "free" society. To cope with their environment, citizens of the postcolonial world need powerful states. While Kohli explores the state capacities of developmental regimes and judges the prospects for democracy to be dim, Tilly examines the causal mechanisms of adversarial democracy and pronounces the state fit for its challenges. Yet Tilly reminds comparativists that Wedeen's creative democratic agency must address Kohli's environmental constraints.

Kohli indeed raises a key issue. In the global south, weakened states coupled to thin democracy are responsible for poorly performing, low-quality, unconsolidated, and incomplete governance. Insecure and at-risk, such states lack the rule of law. When corruption, criminality, and violence are rampant, citizens often seek more accountable and responsible governance. Since citizens react to the outputs of democracy, comparativists should also audit the performance of democracy. The normative implications of empirical theories of democracy can then be addressed in studies that evaluate political performance. What are the implications of "democracy" for "governance"? Does a particular empirical democratic theory produce results that advantage its citizens? Why or why not? If not, what are the implications for its "democracy"? How do these findings tell us what kind of democracy we should value and how we should judge a polity as "democratic"? More generally, scholars should compare and contrast different normative commitments to democracy. Can an author's democracy pass a performance test of its collective agency and deliver the goods it promises? For example, does Acemoglu and Robinson's liberal procedural democracy turn power politics into legitimate, conflict-free authority? Is Wedeen's postmodern democracy indeed a creative problem-solver? Will Kohli's post-colonial socialist democracy successfully confront and accommodate its environmental constraints? Might Tilly's democratic socialist democracy be egalitarian?

Commitment to a type of democracy hinges on such evaluations of its political performance or regime fitness. Comparativists do not value elections for elections' sake, talk for talk's sake, coalitions for coalitions' sake, or contention for contention's sake. Elections, talk, coalitions, and contention are judged by the practical meaning and moral significance they hold for citizens trying to solve their political problems.

Democracies may be evaluated by internal moral desiderata (deontological) and external empirical criteria (teleological). With respect to the latter, "ought" implies "is" because of the consequences of "ought." Theorizing about democratic institutions is often about results, and theorizing about types of democracy often concerns outcomes. As Fung (2007: 444, emphasis in original) writes, "when a conception of democracy has institutional consequences that are consistent with its values I say that it is in *pragmatic equilibrium.*"

The comparative search for criteria – standards and benchmarks – for the optimal performance of democratic institutions began in earnest with Dahl (1971), Eckstein and Gurr (1975), Lijphart (1975), and Powell (1982). Comparativists today debate such institutions as federalism, consociationalism, multiple parties, independent courts, central banks, factionalism, veto players, voluntary associations, and electoral rules. They examine such consequences as efficiency, equity, justice, freedom, liberty, the public good, and social welfare. In their own ways, the authors under review here evaluate the real-world performance of procedural, discursive, contentious, and coalitional democracy.

If democratic theory expresses a consequentialist morality, then causal methodology surely matters. There is, however, a complication: endogeneity. Since the early work on democratic stability, comparativists have explored the social conditions that support political democracy. Change the enabling conditions and one changes the chances for democracy. Is democracy found in a diverse and individualistic culture, or in a homogeneous and holistic culture? Is democracy found in a country open to foreign trade, or in one whose economic development is autarkic? In today's world, democracies confront several external challenges to building free and rational societies. Geopolitical environments and interstate competition, for example, still shape nationalism and state building, and thereby influence normative visions of democracy.

Thick democracy has thick internal foundations. On a loose leash, the environment yields potentials and possibilities. Such a democracy can adapt to changing external circumstances, and hence is probably sustainable. Put differently, thick democracy is its own self-generating cause. On the other hand, thin democracy has thick external requirements. On a tight leash, its environment is determinative. Such a democracy lacks the capability of adapting to new conditions, and hence is less likely to endure. Put otherwise, thin democracy contains the seeds of its own destruction.

The selection of democracy implies the victory of one regime over another. Contingency in origins has consequences for the operation of democracy – its capacities, powers, and processes. Because types of democracy influence performance, democratic performance is also contingent on environment. Given that democracy has no practical significance of its own, comparativists must examine how the environment shapes, impedes, or challenges its mechanisms, institutions, and activities. To evaluate democratic theory comparativists thus need to study the context in which democracy emerges. To understand the outcomes of democracy comparativists must understand the causes of democracy. How is procedural, discursive, multiclass, and contentious democracy possible?

In sum, if democratic theory expresses a teleological morality – democracy is a conditionally value good that is valid under certain circumstances and invalid under others – comparativists should apply the consequentialist test and address a key question about democratic performance: in building a democratic state, which democracy under which conditions is best, and how might it be achieved? However, propositions about how democracy operates, hypotheses about what democracy produces, and laws about when democracy endures are related to theories of why states achieve democracy in the first place. Moreover, the thinner the democracy, the more evaluation involves etiology. Comparativists thus need to reason backward to causes and forward to consequences.

A research agenda that evaluates the fitness of democratic governments compared to autocratic and hybrid regimes, and judges the performance of different democratic institutions, suits academics concerned with policy relevance. Foreign-policy makers in the United States, especially neoliberal interventionists, regularly become engaged in nation building, state building, economic development, and social transformation in the global south. Based on implicit expectations or explicit philosophies, they design real-world democratic institutions. Deeper knowledge about the origins, operations, and outcomes of democracy, and especially about how democracy is controlled and constrained, might temper their efforts to create democracy and qualify their attempts to improve democratic performance. While democracy is a political institution subject to (re)construction, when democratic theory meets causal methodology beliefs in the good society and the best government, even those held by great powers, are put to the tests of social engineering and practical constitutionalism.

Comparativists do not need other-worldly justifications for such democratic values as liberalism and justice. Nor do they require permanent truths about all democracies every place and every time. The search for necessary and sufficient presuppositions about the essence of democracy is a chimerical search for certainty.

Justifications of democratic theory need not rest on the speculative metaphysics of transcendent principles derived from abstract theories of human nature and of the good society. Abstract normative commitments to democratic theories eventually come to rest on the validity of empirical claims about causal human psychology – humans-as-they-happen-to-be – and about causal social interactions – humans-as-they-happen-to-become. As much as our moral intuitions motivate our normative commitments, concrete empirical claims drive our theoretical beliefs. Instead of proposing a freestanding moral language about democracy, comparativists therefore should investigate the empirical upshot of its normative principles. Put otherwise, causal methodologies can ground democratic theories. To further their critical, normative, and policy purposes, comparativists can produce knowledge claims about the conditions, settings, and contexts that make democracy possible and viable. As Shapiro (1990: 223) writes, "What is so frustrating about much of the turn away from neo-Kantian theory is that for all the appeal to historical specificity by which it is often motivated there has been little serious grappling with empirical complexity and causal argument."

9.2. COMPARATIVE POLITICS

Barrington Moore ended in the midst of an ought/is dilemma, boldly holding "reality and justice in a single vision" (William Butler Yeats, cited in Rorty 1999: 7), audaciously coupling an ethics of responsibility to an ethics of conviction (Weber 1946a). As the debate between normative and empirical theorists of democracy is revisited four decades after the 1960s, modern comparative politics finds itself constituted by Moore's classic. The Barrington Moore Problem Situation – how alternative modernities challenge liberalism, how state building occurs amid contentious world politics, and how institutions arise, persist, and change – still define comparative politics. Yet the Barrington Moore Problem – the affinities of democratic theories and causal methodologies – that once energized classics like Barrington Moore's tarries behind as the new classics of Daron Acemoglu

and James A. Robinson, Lisa Wedeen, Atul Kohli, and Charles
Tilly take center stage. Democratic theories and causal methodologies have advanced since Moore's time, yet the problem of
moral agency and political democracy in a causal world remains
unexplored and the Moore Curve remains undertheorized.

While much has been gained, some of the earlier scholarly
world thus has been lost. Political theory and comparative politics
have become highly specialized fields separated by a division of
labor. Democratic theorizing and causal methodology now proceed on two very separate tracks. There is a normative and
an empirical literature, and the trains almost never meet.
Nevertheless, a key finding about deliberative democracy is that
deliberation's success or failure depends on context (Thompson
2008: 499). Context must also be the key to the success of procedural, class coalitional, and contentious democracy.

Moore's Problem remains the benchmark of our progress as a
political science and as a humanist endeavor. Moore ended not
with a solved problem but with a better understanding of the
antinomies that challenge comparativists to revist the issue.

Comparativists nowadays routinely call for multimethod –
qualitative and quantitative – research. This book has demonstrated that progress will also occur through multitheory – research
schools and democratic theories – research. A multitheory- and
multimethod-study of democracy is an intellectually exciting and
potentially productive scholarly adventure. Comparativists
should stay attuned to developments in both theory and method.
Demolishing the barriers that have separated the two research
traditions would turn hostile strangers into friendly partners in
their common quest to understand democratization.

References

Abbott, Andrew. 2001. *The Chaos of Disciplines*. Chicago: University of Chicago Press.

Acemoglu, Daron and James A. Robinson. 2006. *Economic Origins of Dictatorship and Democracy*. Cambridge: Cambridge University Press.

Aldrich, John H., James E. Alt, and Arthur Lupia. 2008. "The EITM Approach: Origins and Interpretations." In Box-Steffensmeier, Janet M., Henry E. Brady, and David Collier, Eds. *The Oxford Handbook of Political Methodology*. Oxford: Oxford University Press, pp. 828–843.

Almond, Gabriel. 1988. "Separate Tables: Schools and Sects in Political Science." *PS* 21, no. 4: 828–842.

Almond, Gabriel A. and G. Bingham Powell, Jr. 1966. *Comparative Politics: A Developmental Approach*. Boston: Little, Brown.

Almond, Gabriel A. and Sidney Verba. 1963. *The Civic Culture: Political Attitudes and Democracy in Five Nations*. Princeton: Princeton University Press.

Arendt, Hannah. 1958. *The Human Condition*. Second Ed. Chicago: University of Chicago Press.

Aristotle. 1981. *The Politics*. Revised Ed. New York: Penguin.

Arrow, Kenneth J. 1951. *Social Choice and Individual Values*. Second Ed. New Haven: Yale University Press.

Barber, Benjamin. 1988. *The Conquest of Politics: Liberal Philosophy in Democratic Times*. Princeton: Princeton University Press.

Barry, Brian. 1970. *Sociologists, Economists, and Democracy*. Chicago: University of Chicago Press.

Bendix, Reinhard. 1969. *Nation Building and Citizenship: Studies of Our Changing Social Order*. Garden City, NY: Anchor.

220

References

Benhabib, Seyla. 1995. "Response." *Political Theory* 23 (November): 674–681.

Berlin, Isaiah. 1958. "Two Concepts of Liberty." In Berlin, Isaiah. *Liberty: Incorporating Four Essays on Liberty*. 2002. Second Ed. London: Oxford University Press, pp. 166–217.

Bevir, Mark. 2008. "Meta-Methodology: Clearing the Underbrush." In Box-Steffensmeier, Janet M., Henry E. Brady, and David Collier, Eds. *The Oxford Handbook of Political Methodology*. Oxford: Oxford University Press, pp. 48–70.

2010. *Democratic Governance*. Princeton: Princeton University Press.

Box-Steffensmeier, Janet M., Henry E. Brady, and David Collier. 2008. "Political Science Methodology." In Box-Steffensmeier, Janet M., Henry E. Brady, and David Collier, Eds. *The Oxford Handbook of Political Methodology*. Oxford: Oxford University Press, pp. 3–34.

Brady, Henry. 2008. "Causation and Explanation in Social Science." In Box-Steffensmeier, Janet M., Henry E. Brady, and David Collier, Eds. *The Oxford Handbook of Political Methodology*. Oxford: Oxford University Press, pp. 217–270.

Cartwright, Nancy. 1989. *Nature's Capacities and Their Measurement*. Oxford: Oxford University Press.

Chomsky, Noam. 1959. "Review of Verbal Behavior," *Language*, 35: 26–58.

Cleary, Mathew R. and Susan C. Stokes. 2006. *Democracy and the Culture of Skepticism: Political Trust in Argentina and Mexico*. New York: Russell Sage.

Collier, David and Colin Elman. 2008. "Qualitative and Multimethod Research: Organizations, Publication, and Reflections on Integration." In Box-Steffensmeier, Janet M., Henry E. Brady, and David Collier, Eds. *The Oxford Handbook of Political Methodology*. Oxford: Oxford University Press, pp. 779–795.

Collins, Randall. 1998. *The Sociology of Philosophies: A Global Theory of Intellectual Change*. Cambridge, MA: Harvard University Press.

Dahl, Robert A. 1956. *A Preface to Democratic Theory*. Chicago: University of Chicago Press.

1957. "The Concept of Power." *Behavioral Science* 2 (July): 201–215.

1971. *Polyarchy: Participation and Opposition*. New Haven: Yale University Press.

Dahl, Robert A. and Charles E. Lindblom. 1953. *Politics, Economics, and Welfare: Planning and Politico-Economic Systems Resolved into Basic Social Processes*. New York: Harper Torchbooks.

Deutsch, Karl. 1966. *The Nerves of Government: Models of Political Communication and Control*. New York: Free Press.

Downs, Anthony. 1957. *An Economic Theory of Democracy*. New York: Harper & Row.

Dunn, John. 1999. "Democracy and Development?" In Ian Shapiro and Casiano Hacker-Cordón, Eds. *Democracy's Value*. Cambridge: Cambridge University Press, pp. 132–140.

Durkheim, Emile. [1893] 1933. *The Division of Labor in Society*. New York: Free Press.

Eagleton, Terry. 2008. *Literary Theory: An Introduction*. Anniversary Edition. Malden, MA: Blackwell.

Easton, David. 1953. *The Political System*. Chicago: University of Chicago Press.

Eckstein, Harry. 1966. *Division and Cohesion in Democracy: A Study of Norway*. Princeton: Princeton University Press.

   1971. *The Evaluation of Political Performance: Problems and Dimensions*. Beverly Hills: Sage.

   1980. "Theoretical Approaches to Explaining Collective Political Violence." In Ted Robert Gurr, Ed. *Handbook of Political Conflict: Theory and Research*, New York: Free Press, pp. 135–165.

Eckstein, Harry and Ted Robert Gurr. 1975. *Patterns of Authority: A Structural Basis for Political Inquiry*. New York: Wiley.

Elster, Jon. 2007. *Explaining Social Behavior. More Nuts and Bolts for the Social Sciences*. Cambridge: Cambridge University Press.

Fish, Stanley. 2011. *How To Write a Sentence and How To Read One*. New York: Harper.

Friedman, Thomas. 2005. "The Country We Got." *New York Times*, 1/6/05, p. A27.

Fung, Archon. 2007. "Democratic Theory and Political Science: A Pragmatic Method of Constructive Engagement." *American Political Science Review* 101 (August): 443–458.

Gellner, Ernest. 1995. *Anthropology and Politics: Revolutions in the Sacred Grove*. Oxford: Blackwell.

Goodin, Robert E. and Charles Tilly, Eds. 2006. *Oxford Handbook of Contextual Political Analysis*. Cambridge: Cambridge University Press.

Gurr, Ted Robert. 1974. "Persistence and Change in Political Systems: 1800–1971." *American Political Science Review* 68 (December): 1482–1504.

Hamilton, Alexander, John Jay, and James Madison. [1787–88] 1961. *The Federalist: A Commentary on the Constitution of the United States*. New York: Random House.

Habyarimana, James, Macartan Humphreys, Daniel N. Posner, and Jeremy M. Weinstein. 2009. *Coethnicity: Diversity and the Dilemmas of Collective Action*. New York: Russell Sage.

Habermas, Jürgen (1989). *The Structural Transformation of the Public Sphere: An Inquiry into a Category of Bourgeois Society.* Trans. Thomas Burger, Cambridge, MA: The MIT Press.

Hacking, Ian. 1983. *Representing and Intervening: Introductory Topics in the Philosophy of Natural Science.* Cambridge: Cambridge University Press.

Hobbes, Thomas. [1651] 1988. *Leviathan.* London: Penguin.

Holland, Paul W. 1986. "Statistics and Causal Inference." *Journal of the American Statistical Association* 81 (December): 945–960.

Huntington, Samuel P. 1968. *Political Order in Changing Societies.* New Haven: Yale University Press.

Ingelhart, Ronald and Christian Welzel. 2005. *Modernization, Cultural Change, and Democracy: The Human Development Sequence.* Cambridge: Cambridge University Press.

Kalyvas, Stathis N. 2006. *The Logic of Violence in Civil War.* Cambridge: Cambridge University Press.

Katznelson, Ira. 2003. *Desolation and Enlightenment. Political Knowledge After Total War, Totalitarianism, and the Holocaust.* New York: Columbia University Press.

2009. "Strong Theory, Complex History: Structure and Configuration in Comparative Politics Revisited." In Mark Irving Lichbach and Alan Zuckerman, Eds. *Comparative Politics: Rationality, Culture, and Structure.* Second Ed. Cambridge: Cambridge University Press, pp. 96–116.

Kern, Stephen. 2004. *A Cultural History of Causality.* Princeton: Princeton University Press.

King, Gary, Robert O. Keohane, and Sidney Verba. 1994. *Designing Social Inquiry: Scientific Inference in Qualitative Research.* Princeton: Princeton University Press.

Kohli, Atul. 2004. *State-Directed Development: Political Power and Industrialization in the Global Periphery.* Cambridge: Cambridge University Press.

Kuhn, Thomas S. 1970. *The Structure of Scientific Revolutions.* Second Ed., enlarged. Chicago: University of Chicago Press.

Kurki, Milja. 2008. *Causation in International Relations: Reclaiming Causal Analysis.* Cambridge: Cambridge University Press.

Laitin, David D. 2007. "Culture, Rationality, and the Search for Discipline." In Gerardo L. Munck and Richard Snyder, Eds. *Passion, Craft, and Method in Comparative Politics.* Baltimore: Johns Hopkins University Press, pp. 601–648.

LaPalombara, Joseph. 1970. "Parsimony and Empiricism in Comparative Politics: An Anti-Scholastic View." In Robert H. Holt and John E. Turner, Eds. *The Methodology of Comparative Research.* New York: Free Press, pp. 123–149.

Lasswell, Harold Dwight. 1950. *Politics: Who Gets What, When, How.* New York: P. Smith.

Lichbach, Mark. 1995. *The Rebel's Dilemma.* Ann Arbor: University of Michigan Press.

2003. *Is Rational Choice Theory All of Social Science?* Ann Arbor: University of Michigan Press.

2005. "How to Organize Your Mechanisms: Research Programs, Stylized Facts, and Historical Narratives." In Christian Davenport, Hank Johnston, and Carol Mueller, Eds. *Repression and Mobilization,* Minneapolis: University of Minnesota Press, pp. 227–243.

2008. "Modeling Mechanisms of Contention: McTT's Positivist Constructivism." *Qualitative Sociology* 31 (December): 345–354.

2009. "Thinking and Working in the Midst of Things: Discovery, Explanation, and Evidence in Comparative Politics." In Mark Irving Lichbach and Alan S. Zuckerman, Eds. *Comparative Politics: Rationality, Culture, and Structure,* Second Ed. Cambridge: Cambridge University Press, pp. 18–71.

2010. "Charles Tilly's Problem Situations: From Class and Revolution to Mechanisms and Contentious Politics." *Perspectives on Politics* 8 (June): 543–549.

Lichbach, Mark Irving and Jeffrey Kopstein, Eds. 2009. *Comparative Politics: Institutions, Identities, and Interests in Today's Small World.* Third Ed. Cambridge: Cambridge: University Press.

Lichbach, Mark Irving and Ned Lebow, Eds. 2007. *Theory and Evidence in Comparative Politics and International Relations.* New York: Palgrave-Macmillan.

Lichbach, Mark Irving and Adam Seligman. 2000. *Market and Community: The Bases of Social Order, Revolution, and Relegitimation.* University Park: Pennsylvania State University Press.

Lichbach, Mark Irving and Alan Zuckerman. 2009. *Comparative Politics: Rationality, Culture, and Structure.* Second Ed. Cambridge: Cambridge University Press.

Lijphart, Arend. 1975. *The Politics of Accommodation: Pluralism and Democracy in the Netherlands.* Second Ed. Berkeley: University of California Press.

1999. *Patterns of Democracy: Government Forms and Performance in Thirty-Six Countries.* New Haven: Yale University Press.

Linz, Juan J. [1975] 2000. *Totalitarian and Authoritarian Regimes.* Boulder, CO: Lynne Rienner.

Lipset, Seymour Martin. 1963. *Political Man: The Social Bases of Politics.* New York: Anchor Books.

Lipset, Seymour Martin and Stein Rokkan. 1967. "Cleavage Structures, Party Systems, and Voter Alignments: An Introduction." In Seymour Martin Lipset and Stein Rokkan, Eds. *Party Systems and Voter Alignments*. New York: Free Press, pp. 1–64.

Locke, John. 1988. *Two Treatises of Government*. Peter Laslett, Ed. Cambridge: Cambridge University Press.

Lukes, Steven. 1985. *Emil Durkheim His Life and Work: A Historical and Critical Study*. Stanford, CA: Stanford University Press.

MacCallum, Gerald C. Jr., 1967. "Negative and Positive Freedom." *Philosophical Review* 76 (July): 312–334.

Machiavelli, Niccolo. [1514] 1961. *The Prince*. London: Penguin.

Madison, James, Alexander Hamilton, and John Jay. [1788] 1987. *The Federalist Papers*. Issac Kramnick, Ed. New York: Penguin.

Mansbridge, Jane J. 1980. *Beyond Adversary Democracy*. Chicago: University of Chicago Press.

  1996. Using Power/Fighting Power: The Polity. In Seyla Benhabib, Ed. *Democracy and Difference: Contesting the Boundaries of the Political*. Princeton: Princeton University Press, pp. 46–66.

Marx, Karl. [1845] 1998. *The German Ideology, Including Theses on Feuerbach*. New York: Prometheus Books.

  [1869] 1963. *The 18th Brumaire of Louis Bonaparte*. New York: International Publishers.

May, Kenneth O. 1952. "A Set of Independent, Necessary and Sufficient Conditions for Simple Majority Decision." *Econometrica* 20 (October): 680–684.

McAdam, Doug, Sidney Tarrow, and Charles Tilly. 2001. *Dynamics of Contention*. Cambridge: Cambridge University Press.

Menard, Louis. 2001. *The Metaphysical Club: A Story of Ideas in America*. New York: Farrar, Straus and Giroux.

Michels, Robert. [1919] 1962. *Political Parties: A Sociological Study of the Oligarchical Tendencies of Modern Democracy*. New York: Free Press.

Montesquieu. 1989. *The Spirit of Laws*. Cambridge: Cambridge University Press.

Moore, Barrington, Jr. 1966. *Social Origins of Dictatorship and Democracy: Lord and Peasant in the Making of the Modern World*. Boston: Beacon Press.

  1978. *Injustice: The Social Bases of Obedience and Revolt*. White Plains, NY: M. E. Sharpe.

  2007. "The Critical Spirit and Comparative Historical Analysis." In Gerardo L. Munck and Richard Snyder, Eds. *Passion, Craft, and Method in Comparative Politics*. Baltimore: Johns Hopkins University Press, pp. 86–112.

Mosca, Gaetano. 1939. *The Ruling Class.* Trans. Arthur Livingston. New York: McGraw-Hill.

Neiman, Susan. 2009. *Moral Clarity: A Guide for Grown-Up Idealists.* Revised Ed. Princeton: Princeton University Press.

North, Douglass C. and Barry R. Weingast (1989). "Constitutions and Commitment: The Evolution of Institutions Governing Public Choice in Seventeenth-Century England." *Journal of Economic History* 49 (December): 803–832.

Olson, Mancur, Jr. 1965. *The Logic of Collective Action: Public Goods and the Theory of Groups.* Cambridge, MA: Harvard University Press.

Ostrom, Elinor. 1990. *Governing the Commons: The Evolution of Institutions for Collective Action.* Cambridge: Cambridge University Press.

Pareto, Vilfredo. [1920] 1980. *Compendium of General Sociology.* Abridged by Giulio Farina, Edited by Elisabeth Abbott. Minneapolis: University of Minnesota Press.

Parsons, Talcott. 1951. *The Social System.* New York: Free Press.

Pettit, Philip. 1997. *Republicanism: A Theory of Freedom and Government.* Oxford: Oxford University Press.

Pitkin, Hanna. 1967. *The Concept of Representation.* Berkeley: University of California Press.

Plato. 1974. *The Republic.* Second Ed. New York: Penguin

Powell, G. Bingham, Jr. 1982. *Contemporary Democracies: Participation, Stability, and Violence.* Cambridge, MA: Harvard University Press.

Przeworski, Adam. 2007. "Is the Science of Comparative Politics Possible?" In Carles Boix and Susan C. Stokes, Ed. *Oxford Handbook of Comparative Politics.* Oxford: Oxford University Press, pp. 147–171.

2010. *Democracy and the Limits of Self-Government.* Cambridge: Cambridge University Press.

Przeworski, Adam, Michael E. Alvarez, José Antonio Cheibub, and Fernando Limongi. 2000. *Democracy and Development.* Cambridge: Cambridge University Press.

Rapoport, Anatol. 1960. *Fights, Games, and Debates.* Ann Arbor: University of Michigan Press.

Rawls, John. 1971. *A Theory of Justice.* Cambridge, MA: Harvard University Press.

1993. *Political Liberalism.* New York: Columbia University Press.

Riker, William H. 1982. *Liberalism Against Populism: A Confrontation Between the Theory of Democracy and the Theory of Social Choice.* San Francisco: W. H. Freeman.

226   References

Rorty, Richard. 1982. *Consequences of Pragmatism (Essays, 1972–1980)*. Minneapolis: University of Minnesota Press.
  1999. *Philosophy and Social Hope*. Harmondsworth, UK: Penguin.
Rousseau, Jean-Jacques. [1762] 1968. *The Social Contract*. New York: Penguin.
Rubin, Donald B. 1974. "Estimating Causal Effects of Treatments in Randomized and Nonrandomized Studies." *Journal of Educational Psychology* 66: 688–701.
Samuelson, Paul A. 1947. *Foundations of Economic Analysis*. Enlarged Ed. Cambridge, MA: Harvard University Press.
Schmitter, Philippe C. 2007. "Corporatism, Democracy, and Conceptual Traveling." In Gerardo L. Munck and Richard Snyder, Eds. *Passion, Craft, and Method in Comparative Politics*. Baltimore: Johns Hopkins University Press, pp. 305–350.
Schotter, Andrew and G. Schwödiauer. 1980. "Economics and the Theory of Games: A Survey. *Journal of Economic Literature* 18 (June): 479–527.
Schumpeter, Joseph A. 1950. *Capitalism, Socialism and Democracy*. Third Ed. New York: Harper & Row.
Schwartz, Barry. 2004. *The Paradox of Choice: Why More Is Less*. New York: ECCO.
Schweinitz, Karl de., Jr. 1964. *Industrialization and Democracy*. New York: Free Press.
Scott, James C. 1985. *Weapons of the Weak: Everyday Forms of Peasant Resistance*. New Haven: Yale University Press.
Shapiro, Ian. 1990. *Political Criticism*. Berkeley: University of California Press.
  2002. "The State of Democratic Theory." In Ira Katznelson, and Helen V. Milner, Eds. *Political Science: The State of the Discipline*. New York: W.W. Norton & Company, pp. 235–265.
  2003. *The State of Democratic Theory*. Princeton: Princeton University Press.
  2005. *The Flight From Reality in the Human Sciences*. Princeton: Princeton University Press.
Shaw, George Bernard. [1902] 2010. *Man and Superman*. New York: Create Space.
Shklar, Judith. 1984. *Ordinary Vices*. Cambridge, MA: Harvard University Press.
Skinner, Quentin. 1974. "Some Problems in the Analysis of Political Thought and Action." *Political Theory* 2 (August): 277–303.
Skocpol, Theda. 1979. *States and Social Revolutions: A Comparative Analysis of France, Russia and China*. Cambridge: Cambridge University Press.

Sniderman, Paul M. and Louk Hagendoorn. 2007. *When Ways of Life Collide: Multiculturalism and Its Discontents in the Netherlands*. Princeton: Princeton University Press.

Stinchcombe, Arthur L. 2005. *The Logic of Social Research*. Chicago: University of Chicago Press.

Stokes, Susan C. 2001. *Mandates and Democracy: Neoliberalism by Surprise in Latin America*. Cambridge: Cambridge University Press.

Tarrow, Sidney G. 2011. *Power in Movement: Social Movements and Contentious Politics*. Revised and Updated Third Ed. Cambridge: Cambridge University Press.

Taylor, Charles. 1985. "Philosophy and the Human Sciences." *Philosophical Papers 2*. Cambridge: Cambridge University Press.

Thompson, Dennis F. 2008. "Deliberative Democratic Theory and Empirical Political Science." *Annual Review of Political Science* 11: 497–520.

Tilly, Charles. 1975. "Reflections on the History of European State-Making." In Charles Tilly Ed. *The Formation of National States in Western Europe*. Princeton: Princeton University Press, pp. 3–83.

2003. *The Politics of Collective Violence*. Cambridge: Cambridge University Press.

2004. *Social Movements, 1768–2004*. Cambridge: Cambridge University Press.

2007. *Democracy*. Cambridge: Cambridge University Press.

2008. *Contentious Performances*. Cambridge: Cambridge University Press.

Tilly, Charles and Sidney Tarrow. 2007. *Contentious Politics*. Boulder, CO: Paradigm.

Tocqueville, Alexis de. [1850] 1969. *Democracy in America*. George Lawrence, Trans. New York: Anchor Books.

Trotsky, Leon. [1932] 1980. *The History of the Russian Revolution*. New York: Pathfinder.

Tsai, Lily L. 2007. "Solidarity Groups, Informal Accountability, and Local Public Goods Provision in Rural China." *American Political Science Review* 101 (May): 355–372.

Unger, Roberto Mangabeira. 1987. *Social Theory: Its Situation and Its Task*. London: Verso.

Vonnegut, Kurt. 1966. *Mother Night*. New York: Avon.

Weber, Max. [1924] 1968. *Economy and Society*. Two volumes. Berkeley: University of California Press.

1946a. "Politics as a Vocation." In H. H. Gerth and C. Wright Mills, Eds. *From Max Weber: Essays in Sociology*. New York: Oxford, pp. 77–128.

1946b. "Science as a Vocation." In H. H. Gerth and C. Wright Mills, Eds. *From Max Weber: Essays in Sociology.* New York: Oxford, pp. 129–156.

1946c. "Religious Rejections of the World and Their Directions." In H. H. Gerth and C. Wright Mills, Eds. *From Max Weber: Essays in Sociology.* New York: Oxford, pp. 323–359.

Wedeen, Lisa. 2004. "Concepts and Commitments in the Study of Democracy." In Ian Shapiro, Rogers Smith, and Tarek E. Masoud, Eds. *Problems and Methods in the Study of Politics.* Cambridge: Cambridge University Press, pp. 274–306.

2008. *Peripheral Visions: Publics, Power, and Performance in Yemen.* Chicago: University of Chicago Press.

Wittgenstein, Ludwig. 2009. *Philosophical Investigations.* Fourth Ed. P. M. S. Hacker and Joachim Schulte, Eds. and Trans. Oxford: Wiley-Blackwell.

Wolin, Sheldon S. 1996. "Fugitive Democracy." In Seyla Benhabib, Ed. *Democracy and Difference: Contesting the Boundaries of the Political.* Princeton: Princeton University Press, pp. 31–45.

Zuckerman, Alan S. 1975. "Political Cleavage: A Conceptual and Theoretical Analysis." *British Journal of Political Science* 5 (April): 231–248.

1989. "The Bases of Political Cohesion: Apply and Reconstructing Crumbling Theories." *Comparative Politics* 21 (July): 473–495.

Index